Working with Disabled People in Policy and Practice

Interagency Working in Health and Social Care
Edited by Jon Glasby

Aimed at students and practitioners, this series provides an introduction to inter-agency working across the health and social care spectrum, bringing together an appreciation of the policy background with a focus on contemporary themes. The books span a wide range of health and social care services and the impact that these have on people's lives, as well as offering insightful accounts of the issues facing professionals in a fast-changing organizational landscape.

Exploring how services and sectors interact and could change further, and the evidence for 'what works', the series is designed to frame debate as well as promote positive ways of interdisciplinary working.

Published titles

Kellett: *Children's Perspectives on Integrated Services: Every Child Matters in Policy and Practice*
French/Swain: *Working with Disabled People in Policy and Practice*

Forthcoming titles

Williams/Johnson: *Learning Disability and Inclusion*
Baggott: *Public Health and Wellbeing*

Working with Disabled People in Policy and Practice
A Social Model

Sally French and John Swain

First published 2012 by
PALGRAVE MACMILLAN

Palgrave Macmillan in the UK is an imprint of Macmillan Publishers Limited, registered in England, company number 785998, of Houndmills, Basingstoke, Hampshire RG21 6XS

Palgrave Macmillan in the US is a division of St Martin's Press LLC, 175 Fifth Avenue, New York, NY 10010.

Palgrave Macmillan is the global academic imprint of the above companies and has companies and representatives throughout the world.

Palgrave® and Macmillan® are registered trademarks in the United States, the United Kingdom, Europe and other countries.

ISBN: 978–0–230–58078–7

This book is printed on paper suitable for recycling and made from fully managed and sustained forest sources. Logging, pulping and manufacturing processes are expected to conform to the environmental regulations of the country of origin.

A catalogue record for this book is available from the British Library.

A catalog record for this book is available from the Library of Congress.

10 9 8 7 6 5 4 3 2 1
21 20 19 18 17 16 15 14 13 12

Printed and bound in Great Britain by the MPG Books Group,
Bodmin and King's Lynn

Contents

List of Boxes and Figures

Figures

Acknowledgements

The authors and publishers are grateful to the following organizations for granting permission to reproduce copyright material: Candoco Dance Company (www.candoco.co.uk) for the two photographs featured in Figure 1.2, which they have kindly provided from their tour archive; Institute of Futures Studies, Stockholm for Figure 8.1, originally from Dahlgren, G. and Whitehead, M. (1991) *Policies and Strategies to Promote Social Equality in Health*; Stockholm, Sweden: Institute of Futures Studies.

Every effort has been made to contact all the copyright holders, but if any have been inadvertently omitted the publishers will be pleased to make the necessary arrangements at the first opportunity.

All internet references were accurate at the time of going to print – but details of individual sites are likely to change.

Introduction

In this Introduction we would like to say a little about the what, the why and the how of this book. This book presents the academic field of disability studies, as it relates to health and social care policy and practice. Disability studies is concerned with the social, political and cultural analysis of disability. It has at its heart the social model of disability which views disability in terms of environmental, structural and attitudinal barriers that deny disabled people full participation in society and full citizenship rights. The book supports health and social care professionals, and students of these professions, in critical reflection on the provision of services to disabled people with the social model of disability as the underlying theoretical framework.

In accord with the orientation of the book, we prioritize the views and experiences of disabled people, as expressed by disabled people themselves. In doing so we have drawn on research that we have conducted or been involved in, such as the oral history of the education of visually impaired people and the narratives of disabled people sexually abused as children.

In line with the aims of the series, this book will aim to:

- Provide a clear exposition of relevant policy, history and underlying themes for the future, as they affect the working practices of all those concerned with disabled people
- Outline the roles played by the various professionals involved in the support of disabled people and their families
- Focus on partnership or inter-agency working to provide more personalized services, with a particular emphasis on looking beyond 'special' and into ordinary, mainstream services
- Highlight examples of positive, evidence-based practice in working with disabled people throughout the life course

Central to this text is the promotion of full active participatory citizenship and health and social work policy and practice that is informed by disabled people themselves. The underlying theme is the struggle of how to develop inter-agency practice, given that the social model does not provide a prescribed, 'recipe book' approach. It is recognized that the social model centrally underpins a critically reflective stance towards the dominant individual model within professional policy and practice. We include Reflective Exercises with each chapter and hope that the book will be read critically, constantly questioning the arguments and their implication for practice both in your own and other professional agencies. This book is intended to stimulate thought and if you read it critically, you will no doubt find much with which you disagree, and in the process you will clarify your own beliefs.

1 Modelling Disability and Impairment

In this chapter we discuss:

- The individual model of disability
- The social model of disability
- Long term conditions
- The tragedy model of disability
- The affirmative model of disability
- Implications for policy and practice

In this chapter we will examine two central models of disability, the individual model and the social model, to illustrate the ways in which underlying ideas and concepts can shape policy and practice in health and social care. We will also consider the tragedy model and the affirmative model, which are closely associated with the individual and social models of disability. Some consideration will also be given to the term 'long term conditions', which is frequently used alongside 'disability' in research and policy documents.

A model can be defined as a conceptual framework for understanding causal relationships. It usually lies within the framework of a broader theory (Brown, 2009). For example, an inability to move around in the environment may be thought to be caused by physical impairment. Within every society there are competing models of disability, with some being more dominant than others at different times (Oliver, 2004; Wilder, 2006). In earlier centuries, for example, models of disability were based upon religion (Whalley Hammell, 2006). Although often in conflict, models of disability may gradually influence and modify each other. The models put forward by powerful groups within society, such as the medical profession, tend to dominate the models of less powerful groups, such as those of disabled people themselves (French and Swain, 2002).

It is essential to explore these models of disability, for attitudes and behaviour towards disabled people, policy, professional practice, and the running of institutions, including hospitals, rehabilitation centres and social service departments, are based, at least in part, upon them. As Oliver states:

> The 'lack of fit' between able-bodied and disabled people's definitions is more than just a semantic quibble for it has important implications both for the provision of services and the ability to control one's life. (1993a, p. 61)

Even the ways in which single words are defined can shape both policy and practice. The word 'independence' is an example.

Box 1.1	What is independence?

The predominant meaning of independence among health and social care professionals is the ability to do things for oneself. This definition has, however, been challenged by disabled people who view independence in terms of self-determination, control and managing and organizing any assistance that is required. Ryan and Holman state that, 'independence is not necessarily about what you can do for yourself, but rather about what others can do for you, in ways that you want it done' (1998, p. 19).

Additionally, some cultures have a collectivist orientation and do not value independence as much as others. In a very real sense, we are all dependent on each other for our survival so nobody is truly independent.

The individual model of disability

The most widespread view of disability at the present time, at least in the Western world, is based upon the assumption that the difficulties disabled people experience are a direct result of their individual physical, sensory or intellectual impairments (Oliver and Sapey, 2006; French and Swain, 2008). Problems are thus viewed as residing *within* the individual. The individual model of disability is deeply ingrained and 'taken as given' in the medical, psychological and sociological literature. Even in the literature on the sociology of health and illness, disability as a social problem is rarely acknowledged (Barnes and Mercer, 1996; Swain et al., 2003).

The medical model can be regarded as a subcategory of the overarching individual model of disability where disability is conceived as part of the disease process, abnormality and individual tragedy – something that happens to unfortunate individuals on a more or less random basis. Treatment, in turn, is based upon the idea that the problem resides within the individual and must be overcome by the individual's own efforts. Disabled people have, for example, been critical of the countless hours they have spent attempting to learn to walk or talk at the expense of their education and leisure (Oliver, 1993b; French and Swain, 2008). According to this perception of disability, disabled people have something wrong with them that needs to be corrected so that they can be as much like other people as possible.

The predominance of medicine in the lives of disabled people, especially when they are young, has been criticized by disabled people. Mason and Rieser state:

> For young people the disadvantages of medical treatment need to be weighted against the possible advantages. Children are not usually asked if they want speech therapy, physiotherapy, orthopaedic surgery, hospitalisation, drugs or cumbersome and ugly 'aids and appliances'. We are not asked whether we want to be put on daily regimes or programmes which use hours of precious play-time. All these things are just imposed on us with the assumption that we share our parents' or therapists' desire for us to be more 'normal' at all costs. We are not even consulted as adults as to whether we think those things had been necessary or useful. (1992, p. 82)

Individualistic definitions of disability certainly have the potential to do serious harm. The medicalization of learning disability, whereby people were institutionalized and abused, is one example (Potts and Fido, 1991; Atkinson et al., 2000). Other examples are the practice of oralism, where deaf children were prevented from using sign language and punished for using it (Humphries and Gordon, 1992; Dimmock, 1993), and 'sight-saving' schools where visually impaired children were prevented from using their sight and, in consequence, were denied a full education (French, 2005). Research about disabled people is also underpinned by the individual model. It is usually medical or psychological in orientation, rather than social and political, which has serious implications for disabled people as research knowledge underpins both policy and practice (Barnes and Mercer, 1997; Swain and French, 2004).

None of these arguments imply that considering the medical or individual needs of disabled individuals is wrong. Disabled people, like everyone else, require an excellent health and social care service that may free them of symptoms, assist with independence and even save their lives. Insulin, for instance, has saved the lives of people with diabetes and an in-dwelling shunt has saved the lives of babies with hydrocephalus. Similarly, visually impaired people with glaucoma may have their sight preserved by eye drops or surgery and social assistance may enable disabled people to live fuller lives. The problem with the individual model is that it has been used to interpret disabled people's needs and to dominate their lives. The effect of the physical, attitudinal and social environment on disabled people has been largely ignored or regarded as relatively fixed, which has maintained the status quo and kept disabled people in their disadvantaged state within society (Oliver and Sapey, 2006). Thus the onus has been on disabled people to adapt to a disabling environment (Swain, French, Barnes et al., 2004). This is something that disabled people have increasingly joined forces to challenge. As Oliver states:

The disability movement throughout the world is rejecting approaches based upon the restoration of normality and insisting on approaches based upon the celebration of difference. (1996a, p. 44)

The social model of disability

The social model of disability is often referred to as the 'barriers approach' where disability is viewed not in terms of the individual's impairment, but in terms of environmental, structural, and attitudinal barriers which impinge upon the lives of disabled people and which have the potential to impede their inclusion and progress in many areas of life, including employment, education, housing and leisure, unless they are minimized or removed (Oliver, 1996a). The social model of disability has arisen from the thinking, writings and growing cultural identity of disabled people themselves (Swain, French, Barnes et al., 2004).

The definition of impairment and disability shown in Box 1.2 is that of the Union of the Physically Impaired Against Segregation (UPIAS), which was an early radical group of the Disabled People's Movement. Its major importance is that it breaks the causal link between impairment and disability.

 Box 1.2 **Impairment and disability**

Impairment

'Lacking part or all of a limb, or having a defective limb, organ or mechanism of the body.'

Disability

'The disadvantage or restriction of activity caused by a contemporary social organisation which takes no or little account of people who have physical impairments and thus excludes them from participation in the mainstream of social activities. Physical disability is therefore a particular form of social oppression.'

(UPIAS, 1976, p. 14)

The word 'physical' has now been removed from this definition so as to include people with learning difficulties and users of the mental health system. This and similar definitions break the connection between impairment and disability, which are viewed as separate entities with no causal link. This is similar to the distinction made between sex (a biological entity) and gender (a social entity) in the women's movement (Gove and Watt, 2004).

The World Health Organization's *International Classification of Impairments, Disabilities and Handicaps* (ICIDH) (1980) and the revised version (ICIDH-2) (2001) have been rejected by the Disabled People's Movement because, despite taking social and environmental factors into account, the meaning of disability is still underpinned by the individual model and the causal link between impairment and disability remains intact (Pfeiffer, 2000; Hurst, 2000).

Disability is viewed within the social model in terms of barriers (French, 2004a). There are three types of barriers, which all interact (see Box 1.3).

Box 1.3   **Disabling barriers**

- **Structural barriers** – which refer to the underlying norms, mores and ideologies of organizations and institutions, which are based on judgements of 'normality' and which are sustained by hierarchies of power.
- **Environmental barriers** – which refer to physical barriers within the environment, for example steps and cluttered pavements, and to lack of resources for disabled people, for example lack of Braille and lack of sign language interpreters. It also refers to the ways things are done which may exclude disabled people, for example the way meetings are conducted and the time allowed for tasks.
- **Attitudinal barriers** – which refer to the adverse attitudes and behaviour of people towards disabled people.

These three types of barriers interact to give rise to economic, political and cultural disadvantage at every level in society.

It can be seen that the social model of disability locates disability not within the individual disabled person, but within society. Thus the person who uses a wheelchair is not disabled by paralysis but by building design, lack of lifts, rigid work practices, and the attitudes and behaviour of others. Similarly, the visually impaired person is not disabled by lack of sight, but by lack of Braille and large print, cluttered pavements, and stereotypical ideas about blindness. Finkelstein (1998) has argued that non-disabled people would be equally disabled if the environment were not designed with their needs in mind, for example if the height of doorways only accommodated wheelchair users. Human beings fashion the world to suit their own capabilities and limitations and disabled people want nothing more than that.

The social model of disability highlights the social and political nature of disability. It has been formulated by the Disabled People's Movement and has gathered strength over the past thirty-five years as the movement has grown and developed. It contributed to the passing of the Disability Discrimination Act 1995 and subsequent changes to the built environment such as ramps and bleeper crossings. The social model of disability did not, however, arise in a vacuum. Radical groups, such as the National League of the Blind, which was founded in 1890 and affiliated to the TUC, protested about unemployment and campaigned for statutory assistance. The coming together of disabled people with different impairments has, however, been a fairly recent development that was necessary to build the Disabled People's Movement.

Challenges to the social model of disability

Over the years, a number of disabled people have pointed out some limitations of the social model of disability and have sought to extend it. Their major concern has been the neglect of impairment (Morris, 1991; Crow, 1996; Thomas, 2007; Hughes, 2009). Hughes and Paterson (1997) and Hughes (2004) have been critical of the neglect of the body in the social model of disability on the grounds that the body can be viewed in psychological, social, historical and cultural terms and is not, therefore, merely a biological entity. Just as height, weight, age, skin colour and physique have social and cultural dimensions, so too does impairment. Wendell (1997) draws parallels between the oppression of women and the oppression of disabled people, which is built around attitudes towards the body in patriarchal society – attitudes that Hughes and Paterson (1997) refer to as 'tyrannies of perfection'. Wendell (1997) believes that in a society that idealizes the body, physically disabled people are marginalized and that disabled women are the most likely to be affected, as women are judged by their bodies more than men. The fitness and health of the body are also greatly valued in our society today, which may serve to oppress disabled people, for example in their employment, if their bodies do not meet these ideals. Wendell explains:

> When you listen to this culture in a disabled body you hear how often physical health and vigour are talked about as if they were moral virtues. People constantly praise others for their 'energy', their stamina and their ability to work long hours ... when health is spoken of as a virtue, people who lack it are made to feel inadequate. (1997, p. 260)

Hughes and Paterson go as far as to argue that 'there is a powerful convergence between biomedicine and the social model of disability with respect to the body. Both treat it as a pre-social, inert, physical object' (1997, p. 329). They believe that impairment structures the experience of disabled people and that they encounter impairment and disability 'as part of a complex interpenetration of oppression and affliction' (1997, p. 335). Crow agrees, and states that, 'external disabling barriers may create social and economic disadvantage but our subjective experience of our bodies is also an integral part of our everyday reality' (1996, p. 210). In addition, Thomas (1999, 2007) believes that an undermining of disabled people's psycho-emotional well-being, which can be caused by both impairment and barriers within society, has been neglected within the social model and needs to be addressed.

Impairment cannot be divorced from social factors. It is frequently produced by poverty and poor working conditions and can be made worse by disabling barriers within society. Some impairments only arise when society changes. For instance, dyslexia was not labelled as an impairment before employment and social interaction made reading and writing necessary. Furthermore, the attitudes and personality of the disabled person can be important in deciding what is and what is not a barrier and how it should be addressed. In a study by French (2001) on the employment experiences of visually impaired physiotherapists, for instance, barriers were perceived and responded to differently even by people with the same type and level of impairment.

Crow (1996) is of the opinion that it has been necessary for disabled people to provide a clear, unambiguous model of disability to bring about political change. Admitting that there may be a negative side to having an impairment or being disabled, or highlighting problems that cannot be readily solved by social and environmental manipulation, may undermine the campaign. This, it is argued, has led to disabled activists ignoring impairment, which has become something of a taboo subject. As Hughes and Paterson state:

> [T]he social model has succeeded in shifting debates about disability from biomedically dominated agendas to discourses about politics and citizenship. However, debates about the body and impairment are beginning to re-emerge within the disability movement ... This is a highly contentious debate since it tugs – somewhat disconcertedly – at the key conceptual distinction which lies at the heart of the transformation of disability discourse from medical problems to emancipatory politics. (1997, p. 326)

One reason for the neglect of impairment by the Disabled People's Movement, and its concentration on disabling barriers, is that the latter has the potential to draw them together into a powerful political force. This is particularly important as the diversity of impairment is often used as a reason for leaving disabling barriers intact (Barnes, 1991). However, barrier removal is highly complex especially when considering conditions such as autism, mental health problems and severe learning difficulties. Indeed, it can be argued that the social model of disability has tended to concentrate on barriers experienced by people with physical and sensory impairments, which, though still highly complex, are easier to understand and remove. Nevertheless, the social model of disability has been used to change practice and improve the lives of disabled people with diverse impairments. Pound (2008), for instance, has used the insights of the social model of disability in her work with people with aphasia.

The representativeness of the Disabled People's Movement, and hence the consensus among disabled people concerning the meaning of disability, has also come under scrutiny. The Disabled People's Movement was initially fashioned by men, particularly men with motor impairments (Morris, 1991). This may be one reason why the more personal aspects of disability and impairment have been neglected. It has largely been feminists who have emphasized personal experience and its important role in political analyses. As Morris states:

> Like other political movements, the disability movement both in
> Britain and throughout the world, has tended to be dominated by men
> as both theoreticians and holders of important organisational posts.
> Both the movement and the development of a theory of disability has
> been the poorer for this as there has been an accompanying tendency
> to avoid confronting the personal experience of disability. (1991, p. 9)

Not all disabled people are well represented in the Disabled People's Movement, for example old people and people with learning and communication disabilities, and for this reason it has been accused of elitism and of failing to represent the views of all disabled people (Oliver, 1996a). In addition, some people in the deaf community do not regard themselves as disabled but as a linguistic minority (Ladd, 1990). Most disabled people are not actively involved in disability politics and some may view disability in a similar way to many non-disabled people – that is, as an individual problem. This has led to questions concerning the right of the Disabled People's Movement to represent the views and interests of disabled people. Bury states, for example, that 'disability theorists are themselves arguing a case which reflects the experiences of a small and unrepresentative minority of the disabled' (1997, p. 139). Oliver, however, challenges such arguments. He states:

> In representative democracies, representation is always less than perfect.
> The Conservative Party does not represent all conservative voters nor
> does the British Medical Association represent all doctors ... and yet
> the right of the Disability Movement to represent disabled people is
> continually questioned by politicians, policy makers and professionals
> alike ... if the legitimate claims of the movement to represent the
> interests of disabled people are denied, who else will represent our
> interests – doctors? politicians? the Royal Institutes and Associations?
> (1996b, p. 150)

Proponents of the social model of disability have also been accused of failing to take account of multiple and simultaneous oppression, for example that regarding black disabled people, disabled women and lesbian and gay disabled people (Stuart, 1993; Vernon, 1996; Banton and Singh, 2004.) These issues are, however, slowly being addressed and their neglect can be explained, at least in part, in terms of the Disabled People's Movement being a young social movement.

It is our view that the social model of disability will continually undergo revisions and developments as disabled people constructively debate the best ways to theorize disability through their writings, conferences and organizations. It is important to realize, however, that although some improvement in barrier removal has occurred the process has only just began. It is still a daily experience for me (Sally), as a visually impaired person, to find steps without white lines, busy roads without crossings, hazardous objects on pavements and inaccessible information. The central message of the Disabled People's Movement, that disabled people are disabled by barriers outside themselves, is, therefore, no less important today than when the social model of disability was formulated.

Long term conditions

The term 'long term condition' is now in common use and is synonymous with the medical terms 'chronic illness' and 'chronic disease', which derive from the Greek 'chronos' meaning 'lasting a long time'. 'Acute illness' is the opposite of 'chronic illness' and is short term, rapid in onset, intense and potentially curable but sometimes fatal – examples are pneumonia and meningitis. The terms 'chronic' and 'acute' are also applied to symptoms, for instance acute and chronic pain, and to mental health problems, where no obvious disease process may be present, for instance acute and chronic schizophrenia and depression.

The term 'long term conditions' is now widely used in medical, research and educational circles. For instance, the University of West England has a 'Long Term Conditions' research programme, the University of Northumbria has a 'Disability and Long Term Conditions' research programme and the University of Nottingham awards a certificate in 'Long Term Conditions'. Various government documents also use this term, for instance the *National Service Framework for Long Term Conditions* (DH, 2005a) and *Supporting People with Long Term Conditions* (DH, 2007c).

Box 1.4 offers various definitions of 'long term conditions' and 'chronic illness and disease' from government and other sources.

Box 1.4	What is a 'long term condition'?

'Long term conditions require ongoing medical care, limit what people can do and are likely to last more than a year.'
(NHS Scotland, www.sehd.scot.nhs.uk)

'A long term condition is one that can not be cured but can be managed through medication and/or therapy.'
(DH, Long Term Conditions, www.dh.gov.uk)

'Chronic diseases are diseases which current medical intervention can only control but not cure. The life of a person with a chronic condition is forever altered. There is no return to normal.'
(Chronic Disease Management: a compendium of information, DH, 2004a, p. 7)

'[Chronic illness is] an illness that is permanent or lasts a long time. It may get slowly worse over time. It may lead to death or it may finally go away. It may cause permanent changes to the body. It will certainly affect the person's quality of life.'
(Chronic Illness Alliance, www.chronicillness.org.au)

Thomas regards chronic illness as a category of impairment. She states:

'Impairments may be life-long or acquired, physical or mental. This approach to impairment is clearly inclusive of diseases that are commonly referred to as "chronic illnesses".'
(Thomas, 2007, p. 14)

The Disability Discrimination Act 1995, in contrast, incorporates impairments and 'long term conditions' within the term 'disability', which is defined as:

'A physical or mental impairment which has a substantial and long term adverse effect on a person's ability to carry out normal day to day activities.'

This adds another layer of confusion, as the term 'disability' in this Act would, as we discussed above, be defined as 'impairment' by the Disabled People's Movement. 'Disability', under the Disability Discrimination Act, includes such conditions as cancer, diabetes, HIV, severe allergies and facial deformity.

Although these definitions are somewhat contradictory, the main features of long term or chronic conditions appear to be that they are long lasting or recurrent, amenable to medical intervention, yet not usually curable, and possibly, though not necessarily, progressive and permanent. They also tend to limit what people can do, which is viewed, in these definitions, in negative terms such as reducing the quality of life.

Most disease in the Western world is chronic and some, for instance AIDS and various forms of cancer, have become chronic as medical intervention has improved. Chronic diseases, such as asthma, rheumatoid arthritis, multiple sclerosis and schizophrenia can, however, have acute episodes. Chronic disease is associated with old age, though by no means entirely; for instance haemophilia, diabetes, schizophrenia, asthma and epilepsy are all defined as chronic diseases yet affect young people. Old age is, however, frequently associated with more than one chronic disease. Conditions such as paraplegia and cerebral palsy are not usually classed as long term or chronic conditions, possibly because there is usually no disease process present, they are not obviously progressive and are not directly associated with illness.

The present concern with long term conditions has probably come about because of the emphasis given to acute medical conditions since the founding of the NHS. Most disease in the Western world is now chronic and yet acute medicine has been deemed more important with disproportionate resources being used to support it (Blakemore and Johnson, 2009). Conditions such as schizophrenia and depression, which 'long term conditions' tends to incorporate, have also been neglected. In this sense the current emphasis on chronic conditions can be welcomed. However, 'long term conditions' is a confusing, and some would say divisive, term to use as an alternative to, or alongside, disability. Many disabled people have their impairments for a lifetime and, as we discussed above, have fought a long political battle to distinguish 'impairment' from 'disability' in order to move disability from a medical to a social and political understanding. Many disabled people, including those who would be classified as having a chronic illness, have also fought hard to distance themselves from the idea that they are ill or in need of medical ministration which may, for instance, have implications for gaining employment (Davis, 2004). Some disabled people have chronic diseases but view the problems they encounter as external to themselves and originating within a disabling society where their citizenship is denied.

It is worthy of note, that the term 'long term conditions' is promoted by government and powerful institutions such as universities, rather than disabled people themselves, which may be an attempt to depoliticize disability. As Swain et al. state, 'labels are usually bestowed by those who have power and authority on those who do not' (2003, p. 12). However, because of the negative connotations of disability that are still prevalent within society, some people prefer to think of themselves as having 'long term conditions' rather than being disabled.

Box 1.5	**Am I Disabled?**

In my late 40s I, John, developed Type 1 diabetes. It began with sores in my mouth and throat and an incredible thirst that I doused with copious amounts of fruit juice, which had a positive side as I enjoy fruit juice. After about a month I visited the GP, having no inkling of what was immediately obvious to him, that I had diabetes. He told me that I had 'sugar coming out of my ears'. At the diabetic clinic I was put on injections of insulin and shown how to measure my blood sugar levels. The consultant reassured me that I could lead a normal life and that many of his patients did the Great North Run. This was not particularly effective reassurance as I do not desire normality and being a marathon runner is not on my wish list.

So I am certainly diabetic; I am impaired but am I disabled? By what criteria might I be categorized as disabled? Severity of impairment is clearly a factor. Besides diabetes itself, the list of dangers of possible further impairments, including heart problems, kidney problems, circulation problems, visual impairment (diabetic retinopathy), impotence and so on, is frightening. Yet this is questionable as a criterion for being categorized as disabled. I am short and long-sighted but this is easily corrected by glasses and would not categorize me as disabled. So, if my blood sugar levels are well controlled by insulin, as they generally are, am I therefore non-disabled? Would others view me as disabled? Many disabled people, it seems, do. The reaction of a disabled friend, being told I have diabetes, was that she was pleased that I had 'come over to the other side'. The views of non-disabled people, however, are generally that I am non-disabled. By this criterion I seem to sit in both camps; seen as disabled by disabled people, and non-disabled by non-disabled people.

What about the legal situation? According to the Disability Discrimination Act, for instance, I am disabled. This can be an important criterion for some disabled people, for instance to be registered as blind or partially sighted can be a step across the non-disabled/disabled divide and may entitle the person to various benefits.

Am I discriminated against because I am impaired? This is a key criterion within the social model of disability. There are certain things that can be pointed to such as the general lack of knowledge about diabetes. One work colleague offered to help me with my injections – an offer I declined. However, it is difficult for me to point to specific instances where I have experienced discrimination. For instance, I have no access problems. Occasionally I have come across 'no food or drink allowed' signs but this has been easily overcome by stating that I have diabetes.

So am I disabled? Personally speaking my answer is that, yes, I am.

I have three main reasons for affirming a disabled identity. The first is that I am certainly impaired. I also have a long-term health condition but find this meaningful only as a description of my impairment and meaningless as a label. The second is that I have to deal regularly with professional and service providers. Without going into detail, this is an ongoing battle within service user/provider power relations. Almost every time I have my annual check-up and follow-ups I have a different doctor. I get conflicting information. One doctor told me that I am hypoglycaemic whenever my blood sugar levels are below 4 (which is quite often), but another doctor denied this. Another doctor put me on statins to reduce my cholesterol levels. Following this, I experienced disastrous side effects including loss of appetite, nausea and tinnitus. I took myself off the statins and the next doctor told me I was quite right to do so and that he didn't know why I had been put on them in the first place. Furthermore, my driving licence has to be renewed every three years and requires a report from my GP. My third reason is simply that I identify with disabled people and I am accepted by disabled people as disabled. This for me is a significant statement: I am disabled and I stand (metaphorically speaking!) with disabled people.

Am I disabled?

I, Sally, was born with a visual impairment caused by the absence of the macula on the retina of both eyes. The macula is a small group of cells (cones) which are responsible for visual acuity, central vision and colour vision. The visual impairment that results from this condition is severe and cannot be corrected. I am colour-blind, can barely read the top letter of the optician's chart with maximum correction and have no central vision. I also see very little in sunlight. Although I have very useful vision, I am registered blind and use visual aids such as strong magnifying glasses and a monocular (small telescope). I use a white stick in certain situations, such as crossing roads, getting through crowds and when I need help, and I am eligible for a guide dog. The condition is non-progressive, with no medical treatment available. It is not associated with pain or any symptoms of illness. Although I have been visually impaired all my life, it has never been termed a 'long term condition'.

I have always considered myself to be disabled. Until I was nine, I attended a mainstream school – a tiny one with just 30 pupils – but my mother, aware that I would eventually be sent to a special residential school, prepared me for this prospect from an early age and was careful to explain why I would have to go. I knew I was different from other children as I found some things that they found easy, difficult or impossible and I was able to interpret this as due to lack of sight. Ophthalmologists were very influential in sending me to a special residential school for visually impaired children even though I was managing well in my little mainstream school.

At the special school I attended we were regularly seen by an ophthalmologist but, as there was no medical treatment possible for my impairment (or for that of most of the other children), nothing of any consequence resulted. I remember repeatedly saying that I could not see in the sunshine but tinted lenses (which some of the other children had) were always denied and it was not until I left school, and could take matters into my own hands, that I discovered how helpful they would be. Contact lenses and low vision aids were both in their infancy at this time and we were used as experimental subjects – rarely to our advantage. There was no consultation with us nor recognition of our own considerable experience of visual impairment. After leaving school, the only time I saw ophthalmologists was in their 'gate-keeper' role to obtain visual aids from the NHS. This, however, was so time-consuming and frustrating that for many years I have purchased my own – an option that would not be available to all visually impaired people, as they are expensive.

The experience of spending much of my childhood in blindness institutions has been an important part of my lifelong identity. We were very cut off from the 'normal' world, which we only ventured into during holiday times. This was continued, to some extent, when I trained at a special physiotherapy college for visually impaired students. In these segregated situations, strong friendships were forged which have lasted throughout my life. I feel part of a community where understanding, loyalty and trust are high.

I am aware of encountering barriers every day of my life which include roads I cannot cross, notices I cannot read, difficulties in finding buildings and not being able to recognize people. I get around well but it takes considerable concentration, energy and effort. Some of these barriers could be rectified relatively easily – and some improvements have been made – but other problems, for example the dazzling sunlight, taking longer to do some things such as read and not being able to recognize people, are less easy to overcome. However, some people are more forthcoming than others at 'making themselves known' and the recent commercial development of sunglasses that fit over ordinary glasses and which screen out light from the top and the sides has enhanced my sight and functioning more than any medical consultation or optician's prescription ever has.

I have never had any doubt that I am disabled and have only occasionally had difficulty convincing other people that I am.

The tragedy model of disability

The tragedy model, as its name implies, depicts impairment and disability as a personal, individual tragedy rather than a social and political issue. As French and Swain state:

> In the personal tragedy theory, disability, or rather impairment – which is equated with disability – is thought to strike individuals at random, causing suffering and blighting lives. (2004, p. 34)

The tragedy model portrays disability as a biological condition and a limitation' (Saxton, 2000), 'as a deficit, a personal burden and a tragedy' (Wilder 2006, p. 2), as an enemy (M. Mason, 2000), as 'abject and abhorrent' (Darke 2004, p. 103), and as '"abnormal" and something to be avoided at all costs' (Oliver and Barnes, 1998, p. 66). Disabled people are perceived as being robbed of any enjoyment in life and as a burden to society (Saxton, 2000). Parens and Asch state:

> There are many widely accepted beliefs about what life with disability is like for children and their families ... They include assumptions that people with disabilities lead lives of relentless agony and frustration and that most marriages break up under the strain of having a child with a disability. (2000, p. 20)

Despite some variation, the tragedy view of disability is widespread across cultures (Ingstad and Reynolds Whyte, 1995; Stone, 1999a) and throughout history (Stiker, 1997; Longmore and Umanski, 2001; Borsay, 2005) and remains so entrenched in society today it has become an ideology. Oliver explains that:

> [I]deologies are so deeply embedded in social consciousness generally that they become 'facts'; they are naturalised. Thus everyone knows that disability is a personal tragedy for individuals so 'affected'; hence ideology becomes common sense. (1993a, p. 50)

Box 1.6	The impact of the tragedy model on disabled children

Many disabled children grow up with parents who believe that impairment is a tragedy. This can result in a lowering of self-esteem and in the denial of their needs and an important part of their identity. Katrina, a visually impaired woman, recalled:

> 'My mother never accepted me, ever. She couldn't cope with the fact that she had a disabled child. She denied it and expected me to be like everyone else ... even when she had reached old age she hadn't accepted it.'
> (French et al., 2006, p. 321)

Abelow Hedley recalls her own similar reaction to the birth of her daughter who has achondroplasia (restricted growth):

> 'When our LilyClaire was born ten years ago, everything was confusion: how to react, how to proceed, what to do. As the frantic first days unfolded it seemed that all we could focus on was how to repair the flaws, and we would listen to anyone from a faith healer to a surgeon if we thought that there was a "fix" for her in it. I remember thinking: we can put men in space, surely we can fix this.'
> (2006, p. 43)

Health and social care professionals also have a tendency to regard impairment as tragic and undesirable and their power within society has perpetuated this view (French and Swain, 2001). As Morris, a woman born with a Y chromosome and mixed reproductive organs states, 'my diagnosis was considered a tragic mistake of nature by both my physicians and my parents' (2006, p. 4).

The words used to describe disabled people are invariably negative or passive. Many words in common use, for example short-sighted, meaning lack of insight, show how deeply rooted negative perceptions of disability are. The very words 'disabled' (not able) and 'invalid' (not valid) indicate the lowly status disabled people have within society. This denigration and misrepresentation of disabled people in language is very widespread across the world. Stone (1999b), for instance, found similar conceptions of disabled people in her studies of ancient Chinese script. For example, the character for 'blind' comprises the characters for 'eye' and 'drum', depicting blind people as musicians, and the character for physical deformity contains that of a worm.

Descriptions of disabled people frequently have tragic overtones, for example 'sufferers' and 'victims'. Disabled people are often spoken of as a homogeneous group rather than as individuals, for example 'the disabled' and 'the blind'. This is reflected in the titles of many charities such as the Guide Dogs for the Blind Association and Riding for the Disabled – although some have recently changed, for example the Royal National Institute for the Blind has become the Royal National Institute of Blind People – with 'of' rather than 'for' implying that blind people are now substantially involved in running the organization. Disabled people are repeatedly labelled by their impairments ('he's a paraplegic', 'she's an amputee') as if the 'tragedy' of impairment renders everything else about them irrelevant and gives them, as Goffman (1963) explained, a 'master status'. This language also stereotypes disabled people rather than regarding them as unique individuals.

The labels ascribed to disabled people sometimes appear, on the surface, to be very positive. For instance, disabled people may be described as cheerful, clever and courageous: indeed, it is not unusual for disabled people to be regarded as courageous simply for living with an impairment – as television programmes such as *Children of Courage* and *Children in Need* illustrate. The assumption embedded within these 'positive' labels is that disabled people are a group 'apart' who are largely incapable of achieving everyday tasks or attaining a positive state of mind so that when they do it is a huge surprise. As a blind physiotherapist remarked:

'Many people are surprised that we can actually do the job and be good at it. I think it's because they think we are fairly good if we can put one foot in front of the other!' (French, 1990, p. 3)

In a similar way, parents of disabled children are often perceived as extraordinary and almost saintly, and are commended for 'making light' of disability. Kent, a blind woman states, 'As I was growing up people called my parents "wonderful". They were praised for raising me "like a normal child"' (2000, p. 57).

The tragedy model assumes that impairment and disability are about loss (with no possibility of gain) and that disabled people, without exception, want to be other than as they are (Swain et al., 2003). It is not surprising, therefore, that a central tenet of the tragedy model, as well as the individual model, is that disabled people should strive to be 'normal' and 'independent', whatever the cost to themselves, in order to reduce the 'tragedy' that has befallen both them and their families (French, 1994). Lapper, who was born with no arms and short legs, recalls the obsession with 'normality' at the residential home and school she attended:

> 'The staff were very keen that we all became proficient in the use of our artificial limbs. The add-on limbs were considered a fundamental aspect of our being able to function properly and fulfil the ultimate aim of the home … they had great faith in those artificial limbs and thought that if we would only practice and use them regularly we would soon be picking up even the most delicate items without breaking or damaging them. But we all instinctively knew those sorry bits of metal were never going to fulfil their hoped-for potential.'
> (2005, p. 35)

Similarly, a disabled woman, talking of her experiences as a patient, states:

> 'What concerns me most of all is this focus on trying to make me "normal". I get that from all the therapists … They had a massive case conference before the adaptations – it was a case of "how normal can we make her first? Are the adaptations necessary?"' (French 2004b, p. 203)

Charities have been, and are, powerful portrayers of impairment and disability and are strongly rooted in the tragedy model. The images and language that are used have built upon, promoted and helped to create stereotypes of disabled people as dependent and tragic (Taylor, 2008). Drake (1996) contends that charity advertising presents impairment as undesirable and a personal misfortune and disabled people as helpless, dependent and pitiable and Barnes believes that, 'By emphasising the "tragedy" of disability these advertisements perpetuate the assumption that living with impairment is a life shattering experience' (1994, p. 38). Figure 1.1 shows an example of charity advertising from the Muscular Dystrophy Campaign, which depicts a young boy sitting in a wheelchair with his hands clasped and a very sad expression on his face. You will note that the photograph is in black and white with a featureless background and the boy is completely alone. The slogan, which likens his wheelchair to a pushchair, emphasizes his dependency and implies that a wheelchair is an undesirable object.

This view of disability has now been seriously challenged by the collective voice of disabled people and charity advertising has become more positive in recent years. On the current website of the Muscular Dystrophy Campaign there is plenty of colour and lots of smiling faces (www.muscular-dystrophy.org).

The media (for instance television, radio, newspapers and magazines) are also powerful in portraying disability and impairment and are deeply rooted in the tragedy model (Taylor, 2008). Barnes et al. (1999) contend that televi-

Figure 1.1	An example of charity advertising

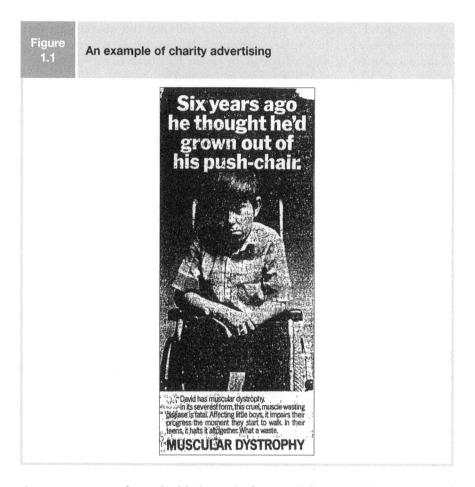

Six years ago he thought he'd grown out of his push-chair.

David has muscular dystrophy. In its severest form, this cruel, muscle-wasting disease is fatal. Affecting little boys, it impairs their progress the moment they start to walk. In their teens, it halts it altogether. What a waste.

MUSCULAR DYSTROPHY

sion programmes about disabled people focus mainly on medicine, cure and 'special achievements' and that disabled people are depicted as criminal, powerless and pathetic in order to, 'contribute to an atmosphere of mystery, deprivation and menace' (1999, p. 192). Barnes states:

> [D]isability in the mass media is extremely negative. Disabling stereotypes which medicalise, patronise, criminalise and dehumanise disabled people abound in books, films, on television and in the press. They form the bedrock on which the attitudes towards, assumptions about and expectations of disabled people are based. (1994, p. 45)

Darke considers that, 'The representation of disability in the media in the last ten years is pretty much the same as it has always been: clichéd, stereotyped and archetypal' (2004, p. 100).

Throughout history and across cultures, disabled people have experienced persecution, abuse and discrimination (Oliver and Barnes, 1998; Stiker, 1997). The Romans, for example, practised infanticide on disabled infants and in medieval Europe disability was linked with evil and witchcraft, which frequently led to murder of those convicted (Barnes, 1994). A stark example of the persecution of disabled people in recent European history is the Nazi regime of the 1930s and 1940s, which was fuelled by the eugenic movement. The word 'eugenics', which means 'well born', was coined by Sir Francis Galton in 1869. The eugenics movement advocated 'improving the human race' by the sterilization, incarceration, surveillance and elimination of those deemed to be 'unfit' (Snyder and Mitchell, 2006). Such ideas and practices were prevalent throughout Europe at this time and were supported by politicians of all persuasions as well as leading doctors and scientists (Kerr and Shakespeare, 2002; Evans, 2004). Micheline Mason states:

> The overall image that was created of disabled people was of being a burden that society could not afford. This reached its peak in Germany in the late 1930s when Hitler's Third Reich issued leaflets comparing the costs of caring for a disabled child with a 'normal' child, proclaiming them to be 'useless eaters'. (2000, p. 29)

Approximately 375,000 disabled people were sterilized by the Nazi regime between 1933 and 1939, including those with learning difficulties, epilepsy, mental health problems and hereditary deafness and blindness (Kerr and Shakespeare, 2002). Sterilization Acts were passed in many countries at this time including Finland, Iceland, Sweden, Norway, Denmark, Switzerland, some states of the USA and Japan (Evans, 2004). Many of these countries continued sterilizing disabled people until the 1970s and, in the case of Japan, until 1996 (Russell, 1998).

Evans (2004) estimates that approximately three-quarters of a million disabled people were murdered by the Nazi regime, including those with cleft lips, stutters and minor deformities. So many deaf people were sterilized or murdered that deaf culture in Germany was almost obliterated (Dimmock, 1993; Evans, 2004). Disabled people were also subjected to brutal experimentation before they were killed (Evans, 2004). It has only been in recent times, however, that the plight of disabled people under the Nazis has been acknowledged (Morris, 1991). Kerr and Shakespeare state that:

> A key point to remember about Nazi euthanasia is the central involvement of scientists and doctors. It is impossible to write off what happened as the aberrant behaviour of a group of thugs, fanatics and ideologues. It was doctors, not SS men, who killed in the euthanasia centres or on the children's wards. Prejudice against disabled people, and racial minorities, was enshrined in the scientific orthodoxy of the early twentieth century, and most of those involved in killing and sterilising disabled people felt that they were performing a service both to society and even the individuals themselves. (2002, pp. 44–5)

Box
1.7 **Genetic medicine today**

It can be argued that these negative attitudes and behaviours towards disabled people, underpinned by the tragedy model, still operate in society today with practices such as genetic testing, genetic counselling, abortion of impaired foetuses, genetic engineering and euthanasia of disabled people. The Royal College of Obstetricians and Gynaecologists has recently called upon the working party of the Nuffield Council on Bioethics to use active euthanasia on seriously impaired babies, such as those with spina bifida, and has also called for a discussion on the costs of bringing up a severely disabled child (Choppin, 2006; Nuffield Council on Bioethics, 2006). Technology is already in place to screen out impaired foetuses. In a recent newspaper article (Smith, 2006), the mother of twins who undertook this technology to avoid having children with cystic fibrosis states, 'they are designer babies but they are designed for the good of mankind.' Such ideas are being challenged by various groups of disabled people, including the UK group Not Dead Yet, who are opposed to euthanasia and eugenics

Micheline Mason (2000) believes that, 'Human genetic engineering is a continuation in the eugenicist belief in social control through manipulation of the gene pool' (p. 24) and that, 'covert eugenic policies still dominate medical practices' (p. 32). Asch agrees that:

'the vast majority of theorists and health professionals still argue that prenatal testing, followed by pregnancy termination if an impairment is detected, promotes family well-being and the public health. To them it is simply one more legitimate method of averting disability in the world.' (2001, p. 306)

Modern genetic medicine has distanced itself from the ideas of eugenics but it can be argued that political and ethical decision making about who should live and who should die has merely been transferred from the state to the family. Hampton (2005) talks of 'family genetics' and believes that it leads to choices that would have been approved of by early eugenicists. He states that, 'We end up with a situation whereupon a decision is made – be it by an individual or committee – to control who gets born' (2005, p. 556). Duster (1990) talks about 'back door eugenics' while Kitcher (1996) uses the terms 'Laissez-faire eugenics' and 'consumer eugenics'. Appleyard is forthright in stating that, 'The free market takes over where Nazism left off' (1999, p. 86). Disabled People's International (DPI), when talking about the abortion of impaired foetuses, state that:

This is not about treating illness or impairment but eliminating or manipulating foetuses which may not be acceptable for a variety of reasons. These technologies are, therefore, opening the door to a new eugenics which directly threatens our human rights. (DPI, 2000, p. 3)

They warn that the link between eugenics and genetics poses a threat to everybody, not just disabled people, because everybody has genetic 'flaws' of some kind that will eventually become apparent when they are ill. They also believe that:

> Our experience as disabled people places us in a unique position to contribute to a comprehensive, ethical discourse leading to scientific development which respects and affirms the essential diversity of human kind. (DPI, 2000, p. 4)

One of the reasons why large numbers of impaired foetuses are aborted is that life for disabled people is generally thought to be unbearable – literally worse than death. Yet disabled people do not generally consider their lives in that way and, as Shakespeare states, 'The idea of disability as automatically equivalent to ... suffering cannot be sustained empirically ... It would be untrue to claim that people with impairments suffer while people without impairments do not' (Shakespeare, 2008, p. 99).

In British law, abortion is prohibited after 24 weeks of pregnancy except when the foetus is 'seriously handicapped', when no upper limit is stipulated (Kerr and Shakespeare, 2002). There is, however, much evidence from disabled people which shows that 'serious' impairment is not incompatible with happiness and a good quality of life. People who become disabled do often regard it as a tragedy initially but tend to adjust psychologically over time. As Bassett, a medical doctor, explains:

> 'I become quadriplegic following a sporting accident 17 years ago. I was ventilator dependent for a while and said to people "I wish I was dead". I am now extraordinarily glad that assisted dying was not legal. I think the first difficulty I faced is that, like many people, I had a terribly negative image of disability. When you suddenly become severely disabled you still have that viewpoint.' (DRC, 2006, p. 4)

The affirmative model of disability

As noted above, both authors of this book are disabled, Sally from birth and John since middle age, yet neither of us identifies with the notion that our lives are tragic or 'lesser' because of our impairments. In 2000, we formulated the affirmative model of disability, which is in direct opposition to the tragedy model (Swain and French, 2000). This was a response to our own personal experience of disability and that of many other disabled people who view their lives in positive terms rather than in terms of tragedy. This is illustrated in the following quotations from disabled people from many we could have chosen. The first is from a young French woman in the early 19th century which shows that feeling neutral or good about disability is nothing new.

Box 1.8 **Feeling good about disability**

'I have just reached my twenty-second year, and I still don't remember ever forming a single regret concerning the loss of my eyes, a loss that seems to me to be of little importance ... people who see tell me "You don't have the slightest understanding of treasures you have never known" ... which, however, does nothing to persuade me that I am unhappy.'
(Husson, 2001, p. 16)

'I do not wish for a cure for Asperger's Syndrome. What I wish for is a cure for the common ill that pervades too many lives, the ill that makes people compare themselves to a normal that is measured in terms of perfect and absolute standards, most of which are impossible for anyone to reach.'
(Halliday Wiley, 1999, p.96)

'I cannot wish that I had never contracted ME, because it has made me a different person, a person I am glad to be, would not want to miss being and could not relinquish even if I were cured.'
(Wendell, 1996, p. 83)

'I am never going to be able to conform to society's requirements and I am thrilled because I am blissfully released from all that crap. That's the liberation of disfigurement.'
(Shakespeare et al., 1996 p. 81)

'I can't imagine being hearing, I'd need a psychiatrist, I'd need a speech therapist, I'd need some new friends, I'd lose all my old friends, I'd lose my job ... It really hits hearing people that a deaf person doesn't want to become hearing. I am what I am.'
(Shakespeare et al., 1996 p. 184)

'There's nothing about my old life I miss at all, apart from being able to play my guitar. I've discovered that I have an extremely strong marriage and I get far more satisfaction from my work as a counsellor than from any other job I've had. I'm as confident now as I've ever been and my life is so much richer. I've always been a positive person and having a stroke didn't change that.'
(Boazman, 2002 p. 94)

A major theme in the quotations is that being disabled is not necessarily viewed as a problem and that life may become better or be just as good following disablement by the opening of different opportunities, discoveries and insights. None of this is to imply that disability is *never* viewed as a tragedy by disabled people but to challenge the idea that it inevitably is. Neither does the affirmative model deny that living in a disabling environment can be difficult and frustrating. Although the social model of disability – involving changes to the environment and people's behaviour – is relatively easy to grasp, the idea that disability is something to be embraced and celebrated is, we have found, more difficult for non-disabled people to accept.

| Figure 1.2 | Examples of disability art |

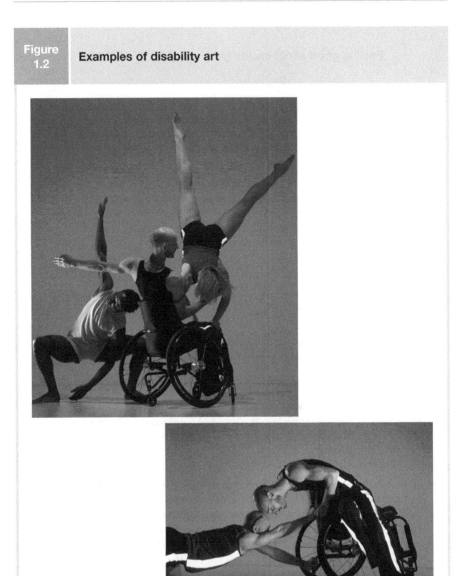

The photographs above are examples of disability art. They show disabled people mixing with others and engaging in creative activity by using their bodies and their wheelchairs. This is in direct contrast to the sad, despondent image of the boy with muscular dystrophy, depicted in Figure 1.1.

Photographer: Hugo Glendinning

Source: Candoco Dance Company (www.candoco.co.uk). Reproduced with kind permission

An important element in the struggle of disabled people for equality and social justice is the disability arts movement. Barnes et al. define disability arts as:

the development of shared cultural meanings and the collective expression of the experience of disability and struggle. It entails using art to expose the discrimination and prejudice disabled people face and to generate group consciousness and solidarity. Disability cabarets can empower people in much the same way as going on a direct action demonstration. (1999, pp. 205–6)

Disability arts is a well-established branch of the Disabled People's Movement. A wide variety of activities are encompassed within disability arts including theatre, dance, poetry, photography, comedy, music and visual art. Although disability arts is concerned with gaining access for disabled people to mainstream artistic facilities and opportunities, its main function is to communicate the distinctive history, skills, customs, experiences and concerns of disabled people, which many believe constitute a distinctive life-style and culture (Vasey, 1992). Disability arts gives disabled individuals the opportunity to express their views and experiences of impairment and disability, which often run counter to mainstream ideas and stereotypes. A central feature of disability arts is, however, collective experience. Disabled people are increasingly coming together to help each other express themselves in art and to share information and ideas.

Disability art is a political as well as an artistic endeavour. It involves making the implicit theories of disability explicit, by exposing the derogatory nature of disablist images and stereotypes and challenging negative attitudes, discrimination and oppression. Through their art, disabled people are promoting very different images of disability. Oliver and Barnes (1998) believe that disability arts produce, at one and the same time, a culture of resistance and celebration.

Implications for policy and practice

Throughout this book we will discuss and examine ways in which the social model and the affirmative model of disability may be put into practice in health and social care. It is necessary to point out, however, that these models are not models of professional intervention. They are, in essence, models of 'the problem' (that is, the disabling society and the dominant presumptions about disabled people and their lives as being tragic). The social and affirmative models of disability provide general principles for the practice of health and social care but are not, in themselves, blueprints for health and social care practice.

Rather than the social model being adopted by health and social care professionals as a foundation for practice, it should be viewed as providing fundamental challenges to generate critical reflection. As Clark, talking about occupational therapy, states 'There is a need to understand the nature of the arguments posed by the disability movement, even if one does not fully accept them, so as to reflect critically on our clinical practice' (2006, p. 243). Critical reflection is vitally important or the principles of the social model of disability can easily become distorted and misunderstood. For instance, taking a 'holistic' approach to health and social care may simply mean extending the individual model to more and more areas of the disabled person's life (French, 2004a).

Applying the social model of disability to practice involves taking a political stand to the situation of disabled people. Many disabled people have criticized the current apolitical stance of health and social care professionals, which, they claim, maintains the status quo. Davis (2004), a disabled activist, for instance, is fervent in his criticism of health professionals' lack of interest and involvement in the disability rights agenda. Similar critiques have been voiced by sociologists such as Illich (1976) and McKnight (1995) and feminists such as Doyal (1991).

Ballantyne and Muir (2008) set out their responses, as occupational therapy educators, to the social and affirmative model of disability and impairment. They argue that if the occupational therapy profession is to change in response to the social model and the affirmative model of disability, then a change of policy is required from the top of the profession. They do not believe that it is possible for individual practitioners to make changes of any magnitude because they are limited by the culture in which they work and the overall policy directives.

Ballantyne and Muir (2008) advocate working with disabled people in an equal partnership in order to bring about social and political change and, in so doing, move away from a client-based model of service towards a citizen-based model where service users are involved in the formulation and running of the services themselves at all stages, including the production of knowledge about what disability is and what services, if any, are required. They believe that, although some of the traditional skills of practitioners are likely to remain useful, professionals need to join disabled people in their ongoing quest for full citizenship and to look outwards to the disabling society. They also need to accept that, as individuals, disabled people may be happy with who they are and have no wish to aspire to 'normality' or to strive for a narrowly defined independence. All the measures in Box 1.9 would help to reduce the power imbalance between professionals and disabled people.

Box 1.9	**Necessary steps to applying the social model of disability to health and social care practice**

- A full understanding of disability by all those who work within health and social care. This should be developed through disability equality training run by skilled disabled people
- The employment of disabled people within the health and social care professions at all levels

- The full involvement of disabled people in curriculum development and education
- Working in partnership with disabled people at all levels of the organization. This will involve professionals in sharing information and expertise and regarding themselves as a resource for disabled people
- Encouraging and enabling disabled people to exercise choice of services appropriate to their desired lifestyles. This would include clarifying the goals to which the disabled person aspires, identifying the barriers that may prevent the realization of those goals, and working towards removing the barriers. This may involve practitioners in both advocacy and counselling skills
- From the perspective of the social model of disability, professional power can be used to highlight the shortfall in resources for disabled people, to ensure that the subjugated voices of disabled people are heard and responded to, and to encourage and support disabled people to assert themselves so that their expertise about disability is at the centre of the development of services and support

Conclusion

Disabled people throughout history and across cultures have been silenced by powerful organizations and institutions (such as government, charities, the church, the medical profession and the media) who have defined them and created and maintained their oppressed position within society. Such a long, repressive history, stretching back centuries, is difficult to dislodge, but in recent years, with the growth of the Disabled People's Movement internationally, disabled people are speaking out, writing their own history, analysing their lives, demanding equal opportunities and anti-discrimination legislation and defining themselves in very different ways.

So where does that leave the health and social care professional? Clearly if the social model and the affirmative model of disability are accepted, the role of health and social care workers, as it presently stands, is seriously challenged but may also open exciting possibilities for change. Twenty-five years ago it would have been difficult to study disability, as disabled people define it, but now there is an abundance of books and articles on which to draw and Disability Studies, as an academic discipline, has been born. This knowledge, which is constantly developing, is available to all those who wish to understand the meaning of disability, as disabled people define it, in our own society and across the world. The challenge to health and social care services is to apply this knowledge appropriately to education, policy, provision and practice.

Reflection exercises

1. Chat informally to any person you know who has an impairment or long term condition. Gauge how far they subscribe to an individual, social, affirmative or tragedy model of disability. Contrast this by asking about the ways they believe they are viewed by other people.

2. With a colleague from another health and social care profession, discuss how far the organizations in which you work have taken heed of the social and affirmative models of disability. What steps can individual practitioners in your two professions take to extend this?

3. How far do you agree with the analysis by Ballantyne and Muir (2008) that substantial change in incorporating the social and affirmative model of disability must come from the top of the profession? What needs to be done to achieve this? How far is it similar or different in your two professions?

Suggestions for further reading

1. Barnes, C. and Mercer, G. (eds) (1996) *Exploring the Divide: Illness and disability*. Leeds, The Disability Press

   Provides a series of chapters that explore the complex relationship between disability, illness and impairment. The following chapters may be particularly useful. Chapter 3 presents a strong defence of the social model of disability in terms of the critiques, while Chapter 4 puts the case for giving more consideration to impairment within Disability Studies. Chapter 7 considers models of disability in relation to users of the mental health system and Chapter 11 takes a detailed look at issues of representation within the Disabled People's Movement.

2. Swain, J. and French, S. (eds) (2008) *Disability on Equal Terms: Understanding and valuing difference in health and social care*. London, Sage

   Edited book, aimed particularly at health and social care workers, explores the tragedy model of disability and challenges it by examining the affirmative model. Chapters 1 and 6 explore the tragedy model and affirmative model of disability, while Chapter 2 examines genetics and eugenics in relation to disabled people. Chapter 3 concerns disability imagery and language, while Chapters 7 and 8 explore the affirmative model of disability. Chapter 10 gives the personal viewpoints of four disabled people concerning their lives and identities. The third section of the book looks at the implications for developing professional practice, provision and policy and is written by a variety of professionals in health and social care.

3. Campbell, J. and Oliver, M. (1996) *Disability Politics: Understanding our past changing our future*. London, Routledge

   Gives a full account of the history and development of the Disabled People's Movement. It is particularly relevant to those who want a detailed understanding of the development of the social model of disability and disability politics.

4. Oliver, M. (2004) If I Had a Hammer: the social model in action, In J. Swain, S. French, C. Barnes and C. Thomas (eds) *Disabling Barriers – Enabling Environments* (2nd edn). London, Sage

   Gives an overview of the social model of disability including the criticisms of it and its practical application.

5. Thomas, C. (2007) *Sociologies of Disability and Illness: Contested ideas in disability studies and medical sociology*. Basingstoke, Palgrave Macmillan

   Examines different theoretical traditions applied to disability and analyses contested topics and debates such as the divide between medical sociology and disability studies and between disability and impairment. It will be of interest to those who want a deeper theoretical understanding of the debates surrounding these issues.

2 The Context: from Segregation to Equal Rights

In this chapter we discuss:

- Words, words, words – independence; normality; informal and formal carers
- Looking back at health and social care – disability history; oral history; policy development
- Looking forward to equal rights – Disabled People's Movement; life and death issues
- Critical reflection

In this context chapter, we look back and look forward at the development of health and social care policy, provision and practice relating to disabled service users. We begin by critically considering some key concepts, such as professional and carer, formal and informal carer, to set the scene for an exploration of the historical context of the work of health and social care professionals with disabled people. This takes us first into the developing history as generated by disabled people themselves, challenging the official history as documented by non-disabled academics and service providers. We then briefly summarize the developments of policy, provision and practice, from the creation of the welfare state, through the NHS and Community Care Act, to the Disability Discrimination Act.

This takes us on to look forward to future change, particularly as generated through the collective voice of disabled people. Here we concentrate specifically on the crucial challenges to life and death decisions of abortion and assisted suicide.

Finally, the chapter turns to the development of present practice and your, the reader's, engagement in changing health and social care. We outline models of critical reflection, raising questions about the processes of professional development and the barriers to change, and set the scene for the promotion of an analytic approach to health and social care practice. In doing so, we hope to provide a bridge between context (professional structures, ethics and values) and health and social care.

Words, words, words

Words have power. They shape and change health and social care. We have only to consider two words that have dominated understandings of disability: normality and independence. These terms have been consistently questioned by disabled people over the past thirty years, not to argue that disabled people really are normal or independent, but to challenge their application to and understanding of disabled people and their lives. The notion of normality stands in stark contrast to that of the celebration of difference. The discourse of difference signifies a rejection of categorization by dichotomies of normal/abnormal and also disabled/non-disabled, to underpin the realization of the diversity and complexity of humanity, and individual and collective identity. The notion too of independence, in the dominant understanding of skills of self-care, has been challenged by notions of shared dependency and the control of support for independent living (see Chapter 5).

The context of health and social care is replete with powerful words that have underpinned the oppression of disabled people. Words too have driven the resistance and resilience of disabled people, not least being the reconceptualization of 'disabled' which is central to the social model (see Chapter 1).

Words encompass and encapsulate the providers, the receivers and the processes of health and social care and are embedded in the development of policy and practice. The main term for providers is, of course, professionals, and probably most people picking up this text will regard themselves as professionals or trainee professionals. There is certainly a plethora of professionals – physiotherapists, occupational therapists, physicians, social workers. The list is seemingly endless, particularly if it includes those who might be deemed to be at the margins of professional status, such as advocates. Simply on this basis, there can indeed be said to be a 'disability industry'. Associated with this is the notion of carers which carries with it the categorization of formal and informal carers: formal mainly encompassing people paid to provide care, and closely associated with the term professional, while informal also encompasses a plethora of people, including immediate family members, wider family members, friends, some volunteers and, perhaps controversially, young people, usually the children of disabled parents.

The power of words is briefly summarized at this point, but will be a recurring theme throughout the book.

Looking back at health and social care

There can be no doubt that the analysis of historical context provides for understanding the present provision of health and social care and for projecting its development. The eugenics movement, for instance, still leaves its mark in the segregation of disabled people and threats to their very existence (as discussed in Chapter 1). As documented by Shakespeare (2008), eugenics thinking was widespread and commonplace in British society before the Second World War. It continues not just within the segregation of disabled people but as a threat to their existence through, for instance, DNR (Do Not Resuscitate) notices feared by disabled people.

Borsay (2005) suggests that there are three main approaches to the history of disability and impairment. There are biographical histories, which supposedly document the contribution of professionals and institutions to the lives of disabled people. In her research into the Barclay school for Partially Sighted Girls, for instance, I (Sally) found a complete difference between the history of this institution in the documents produced by the school and the history in the memories of the women who attended the school (French, 1996). There are, too, empirical histories, or tables of statistics, which we will not reproduce here, that are about the quantity of services provided for disabled people, with quantity interpreted as quality. Finally, there are materialist histories which 'locate past experiences of disability within the economic and political, social and cultural organisations of society' (Borsay, 2005, p. 10). Two clear examples of such histories are the work of Borsay herself (2005) and Oliver and Barnes (1998).

Any attempt to summarize the history relevant to the provision of health and social care is extremely complex. There are fundamental questions ingrained in this whole arena: the who, the what and the why. We would suggest that Borsay generally omits another approach to history, that is, oral history. There is a history, for instance, of the numbers of institutions, the numbers of people catered for in those institutions, the philosophy and biography of the founders of institutions, but where is the history of those incarcerated in the institutions? Such oral history is significant to reflections on health and social care.

Disability history, that is, the life experiences of disabled people at different times and in different places, is a field of enquiry still in its infancy (Hirsch, 1998). Humphries and Gordon state that 'there has been virtually no interest at all in the actual experiences of disabled people' (1992, p. 10). Atkinson suggests that oral history involves people remembering past personal and social events and

> often includes people who have been neglected in traditional history books, such as working class people, women and mental health survivors. (1993, p. 59)

While oral history research has an important role in challenging dominant discourses about disabled people (and other marginalized groups), the telling and reclaiming of personal history also has other, perhaps less obvious, benefits for the participants. Atkinson asserts that:

> Being an oral historian and a contributor to a written history have brought other, less tangible rewards to the people concerned. Their new roles have increased self confidence and an enhanced sense of self

... to have that past put into a written format which can be shown and shared is to gain recognition as a person who matters. (1993, p. v)

There is a growing oral history of disability in the literature now. Campbell and Oliver (1996), for instance, have put together a history of the Disabled People's Movement in the UK based on the testimonies of the activists who witnessed the early days of organizations of disabled people. Of significance too has been the oral history group working at the Open University (Atkinson, 1993; Atkinson et al., 2000). Mitchell et al. (2006) develop this further by providing international examples of accounts of people with learning difficulties who have spoken for themselves and resisted oppression.

We turn, then, to a brief history of the past thirty years, of political and social policy change of particular relevance to disabled people and the provision of health and social care. By the time that Margaret Thatcher was elected as prime minister in 1979, the welfare state was under severe strain due to a number of diverse social and economic factors including those shown in Box 2.1.

Box 2.1	**Social and economic factors**

- An ageing population
- Rising unemployment
- Recession and high inflation
- Shrinkage of the manufacturing industry and the economy generally
- More separation, divorce and lone parents – the welfare state was dependent on the existence of the conventional nuclear family
- More demands for health and social care, as was generally the case in the Western world

The welfare state was also challenged by many new social movements, for example the Women's Movement, the Black Power movement and the Disabled People's Movement, who had not been treated equally and were demanding full citizenship rights. This led in the 1970s to the passing of various Acts including the Sex Discrimination Act 1975 and the Race Relations Act 1976 which made it less acceptable to discriminate against women and people from ethnic minorities in terms, for example, of housing and health and social care. The passing of the Disability Discrimination Act took far longer to achieve and did not reach the statute book until 1995.

A radical new way of thinking, which came to be known as the New Right or Thatcherism, emerged in the 1980s. All areas of public spending were radically reorganized and state involvement in welfare was reduced:

tenants, for example, had the right to buy their council houses and head teachers managed their own budgets. There was a legislative attack on trade unions in order to reduce their power and there were many restrictions placed on local authorities, who were compelled to sell council houses and to put their services (such as the provision of accommodation for old and disabled people) out to competitive tendering (Langan, 1998). State control, it can be said, was, in certain respects, burgeoning – the introduction of the National Curriculum is one example.

The New Right's diagnosis of the problem of the welfare state was that public expenditure had been allowed to grow unchecked. Old virtues of self-help and thrift were espoused rather than relying on the 'nanny state'. Central and local government, as well as professionals, were seen as monopolies that rigidly imposed particular services on people and wasted resources as there was no competition to keep them in check. The roles and expectations of welfare recipients were also challenged, with emphasis being placed on responsibility and individual autonomy rather than deference and dependency within a paternalistic system. This can be summarized under a number of principles that the New Right upheld (Box 2.2).

Box 2.2	**Principles of the New Right**

- **Decentralization** – the state should have a minimal role in welfare provision
- **Privatization** – private companies should own, organize and deliver services
- **Self-help** – people should help themselves and help each other in the community
- **Competition** – services should compete against each other as a means of raising standards and increasing efficiency
- **Freedom of choice** – clients should have choice over which services they receive. This would be encouraged by competition and the reduction of professional and state monopoly
- **Enterprise** – people should be encouraged to be innovative and creative in the services they provide
- **Individualism** – people should be responsible for their own needs including their own care

(From Lovell and Cordeaux, 1999, pp. 175–6)

The New Right dealt with the problem, as they saw it, by introducing ideas from the commercial world. A new kind of management was required which would use business principles to reduce cost and increase efficiency. Such managerialism, it was hoped, would also serve to break down professional control and modify the power of the trade unions. Competition was introduced into the public sector in the belief that it would keep quality up and costs down. Shifts in language accompanied these changes: patients, clients and passengers, for example, became customers, which implied that they had greater choice and control. The discourse was that patients and clients would have more choice, although this was disputed by many including Walmsley who states that, 'The rhetoric of choice has been extensively deployed to justify this marketisation though ... the link between consumer preference and the service provided is often hard to discern' (2006, p. 83).

In 1989, two white papers were published which formed the basis of the NHS and Community Care Act 1990. The white paper *Working for Patients* (Cm 555) dealt with the NHS and set out ways in which competition could be introduced in the form of what is known as an 'internal' or 'quasi' market. District health authorities (DHAs) could 'shop around' among hospitals, rather than being restricted to their own. This created competition among a wide range of NHS and private hospitals. GPs managed their own budgets and had more choice regarding the services they could provide. Self-governing Trust hospitals were also formed which were outside the control of DHAs. In time, community health services and ambulance services also became Trusts (Butler and Calnan, 1999). Services such as laundering, refuge collection, catering and cleaning were put out to competitive tendering and hospitals were encouraged to raise their own resources by, for example, opening flower shops, hair dressers and food outlets on their premises. As K. Jones states:

> [T]he Government's plan for the Health Service, as for other services, involved bringing in the efficiency and competition of the business world, and ultimately breaking up what was seen as a state monopoly in the hands of professional vested interests. (2000, p. 181)

The white paper *Caring for People* (Cm 849) was concerned with services in the community and how market principles would apply there. Before 1990, social service departments both planned and delivered care. They employed their own staff and supplied a limited range of services for their clients. Under the NHS and Community Care Act, however, social service departments became purchasers rather than providers with their role being to assess the needs of clients and issue contracts to others who would supply the services. This division was known as the purchaser–provider split. Those who wished to provide the services were in competition with each other and were obliged to bid for contracts. This resulted in what is referred to as a 'mixed economy of welfare' involving state, voluntary and private providers of services. Under this legislation, clients are allocated a 'care manager' (a professional such as a social worker or occupational therapist) who assesses them and organizes 'packages of care' from a variety of statutory, private and voluntary organizations (Twigg, 1999). A major drive of the NHS and Community Care Act was to close down large institutions, for example psychiatric and mental handicap hospitals, and provide care in the community. In 1990 there were still 32,700 beds in mental handicap hospitals (Walmsley, 2006) but they were gradually reducing.

The NHS and Community Care Act 1990 made it mandatory to involve users in the planning and delivery of services and various charters were drawn up, for example the Patient's Charter (DH, 1991), which were designed to give users more voice, though they carry no legal status. It was thought by many people that these changes would go some way to weakening the monopoly of both the state and professionals, thereby providing disabled people with a greater voice and a greater range and choice of services. It was also envisaged that the 'care manager' would have an overview of the disabled person's needs and would work within a 'needs-led' rather than a 'resource-led' framework. The potential possible benefit for social workers was that they would be working with disabled people in a relationship of greater equality where they could provide more flexible and creative services.

Some people were pessimistic about the changes that the NHS and Community Care Act would bring based upon the beliefs shown in Box 2.3.

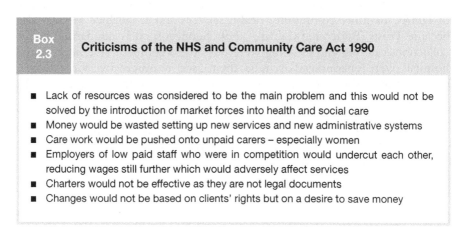

Box 2.3	Criticisms of the NHS and Community Care Act 1990

- Lack of resources was considered to be the main problem and this would not be solved by the introduction of market forces into health and social care
- Money would be wasted setting up new services and new administrative systems
- Care work would be pushed onto unpaid carers – especially women
- Employers of low paid staff who were in competition would undercut each other, reducing wages still further which would adversely affect services
- Charters would not be effective as they are not legal documents
- Changes would not be based on clients' rights but on a desire to save money

As can be seen in Box 2.4, the image of the consumer exercising free choice in health and social care was also viewed as problematic.

Box 2.4	Questioning notions of free choice

- An imbalance of power between those who provide the care and those who receive it
- Finite and limited resources. More customers does not equal more money, as it does in a free market, as customers would be a cost rather than a source of income. Distribution of resources is an act of political will where the interests of individual consumers are juggled against the interests of the community as a whole
- The purchasers of services, for example care managers and GPs, have choice rather than the actual users. They have been termed 'proxy customers' and are usually public sector employees

- Consumerism risks producing social inequalities by focusing on the individual and ignoring wider social factors
- People may not want to be consumers. The choices may be too difficult at times of vulnerability where issues such as trust may be more important

As these policies came into effect, disabled people found that their ideas of independent living in the community clashed with those of Social Service managers and professionals who focused on basic care – bathing, dressing and so on. Furthermore, assessments were geared to available resources rather than being needs led. Over time, 'packages of care' became more restrictive with tighter eligibility criteria and means testing. The emphasis was firmly on 'care' rather than 'quality of life', with few choices and little control. Furthermore, large charities, such as Leonard Cheshire, had the advantage when it came to bidding against smaller organizations, including those that were run by disabled people themselves, with the danger of monopoly and the stifling of innovation (Walmsley, 2006). The unequal power relationship between disabled people and professionals, not least because professionals are the gatekeepers of services, did not fundamentally change with this legislation but, rather, became obscured by notions of consultation and user involvement (French and Swain, 2007).

Some changes that disabled people regard as positive did, however, evolve from the NHS and Community Care Act 1990 and from their own campaigning over many years. The Community Care (Direct Payments) Act 1996, for example, enables local authorities to assess disabled people for a direct payment which they can spend on their own needs including the services of care workers. This effectively gives disabled people the status of employers. The payment made is given following an assessment by a professional, and the disabled person may be monitored, but, nonetheless, many disabled people find direct payment gives them more control over their lives than when they rely on statutory and voluntary services. (This will be discussed in more detail in Chapter 5.)

The Labour government came into power in May 1997 when Tony Blair was elected prime minister. New Labour sought to construct a Third Way between Old Labour and the New Right. New Labour stressed the need to reduce expenditure and increase choice and efficiency, but also emphasized equal opportunities, social justice and social cohesion, having, for instance, strengthened the Disability Discrimination Act. Like the New Right, it stressed individual and family responsibility but placed more emphasis on collective issues within society (Blakemore, 1998), one example being the setting up of the Social Exclusion Unit.

Although the purchaser–provider split remained intact, partnership rather than competition was emphasized, with terms such as 'seamless services' and 'joined up thinking' being used to imply greater collaboration among service providers. Words such as 'partnership' and 'empowerment' peppered policy documents and legislation. Primary care groups, rather than individual GPs, had the responsibility of negotiating with hospital Trusts and competition and contracts were reduced by placing an emphasis on cooperative, long-term arrangements. New Labour also introduced national standards and guidelines in an attempt to enhance quality of health and social care. Organizations such as the National Institute for Clinical Excellence (NICE) and the Social Care Institute for Excellence (SCIE) were set up in an attempt to improve standards. Later renamed the National Institute for Health and Clinical Excellence (while keeping its original acronym), NICE provides guidance, sets quality standards and manages a national database. SCIE aims to identify and spread knowledge about good practice to the social care workforce and support the delivery of personalized social care services. Many of these changes have the potential to improve services for disabled people. For instance, the Disability Discrimination Act now covers education, and notions of a 'seamless service', 'partnership' and 'empowerment' could make services for disabled people more responsive and efficient.

Looking forward to equal rights

In a chapter entitled 'Disability, Struggle and the Politics of Hope', Barton writes:

> [D]isabled people are demanding changes. They are not arguing for sameness, or to become as normal as possible, nor are they seeking an independence without assistance. Their vision is of a world in which discrimination and injustice are removed. They are desirous of the establishment of alternative definitions and perceptions based on a dignified view of difference. The struggle for inclusion is thus disturbing, demanding and developmental. It involves the experience of exercising choices and rights ... (2001, p. 10)

The collective voice of disabled people remains for many, including ourselves, the vanguard of social change for disabled people. The British Council of Disabled People (recently renamed the United Kingdom's Disabled People's Council) is the main umbrella organization of disabled people. The following short extract from their manifesto (April, 2005) refers to the provision of services and support:

> BCODP calls for local authorities and health services to work together where needed to: give disabled people the chance to be responsible for working out and saying what their own needs are. Services should fit around the needs of individual disabled people and give them support to make decisions and to lead full and active lives ... (www.bcodp.org.uk)

One major and controversial arena for various campaigns concerns life and death decisions. Abortion of disabled foetuses is extensive, for instance 90% of foetuses with Down's Syndrome, which is over 1000, are aborted each year in Great Britain and the figure is rising due to more accurate screening techniques (Smith, 2009). Assisted suicide, though still illegal in Britain, is being hotly debated at the present time. This has threatened the security of disabled people and mobilized them into action. For instance, Jane Campbell, a well-known disabled activist, founded and leads Not Dead Yet UK, a campaigning network of disabled people who are against abortion, on the grounds of impairment, and assisted suicide.

The ethical dilemmas relating to abortion and assisted suicide are huge and beyond the scope of this chapter. We intend, therefore, to confine ourselves to the challenges put forward by disabled people and their organizations against the abortion of disabled foetuses and the assisted suicide of disabled people. This is not to imply that every disabled person agrees with these views but they are, nonetheless, held by substantial numbers of disabled people and their organizations, such as Disabled People's International and Not Dead Yet. As Disabled People's International state, 'One of the biggest threats to disabled people this millennium lies within the field of bioethics' (DPI, 2000, p. 2). If you are interested in the recent legal challenges, you could look to cases well featured in the media (guardian.co.uk/society/2009/jul/30/Debbie-purdy-assisted-suicide-legal-victory and news.bbc.co.uk/2/hi/health/1983457'stm (Dianne Pretty's case)).

Despite the importance of bioethical issues to disabled people, it has been argued that their voice has not been heard. Not Dead Yet, talking about assisted suicide, state:

> The collective voice of disabled people on these life-and-death issues
> has not yet been heard by the media, the courts, legislators, the medical
> profession and other policy makers and practitioners. They, and the
> wider public, need to know that the campaign for assisted dying was
> not instigated by the disabled people's movement and does not have
> our support. (www.notdeadyetuk.org/notdeadyet-about.html)

As argued above, the rationale that underlies termination of impaired foetuses is that it is better to be dead than to live as a disabled person (Anstey, 2008). This is a view held by many eminent physicians and scientists, for instance Watson, a scientist who won the Nobel Prize for discovering the structure of DNA, states that, 'Seeing the bright side of handicap is like praising the virtues of extreme poverty' (2000, p. 207) and that:

> There is, of course, nothing pleasant about terminating the existence
> of a genetically disabled fetus. But doing so is incomparably more
> compassionate than allowing an infant to come into the world
> tragically impaired. (2000, p. 225)

Similarly John Sulston, who at the time was the vice-chair of the Human Genetics Commission, stated that parents should not bring a clearly disabled child into the world. Eminent doctors are implying, then, that people who knowingly have disabled children are behaving irresponsibly (cited in DPI, 2000). Rembis (2009) believes that there is a social and cultural bias against genetically disabled children and the Disability Rights Commission, while not opposing genetic research designed to alleviate pain and to provide genuine treatments, believed that these views reduce individuals to their genetic characteristics and reverse the progress which has been made concerning human and civil rights (DRC, 2004b) (see Chapter 1).

Disabled People's International agree that ideas such as those of Watson, Edwards and Sulston foster the belief that disabled people are nothing more than their impairments. They state:

> Many disabled people are only alive today because of scientific progress generally and new medical techniques in particular so of course we wish to promote and sustain such advances where these lead to benefits for everyone. But we want to see research directed at improving the quality of our lives not denying us the opportunity to live. (DPI, 2000, p. 3)

Many disabled people also view disability as 'part of life' and as something which contributes positively to society. As Disabled People's International state: 'Our lives as disabled people celebrate the positive power of diversity. Our experience enriches society. These are our unique gifts to the world' (DPI, 2000, p. 4).

The demand for an accessible and inclusive environment is a central theme in disabled people's arguments against assisted dying. Jane Campbell (2006a) explains this by reference to her own experience:

> 'I benefit from excellent medical care, I live in an adapted bungalow, and my local authority provides proper care support that enables me to choose my own personal assistants. I am not dependent on family and loved ones. I love my good life.'

These points are echoed by those of Not Dead Yet UK who believe individual disabled people's wishes for death often come from a lack of adequate practical, emotional and medical support needed to live dignified lives, rather than any 'suffering' they experience as a result of a medical condition. Lewis (2009) comments on the very different response towards able-bodied people who want to commit suicide and believes that 'The concept of liberating people from suffering by offering them fatal medications is more like an idea from a horror movie than a social polity' (Lewis, 2009, p. 10).

Disabled people are also aware of the risk of exploitation if assisted suicide became legal, including that of cost-cutting practices in contemporary health and social care (Shakespeare, 2008). Now merged into the Equality and

Human Rights Commission, the Disability Rights Commission, for instance, believed that assisted dying could become financially attractive to service providers. Not Dead Yet agrees that:

> In these days of cost cutting in the NHS and social care, assisted dying could all too easily become an attractive 'treatment remedy'... individuals risk being easily exploited by the 'right to die' movement or, worse, by family, friends and health care professionals. Their attitude is not compassionate – it is prejudiced and disablist. (www. notdeadyetuk.org/notdeadyet-about.html)

Campbell (2006a) agrees that the legislating of premature death as a treatment option will place pressures on people near the end of their lives. It can be argued that assisting a disabled person to commit suicide, when they cannot do it themselves, gives them the same opportunities as non-disabled people and yet, as Brignell (2009) argues, what is in the interests of one person may not be in the interests of society as a whole. It is clear from much of the writing from disabled people and their organizations, however, that they are not against assisted suicide per se but only when disabled people are perceived to have no real choice. The Disability Rights Commission, for instance, stated its opposition to assisted suicide all the time there are negative attitudes towards disabled people and all the time that disabled people cannot participate fully and equally in society. Not Dead Yet agrees that real and effective rights to independent living support, as well as palliative care, need to be in place before terminally ill and disabled people would have any real choice. At present, palliative care is mainly confined to people with cancer.

Disabled People's International made the following demands in relation to both assisted suicide of disabled people and the abortion of disabled foetuses (Box 2.5).

Box 2.5	Demands of Disabled People's International

'We demand that:

- the use of new human genetic discoveries, techniques and practices are strictly regulated to avoid discrimination and protect fully, and in all circumstances, the human rights of disabled people
- genetic counselling is non-directive, rights based, widely and freely available and reflects the real experience of disability
- parents are not formally or informally pressured to take pre-natal tests or undergo 'medical' terminations
- all children are welcomed into the world and provided with appropriate levels of social, practical and financial support

- human diversity is celebrated and not eliminated by discriminatory assessments of quality of life, which may lead to euthanasia, infanticide and death as a result of non-intervention
- organisations of disabled people are represented on all advisory and regulatory bodies dealing with human genetics
- legislation is amended to bring an end to discrimination on the grounds of impairment as exceptional legal grounds of abortion
- there is a comprehensive program of training for all health and social care professionals for a disability equality perspective
- as the human genome is the common property of humanity, no patents are allowed on genetic material
- the human rights of disabled people who are unable to consent are not violated through medical interventions.'

(Disabled People's International, 2000, p. 7)

Critical reflection

 Box 2.6 **Why critical reflection?**

Ghaye (2000) provides a list of the claims of reflective practice. In doing so he uses the plural term 'reflective practices' to emphasize that it covers a number of different approaches rather than just one. There are five claims:

1. Reflective practices improve the quality of care we give.
2. Reflective practices enhance individual and collective professional development.
3. Reflective practices change the 'power' relationship between academics and practitioners by broadening who generates and controls knowledge for safe and competent health care.
4. Reflective practices improve the clinical environment. Within this claim it is suggested that practitioners need to recognize and be critical of organizational structures that condition and shape professional practice.
5. Reflective practices help to build a better world. Here it is suggested that reflective practices 'connect with hopes, intentions and struggles for more just, democratic, compassionate, caring and dignified healthcare systems'.

(Derived from Ghaye, 2000, pp. 70–2)

There is now a plethora of literature by professionals and academics for professionals and academics that takes a broadly reflective practice approach, though there are differences between the specific models used. There is also an abundance of courses, both pre-service and in-service, that wholly or in part embrace reflective practice. At this point we shall look first at the basic principles and a little at where these ideas come from. We will begin by looking towards a definition of reflective practice. Gould writes:

There is considerable empirical evidence, based on research into
a variety of occupations, suggesting that expertise does not derive
from the application of rules or procedures applied deductively from
positivist research. Instead, it is argued that practice wisdom rests upon
highly developed intuition which can be difficult to articulate but can
be demonstrated in practice. (1996, p. 1)

An understanding of professional knowledge as developed by practitioners
themselves through and within their practice and their systematic analysis of
practice is central to the origins of the notion of reflective practice. These
ideas have been developed in different ways and in a variety of contexts.
Ghaye and his colleagues have produced a series of books on reflection for
health care professionals. They offer a framework of twelve principles of
reflection with particular emphasis on the first three (Ghaye and Lillyman,
2000, p. 121):

1. Reflective practice is about you and your work.
2. Reflective practice is about learning from experience.
3. Reflective practice is about valuing what we do and why we do it.

Rolfe, Freshwater and Jasper (2001) in their users' guide for nurses and
'the helping professions' distinguish between macro- and micro- models of
reflective practice. Macro-models address the underlying philosophy of
reflection and possible stages in developing thinking and action. One
example of the work they draw on is Kim (1999) whose model goes
through three phases:

1. Descriptive phase – taking a particular situation, event, encounter, what
   happened?
2. Reflective phase – the practitioner asking 'what did I make of this?'
3. Critical/emancipatory phase – moving the questioning forward to the
   implications for practitioner acting, thinking and feeling differently.

There are models or frameworks of critical reflection that attempt to
address broader questions of good practice. For instance, in the volume
edited by Brechin, Brown and Eby (2000) critical reflection is incorporated
into a broader idea of critical practice. Brechin explains:

The term 'critical' is used here to refer to open-minded, reflective
appraisal that takes account of different perspectives, experiences and
assumptions. (2000, p. 26)

Processes of empowerment and anti-oppression are seen as crucial. She picks
out two overall guiding principles. The first is the principle of 'respecting
others as equals' (2000, p. 31). This is justified, in part, by the 'endemic oppression of less powerful groups in society' (2000, p. 31). The second guiding

principle is openness. This is an acceptance of the position that there is a degree of uncertainty in all professional practice and that professional practice is evolving within the particular social and historical context. Founded on these principles, Brechin goes on to outline three pillars of critical practice: forging relationships, seeking to empower others and making a difference.

In our previous work (Swain, Clark, Parry et al., 2004) we also developed a framework of principles, which shares many of the elements of Brechin's model and attempts to incorporate critical reflection within a broader context of enabling relationships, and empowerment and emancipation. It is summarized in Box 2.7.

Box 2.7 **An enabling relationships framework of principles**

Critical reflection

1. To promote understanding of self and others through personal reflection and through dialogue.
2. To facilitate functional reflection through critical examination of the practice/process of health and social care to reveal its assumptions, values and biases.
3. To develop disciplinary reflection and a critical stance towards broader debates about theory and practice.

Enabling relationships

4. To promote mutual understanding and awareness of others' preferences, wishes and needs through open two-way communication.
5. To facilitate, through working in partnership, a collaborative approach to service organization, planning, delivery and evaluation.

Empowerment and emancipation

6. To facilitate the recognition and questioning of power relations, structures and ideologies that limit people's freedom.
7. To promote people's prediction and control over decision-making processes that shape their lives.
8. To promote people's struggles against repression and 'man-made' sufferings, and support the removal of barriers to equal opportunities and promote full participatory citizenship for all.

(Derived from Swain, Clark, Parry et al., 2004, pp. 90–1)

To engage in critical reflection is to engage with the disabling society in which we all live and to engage with people's lives within the disabling society. It is this that we are exploring within this book.

Conclusion

The process of looking back to look forward, analysing the context, is complex and essentially, as we have tried to convey, a questioning process. It engages with the questioning of key concepts and the criteria for the analysis of health and social care policy, provision and practice. Throughout, the voices of disabled people have been prioritized in our analysis; their experiences and views of the development of health and social care. The engagement with the context in this chapter has been directed towards critical reflection by practitioners, by you the reader, in grappling with the rights of disabled people, justice, and the realization of participatory citizenship.

Reflection exercises

1. What do you consider to be the best term to refer to disabled people who receive services and why? (Service users, patients, customers?)
2. In what ways do you think the views and experiences of disabled service users have directly influenced the development of health and social care policy?
3. At this point, stand back from your practice and consider the following questions as starting points for critical reflection and development:

What are the major characteristics of positive practice that can be built upon? What are the barriers to developing good practice? What strategies are in place for understanding and responding to the experiences and views of disabled service users? What do you think are the specific ways in which these strategies can be strengthened?

Suggestions for further reading

1. Barnes, C. and Mercer, G. (eds) (2004) *Disability, Policy and Practice: Applying the social model of disability*. Leeds, The Disability Press

   Explores the social model of disability as a comprehensive critique of orthodox academic and administrative approaches to the understanding and development of social policy for disabled people. It raises a range of important issues and concerns central to theorizing and researching disability policy and practice, spanning employment, housing, higher education, social care, independent living, leisure and social relations.

2. Brechin, A., Brown, H. and Eby, M.A. (eds) (2000) *Critical Practice in Health and Social Care*. London, Sage

   Reviews the evidence on team and inter-professional working, teasing out the new perspectives and the skills required; examines what professional development entails and what it means in different fields of practice; tackles ethical dilemmas of practice alongside changing concepts in society of accountability; explores current debates about how professionals can be supported in their practice and how their performance is best regulated; and highlights the contribution that practitioners can make – alongside others – to policy development at local level.

3. Swain, J., Clark, J., Parry, K. et al. (2004) *Enabling Relationships in Health and Social Care: A guide for therapists*. Oxford, Butterworth-Heinemann

   Explores the provision and practice of professional support and refers to the processes of enabling relationships between participants: professionals and clients. It also invokes the power of relationships to empower and construct change. It takes a reflective practitioner approach and provides individual and group activities to help the reader relate the ideas discussed in the book to themselves, their practice and the particular context of their work.

3 Disabled People: Health and Social Care

In this chapter we discuss:

- Disabling policy and practice – medical model; disabled people's experiences of medical services
- Inclusion and exclusion – structural; environmental; attitudinal and ideological barriers
- Mainstreaming policy and practice

This chapter looks across the board at services/provision, including education, employment services, transport and housing. In particular, we critically explore key concepts such as inclusion, exclusion, and mainstreaming of policy and practice. As throughout, our concentration is on UK services, though the discussion will draw, as appropriate, on international comparisons to inform the critique.

Disabling policy and practice

As a starting point for analysing disabling policy and practice, it is appropriate to turn to the needs of disabled people as defined by disabled people. There are many possible sources for this, one being CILs (Centres for Independent/Inclusive Living), organizations run by disabled people to provide services for disabled people. Southampton CIL's twelve needs of disabled people provide a relevant example (see Chapter 5). The meeting of these needs is central to equality, inclusion, social justice and citizenship for disabled people. One basic necessity, as for all, is appropriate and accessible health care provision. The available evidence, however, suggests that such provision has not been the experience of many disabled people. Medical practice adopts a functionalist stance to illness, which often equates impairment with deviancy (Oliver, 1998). Functionalism is a broad perspective in sociology and anthropology that sets out to interpret society as a structure with interrelated parts, addressing norms, customs, traditions and institutions. This influences the language used by the medical profession, where the term 'abnormal' is common currency, and interpretations of disabled people's ability are commonly described as deficits (MacKay, 2003). Within medicine, quality of life arguments predominate decision making and resource allocation, and become more salient when medical conditions are seen to deviate from what is considered to be the societal norm (Koch, 2000). For disabled people with severe impairments, many are considered to have a poor or no quality of life (Marks, 1999). This can culminate in a variety of medical practices, some questionable, which are sanctioned by medicine's scientific knowledge base. These practices can include such things as withholding treatment (for example do not resuscitate), aggressively applying treatment to those felt suitable (Koch, 2000) and the utilization of measures designed to eliminate impairment. This latter category can include the following medical procedure: advice about the benefit of undertaking prenatal screening, advice about aborting an unborn disabled baby approaching full gestation, withholding nutrition or treatment and infanticide (Wolfensberger, 1994; Crow, 1996; Marks, 1999) (see Chapter 2).

Within this oppressive medical framework, it can be argued that disabled people's tendency to be objectified and dehumanized becomes heightened, potentially impacting upon the way that their medical treatment is delivered. Here we draw on research conducted by Martina Higgins (Higgins and Swain, 2009). It is based on the narratives of seven disabled survivors of sexual abuse, but also discusses other co-occurring forms of child abuse, and more general breaches of a child's human rights. Participants elaborate on their experiences of organizational systems; health care and educational provision, specialist services and mainstream. Their narrative offers insights for practitioners working in the field and urges for critical analysis of taken-for-granted organizational practices. The research highlights the amalgamation, and destructive impact of two distinct forms of societal oppression; child abuse and disablism, as evident in the following two statements (Higgins and Swain, 2009):

'They tied me into a cot, they put on my right leg what's known as a "Jonathon splint", which stretches and keeps your leg straight. They were also testing me for different things. I was allergic to the plaster they used to attach the splint to my leg, so that when they took that off, it just took off the top layer of my skin, so I had raw wounds from that. I wasn't getting the pain relief that I should have been getting and I wasn't being fed properly. I was hungry and thirsty a lot of the time. I don't know why they tied me into the cot; I think it was to stop me moving about.'

Jean

'A couple of times I was given too much medication and I ended up in a children's hospital because I was a bit dopey. My mum only just told me this. She said that I was half awake, half asleep, "you weren't asleep but you weren't awake." She called it comatose, but it wasn't a coma, obviously. They took me in and changed the pain medication that they had me on. That happened again when I was about eight, over Christmas time, where, again, I was given too much medication.'

Jean

Some disabled people report feeling dissatisfied in the relationship they have with the medical profession (Begum, 1996). This can be an even more significant problem for disabled children. Although research indicates that disabled children have a desire to be informed about medical procedure and included in medical consultations (Garth and Aroni, 2003), other writers propose that disabled children's perspectives continue to be overlooked because of misguided assumptions relating to competency and agency (Davis, 2004). Similar to Jean's narrative, hospitalizations can still be experienced by disabled children as traumatic, despite medical progress. There needs to be recognition of children's need for honest, age-appropriate and sensitively delivered information (Closs, 1998). The process of objectification and the imbalance in power can also be seen in some of the other more routine medical procedures that disabled children are regularly subjected to, as demonstrated in the following two quotations from Higgins' research (Higgins and Swain, 2009):

'In one hospital I was photographed because I'm quite unusual, because I have such extreme symptoms in one joint, and also because after my surgery one of my toes stopped growing; so one of my toes is the same size as it was when I was nine. And they said, "Oh, that's interesting. How did that happen?"'

Jean

'I also think that, like other disabled people, I lacked a sense of my own body belonging to me, and being private, of not having to be touched if I didn't want to be. This came from having to have many visits to the doctors and physiotherapists, and needing help to do things. I remember being paraded in front of doctors with very little on and feeling I was a thing for discussion rather than a person in my own right. This feeling got stronger as I got older. I was thirteen before I was given a choice about whether I kept appointments. When I exercised my choice by not going, then I was made to feel guilty by other professionals, which reinforced my feelings of "what is the point?" This lack of a sense that your body belongs to you is an issue that non-disabled children do not have to face. And, again, I can't say that this makes us more of a target, but it does make us better victims as we are less likely to object or tell.'

May

Begum (1996) found that within a primary care setting, disabled women report experiencing medical practices that were considered to be both offensive and intrusive. Begum highlights a tendency for some doctors to show great curiosity towards a woman's impairment. This could happen even when the individual was visiting the health locality for some other, unrelated medical complaint. This medical curiosity, which in Begum's research was felt to be inappropriate, has the potential to become more flagrantly abusive, particularly in the case of disabled children who have less power to protest. As can be seen, May's quote draws some parallels between a continued process of medical objectification and the potential for later sexual victimization.

Contemporary health care is characterized by an emphasis on the quality of knowledge that is used to inform decisions about care interventions. However, the criteria of quality adopted (that of being research evidenced) privileges the knowledge held by health and social care practitioners and betrays the importance of knowledge held by service users. Those at the receiving end of professional services sometimes find themselves in opposition to professionals. Such people include women who may feel that doctors are taking control of their bodies, in childbirth for example (Doyal, 1991) and people from ethnic minority groups who may perceive professionals as ethnocentric, racist and lacking in cultural awareness and sensitivity (Ahmad and Atkin, 1996). In general terms, disabled people have both good and bad experiences of health care and health care professionals. Reading about their positive experiences is not, of course, difficult but reading about their negative experiences may cause uncomfortable feelings and a tendency to ignore or reject what is said. It is important to remember that while health care professionals are not powerless to bring about changes to the way disabled people are treated, they are, nonetheless, enmeshed in a broad system of oppressive practices and discrimination against disabled people – based, for example, on monetary constraints and historical factors such as institutionalization – of which they have limited responsibility or control as individuals. Reynolds believes that:

> Whilst many individual therapists value empowering relationships,
> they encounter significant barriers because of the ways in which
> health, disability, normality and well-being are defined in the health
> care system, and in Western culture more generally. (2004, p. 17)

Disability Studies (the social, political and cultural analysis of disability) is also virtually absent from the educational curriculum of health care professionals, who, therefore, have little opportunity to learn about the meaning of disability within a formal educational setting (Whalley Hammell, 2006).

We recognize that the readers of this book will be motivated to assist disabled people and to serve as a positive force to improve their lives. To achieve this, we believe that an essential first step is to listen to what disabled people say about their experiences of health care, both good and bad. Unless professionals adapt to the needs and wishes of disabled people and become more involved in their struggle for citizenship, it can be argued that their role is very limited.

Box
3.1 **Problems with health care: disabled people's experiences**

The following quotations are from disabled people talking about their experiences with health and social care services:

'How many hours did I spend in those endless corridors learning to "walk" before returning home and promptly settling into a more active and rewarding life in a wheelchair?'
(Finkelstein, 1990, p. 6)

'After being diagnosed as deaf, I tried to get on with my childhood while being constantly interrupted to sit in a hospital chair straining for the slightest possible noise ... which had no meaning and was not of the slightest interest.'
(Heaton, 1998, p. 12)

'I remember speech therapy being a lot of hard work and I can remember getting extremely fed up. I got to a situation where I hated eating because at every mealtime the speech therapist would come into the dining room to supervise us saying, "Remember what we talked about, remember about your swallowing, remember how to drink" ... OK it's good to do it while you're actually eating something, rather than talking about it in theory, but when you're doing it at every mealtime, and your parents have been told so they do it at home, you get to a point when you think, "Wouldn't it be nice to just sit and enjoy your food!?"'
(French, 2004b, p. 104)

'The arm was better when it was done but as time's gone on it's just gone back to how it was ... what did annoy me to be honest was they never said this could happen, at the beginning it was, oh it will be wonderful. Looking back if I knew then what I know now I would not have had the operation done. It messed up so many things at the time.'
(Middleton, 1999, p. 21)

'I hated learning speech – hated it – I felt so stupid having to repeat the s, s, s ... Every time I got it wrong. I had to do it all over again and I was asking myself, "Why do I have to keep going over and over it? I don't understand what it all means!" ... It was just so stupid, a waste of time when I could have been learning more important things.'
(Corker, 1996, p. 92)

'Their responses towards me varied greatly, some showed great compassion, while others showed complete indifference. I had no way of communicating the fact that I was a bright, intelligent, whole human being. That is what hurt the most.'
(Boazman, 1999, pp. 18–19)

Contained within these quotations are two very strong and persistent themes. The first is that disabled people do not necessarily believe that medical treatment and what it might achieve is the most important thing within their lives. A second theme relates to the lack of power disabled people have over their lives especially during childhood. Despite the distress and disruption medical treatment may cause, disabled people are under considerable pressure to go through with it. If they do assert themselves, they frequently meet with resistance or even hostility as the following quotations illustrate:

'I came to realise that expending energy on having fun and living life are rather more important than preserving all one's energy and motivation for doing therapy and chasing dreams of cure.' (Pound 2004, p. 39)

'About two years ago I realised that my walking ability had deteriorated ... so I talked to my GP who referred me to the physiotherapy department at my local hospital. She said, "We can stop the deterioration provided you're willing to spend an hour a day working at it" and she didn't like it because I said I didn't feel that the work was worth it. I told her that I've got limited energy, some of my functions are not automatic, like when I'm talking I'm also trying to remember to swallow my saliva ... All those things are tiring. I said to her that I'm more interested in doing things that engage my mind and imagination. She didn't like it and she wrote me off as somebody she couldn't help rather than treating me as somebody she had helped by giving me some advice.' (French, 2004b, p. 103)

It should be noted that in the final quotation the disabled person was not dissatisfied with the consultation with the physiotherapist, which he found useful, but he was disappointed in the physiotherapist's response when he declined to take her advice. Not only can important areas of life be disrupted by medical intervention but the treatment itself can be very unpleasant. Furthermore, the results of the treatment are sometimes short lived or less than satisfactory. Middleton states:

What seems to have developed is an attitude towards the use of unproven treatment for disabled children which maintains that it may as well be tried, it can't do any harm since they are already impaired. This ignores the very real pain, discomfort and indignity that children suffer as a result of these experiences ... which non-disabled children would not be expected to. (1999, p. 41)

Middleton is also critical of the way in which parents get caught up in financing and promoting unproven treatment because of a need to 'do all they can' for their disabled child. A recent example is the 'Ashley Treatment', a growth and development stunting treatment that prevents girls from reaching puberty (www.guardan.co.uk/world/2007/jan/08/health.usa).

Inclusion and exclusion

As Barton (2008), along with others, has argued, 'in seeking to understand the nature of inclusion, it is absolutely necessary to examine the ways in which exclusion is defined and experienced in the lives of disabled people in different social contexts' (p. 1). Exclusion is perhaps most commonly defined and experienced in terms of employment, or more precisely lack of employment. The statistics of exclusion from employment continue to speak to analyses of the exclusion of disabled people and to dominate the experiences of many disabled people, with disabled people being twice as likely to be unemployed than non-disabled people (Williams et al., 2007). For disabled people in employment, there is also evidence that they are more likely to be 'underemployed' in lower positions with little job security or chance for advancement (French, 2001). Exclusion can be expressed and experienced too in enforced dependency, being dependent on existing health and social care provision, most clearly through segregated care provision, with lack of support for inclusive living. Perhaps at the heart of exclusion lie issues of power as a set of relations involving the exercise of decision making. Central to the inclusion of disabled people is their inclusion in the decision–making processes that shape, plan, resource and evaluate the notion of an inclusive society.

In a previous publication (Swain et al., 1998), we presented the SEAwall model of institutional discrimination faced by disabled people, which seems to draw together the perspectives on exclusion summarized above. To see discrimination as institutionalized is to recognize that inequalities are woven into the very structure and fabric of British, and indeed Western, society and organizations. People with impairments are disabled by institutionalized barriers that prevent their full participative citizenship in society.

Box 3.2	**The SEAwall of Discrimination**

The SEAwall depicts disabling barriers as the bricks of a wall of institutional discrimination, the wall that excludes and the wall to be broken down to realize inclusion.

The foundations of the wall are built at the **S**TRUCTURAL level. Institutional discrimination is founded on the social divisions in society and, in particular, hierarchical power relations between groups (for example disabled and non-disabled people). Inequalities in the distribution of resources, particularly economic, underpin hierarchical power relations, with many disabled people being marginalized from open employment and condemned to poverty.

The **E**NVIRONMENTAL level of barriers is constructed on these foundations, in the interaction between the individual and the social and physical environment. These, then, are the barriers confronted by disabled people in relation to rules, procedures, patterns of behaviour, shared understandings, timetables and so on (that is, social organization), that are geared to the needs and norms of the non-disabled majority.

> The barriers are also created by aids that are geared to the needs and norms of the non-disabled majority (steps, cars, taps, buses and so on), the needs of disabled people being marginalized to 'special' aids. One major factor for many disabled people, as we have seen, is their relationship with health and social care service provision and professional practice, which can play an important role in shaping their lives and enforcing dependency.
>
> The third layer, **A**TTITUDINAL, which is built on the previous two, is constructed in the direct interactions between disabled and non-disabled people, as individuals or in groups. These barriers are manifest in the attitudes and personal prejudices of non-disabled people, their expectations and actions. This includes the beliefs, feelings and behaviour of individual professionals. These relate to, but can differ substantially from, the collective professional practice, including training, ideology and organizational structures, which we included in the environmental level of this model. Thus, our analysis acknowledges that, despite the constraints, individual professionals can and do support the struggle of disabled people against institutional discrimination.

If each brick of this wall of institutional discrimination was separate from all the others, the process of inclusion could be the dismantling of the wall brick by brick. As the Disabled People's Movement has recognized, however, piecemeal approaches are ultimately ineffective in dismantling institutional discrimination, and it needs to be recognized that all these barriers are closely bound and interrelated. Part of the dynamic of this interlinking is through ideology. Thompson (2006) refers to ideology as the 'glue' that binds together the levels in his model of institutional discrimination. In doing so, a dominant ideology operates in a number of ways:

- Legitimizing social inequalities, power relations and structures
- Establishing what is normal and therefore, by extension, what is abnormal (Thompson, 2006)
- Defining cultural values and desirable goals
- Being 'naturalised, taken for granted and almost all-embracing' (Barnes, 1996, p. 48)

There are a number of dimensions to the ideological basis of institutional discrimination and exclusion, including the individual model in which disability is seen as a problem and the problem is located in the impaired individual. The ideology of normality/abnormality is clearly of central importance here (Whalley Hammell, 2006). Judgements of disabled people are, in Western society at least, in accordance with normative criteria whereby we decide a behaviour or situation is normal or abnormal by comparing it with the behaviour and situation of the majority. Thus a disabled person would be deemed abnormal simply as measured against the non-disabled majority, and a special school regarded as abnormal simply because most schools are mainstream, and indeed they are often referred to as 'normal' schools. The dominance of the ideology of normality/abnormality is such that it is difficult to think of areas of contemporary life in which it is not brought to bear. It is important too to recognize that there is an inherent social value basis in this ideology. Social judgements of normality or abnormality have an inherent value judgement of desirable/undesirable or good/bad. As Drake writes:

> The concept of 'normality', far from describing some natural and preordained state of affairs, instead represents an acknowledgement of the values which have come to dominate in a particular community at any given time. (1996, p. 147)

The ideology of independence is closely associated with that of normality and provides a similar basis for rationalizing and justifying discrimination. Independence is defined, though not by many disabled people, in terms of notions of what people normally do for themselves, and, as with the ideology of normality, has both a value-based dimension (as a 'good') and a conformity dimension (as a 'should'). As Oliver tells us:

> [V]ast numbers of people with impairments are socialised into dependency by key components of the traditional welfare state. Special schools, day centres, residential institutions, social security payments that keep people in care all perform this role. (2009, p. 124)

As Oliver also points out, societies founded on oppression, and indeed exclusion, are characterized by difference: 'differences based on gender, ethnic backgrounds, sexual orientation, abilities, religious beliefs, wealth, age, access or non-access to work and so on' (2009, p. 96). While inclusion for disabled people must involve the dismantling of the SEAwall, it is clearly impossible to imagine a society which is inclusive of disabled people but which is also ageist, sexist, racist and so on. An inclusive society can only be an inclusive society for all (Oliver and Barnes, 1998).

Mainstreaming policy and practice

We turn next to the notion of mainstreaming policy and provision. The participation of disabled people within the whole policy decision-making process is a crucial theme within many sources. The overall principle is stated in different ways but essentially requires the inclusion of representative voices of disabled people as a foundation for developing 'mainstreaming policy'. Much of the literature addresses the complexities of this process, including debates around 'representation' and level of inclusion in policy-making, for example questioning 'consultation' as a low level of service user involvement (see Chapter 7). The following are relevant sources: Williams-Findlay (2003), Wright (1999) and Barnes (2003).

A second major theme is access to and control over the support needed to live independently in the community. Although the notion of independent living is contested within the literature, from the viewpoint of many disabled people it needs to be at the heart of policy development. Central to independent living, as generated by disabled people themselves, is control over their own lives, choices, empowerment, freedom. This theme cuts across a number of different policy areas, including social care, health care, housing, transport and education (Prime Minister's Strategy Unit, 2005).

A third theme is support for families with a disabled member(s). It is helpful to address this as a broad theme, to include families with disabled children as well as issues raised by disabled adults in terms of parenthood. In doing so, the theme incorporates: the challenging by disabled people of the categorization of 'carers' and 'cared for'; issues of transition to adulthood (including awareness that disabled children can be future disabled parents); and issues of right to life (policy relating to the termination of pregnancy whether on the grounds of the foetus or the parent being impaired – or both). Again, in terms of policy, this theme clearly crosses many areas. Indeed it is difficult to specify a policy area that is not relevant (for example Booth and Booth, 1998; Wates, 2002).

Looking from the documented viewpoint of disabled people, then, it can be suggested that the mainstreaming of disability issues in policy has two foundations:

■ The processes of mainstreaming policy need to include the voices of disabled people at all levels and all stages.
■ The focus for mainstreaming policy needs to be as broad as possible, with the initial themes of access to and control over the support needed to live independently in the community and support for families with a disabled member(s).

Conclusion

In conducting research with service users and service providers, we have noticed a common 'finding' that is often inherent in the results of research, but rarely focused on explicitly. When discussing services, services providers will talk of the provision of services, sometimes critically and sometimes less critically. It is our experience, too, that in more recent years, service providers have increasingly emphasized the say that service users have in services at different levels of decision making. Service users themselves, however, usually talk of their use of services in the context of their daily lives. We hope that this more holistic approach has been constructed in this chapter, together of course with the crucial importance of the voices of disabled people in health and social care.

Reflection exercises

1. What are the main questions/problems relating to the mainstreaming of disability issues in policymaking?
2. The following four quotes are from disabled service users from research conducted by French (2004b). As you read them, please make notes on the implications for your practice. Then reflect on the implications for the work of other professional agencies and inter-agency working.

'It was one particular physiotherapist who came in the middle of the night and she was so helpful and made such a difference. She said, "Try dropping your shoulders a little bit" and "If you put a pillow in the back of your neck that will help." I use the techniques all the time now, it seems a very small thing but it made a huge difference. On the whole physiotherapists back away because they think they can't do anything, whereas she approached it in a very different way. She realised that she didn't have to have "hands on" at all, that it was something I could do for myself. It made an enormous difference. They are usually very physical and you are supposed to be very physical. It was a small suggestion together with emotional support. The attitude is usually "We can't rehabilitate you so what's the point?" I'm sure most of them feel that they could use their time better.'

'I liked my speech therapist. She was trying to improve my communication and I remember thinking, "what a fantastic woman, what a fantastic job" ... She showed kindness. Kindness is something that is not acknowledged enough. She was gentle and empathetic, I felt as if she was joining in with my struggle.'

'When she came to see me first of all she told me her name and that's nice, not like "I'm the physio" which I've had before. She said "I'm Mary" and very quickly moved into "how are you feeling?" – not a straight "I'm here to do." She had a really warm manner with her and she said, "Can I sit on the edge, is it all right?" – she didn't make assumptions. She checked that my morphine bracelet was working – all those sorts of things. She really acknowledged what I had been through, how I was feeling and a bit of a warning that the pain would be bad even with the morphine but that there would be a time when it would calm – and I call that respect because there's no denial, it's nice and straight and I value that. I value the information. Mary was concerned with strength and function so I had to do very simple things the first time. She said, "Do the push" and I pushed and I couldn't. I was shocked. I wasn't at all prepared because before I went to sleep for that op I could push myself up with my hands. I lay back down again and I was terribly upset and I had a bit of a panic. She was lovely. She said, "We've done the neurological tests and this is a mixture of post-op weakness and genuine loss most of which we can regain." So I took another breath. She was very honest but she was also very tender. There was something about her presence and her being. I got to know her as a person in a very short time. She was definitely "Mary" and not a physio.'

'One day I went to see her and I felt terrible, very vulnerable, very low self-esteem. I remember wheeling myself into her room and with the good hand I swept everything off her desk on to the floor, the phone and everything, a big drama ... She allowed me to get upset, I was allowed to cry and she was fantastic. She wasn't all, "there, there, here's a hankie" and I poured it all out with broken words. She let me leave without the treatment and I just felt so much lighter, so much better ... She didn't try to pacify me or comfort me, but I didn't want that, I wanted someone to hear me. I trusted her enough to get upset in front of her. I couldn't say what I wanted to say because I didn't have enough speech.'

Suggestions for further reading

1. Clark, A., Giarchi, G.G. and Ford, D. (2010) *Disability, Policy and Practice: Issues for health and social care practitioners.* London, Jessica Kingsley

   Explores the relationship between disability and professional health and social care practice. Arguing that the nature of disability is a holistic construction, a fusion of medical, social and bio-psychosocial models rather than about innate biological defects or limitations, the authors show how professionals must embrace difference in order to generate empowerment and social inclusion for service users.

2. Priestley, M. (1998) *Disability Politics and Community Care.* London, Jessica Kingsley

   Priestley addresses the relationship between the politics of disability and community care policies. Guided by his direct work with representatives of the Disabled People's Movement, he argues that although the ideas behind social policy and practice have started to reflect values such as participation, integration and equality, the current policy and its implementation often undermine those goals.

3. Whalley Hammell, K. (2006) *Perspectives on Disability and Rehabilitation: Contesting assumptions; challenging practice.* Edinburgh, Churchill Livingstone

   Provides an accessible introduction to many of the current theoretical perspectives on disability; enabling readers to challenge the taken-for-granted nature of traditional knowledge and assumptions within the rehabilitation, health and community care industries, and encouraging a more critical approach both to the nature of rehabilitation following injury or illness and to the 'problem' of physical difference and disability.

4 Residential Care

In this chapter we discuss:

- A brief history of residential care – establishment of the welfare state; development of the Disabled People's Movement
- An oral history of residential care – a history of the education of visually impaired people
- Living in residential care: more recent experiences – charity services

This chapter examines the now extensive history of residential care as a discredited provision, whether within the local authority, health service or voluntary sector. We address the concept of autonomy in long-term care as a need and as a right. Within these discussions we shall revisit the continuing issues and controversies of residential/institutional living, including user involvement in controlling people's lifestyles, the rights of disabled people in residential care and resources for residential/institutional living. We shall draw on our own research within a large-scale charity, which examined the views and experiences of disabled people in residential care.

A brief history of residential care

So we begin with a brief history of residential care. It is, indeed, brief and provides only the barest summary culled from a fraction of the relevant literature. We believe, however, that some understanding of where we have come from is essential to understanding where we are now and how policy and practice can be developed. We begin with what might be an unexpected starting point, that is, the role that residential care played in the development of the Disabled People's Movement.

The early 1970s saw the establishment of an organization of disabled people called the Union of the Physically Impaired Against Segregation (UPIAS) (see Chapter 1). This group can be said to be one of the founders of the Disabled People's Movement, as it was to develop in subsequent years in the UK, and also the founders of the social model of disability which would prove so vital to disabled activists (Campbell and Oliver, 1996). The group came into exist-ence around the same time that some of the founders left a Leonard Cheshire care home to establish an early independent living scheme. Leonard Cheshire Disability has now become a large-scale traditional international disabil-ity business/charity. Their principal activities in the UK are the provision of services in support of disabled people in the widest context. These serv-ices include care homes, supported living, domiciliary support, day services, resource centres, rehabilitation, respite care, personal support and training and assistance for those looking for work. The name UPIAS is significant in the context of our present discussions in that they were Against Segregation, and quintessentially segregated residential care provision. This takes us onto a brief history of residential care since the Second World War.

In 1942, resulting from the work of a committee chaired by Sir William Beveridge, the Beveridge Report was published. The Beveridge Report led to the establishment of the welfare state through a raft of social legisla-tion aimed at improving the living conditions of the British population. Health care was much more visible than social care and was said to be the 'jewel in the crown' of the welfare reforms. Social care was not nearly so well thought through or so well financed and far more resources went into 'cure' than into 'care'. When setting up the NHS, the government had to negotiate with the powerful medical profession, who were against it. The result of this was a service with three arms which was highly unequal (Ham, 1999).

| Box 4.1 | **Branches of the NHS** |

The hospital and specialist medical services

This consumed most of the resources. There was, however, a hierarchy of hospitals with the acute hospitals and teaching hospitals being well funded whereas others, such as geriatric hospitals and asylums for people with learning difficulties and mental health problems (which were taken over by the NHS), became 'backwaters'.

Family practitioner services

These included services by GPs, dentists and ophthalmic opticians.

Local authority services

These included services by district nurses, health visitors and social workers and catered for various groups including old, homeless and disabled people.

Part 3 of the National Assistance Act 1948 established welfare departments in local authorities and obliged them to provide accommodation for old, disabled and homeless people over 18 and to promote their welfare. They had few powers or resources, however, to support people at home and it was assumed that much could be left to voluntary services and the family. Little was done apart from providing residential accommodation and a limited home-help service to clean people's homes. The NHS inherited some elements of social care such as the mental handicap asylums and some institutions for old people (Timmins, 2001). These institutions had an appalling history of abuse and neglect which continued under the NHS (Ryan and Thomas, 1990). As Welshman states:

> [T]he powerful sociological critique of institutional care had by the late 1960s been augmented by evidence of scandals relating to ill-treatment, stealing and indifference on the part of staff. (2006, p. 36)

In the 1970s, Young Chronic Sick Units were built in hospital grounds as a way of releasing young disabled people from geriatric and general hospital wards. This measure was, however, opposed by disabled people who already had more ambitious plans to live independently in the community. Even by the 1980s, more than half of disabled people under 64 in residential care were in geriatric wards, hospital wards or old people's homes (Morris, 1991).

The situation was so dire for disabled people following the Second World War that major new charities were founded, particularly by the parents of disabled children. The Spastics Society (later named Scope), for instance, was founded in 1952 and provided residential services, special schools and assessment centres.

Here, then, we can see some of the seeds that were to give rise to the Union of the Physically Impaired Against Segregation, an organization of disabled people, and of the development of policy and subsequent development of the Disabled People's Movement.

An oral history of residential care

The summarized history above is largely one of the formal development of policy and provision rather than that of the experiences of disabled people. History tends to be written by those with power. Disability history is still in its infancy and can explore areas of life that have been barely touched, such as the lives of disabled children:

> There appears to be little historical work in the area of disability and special education which draws on the lives and voices of disabled people themselves. (Armstrong, 2003, p. 71).

French et al. (2006) set out to document the oral history of the education of people with visual impairments, many of whom had experienced residential education. Our aim was to emphasize and promote the voices of people with visual impairments. As Thompson states:

> [O]ral history is not simply a question of adding a complementary source to match documentary evidence, it is more likely to challenge and subvert understandings of care and control. (2000, p. 8)

Oral history is political as it can give rise to group solidarity and individual empowerment (see Chapter 2). It is a way of affirming oneself and claiming one's history. It can challenge assumptions, develop a fuller, more rounded account and may even transform history. It captures great variety and the 'messiness' of history. We concentrate here on the 1944–1981 era and participants' experiences of residential care. We begin with experiences of what can be called abuse. Abuse is a broad and highly complex theme that takes many manifestations within these stories.

Of all the themes within the stories from this era, examples of physical and emotional abuse are the most deeply ingrained and there are numerous accounts of specific experiences. This begins with lack of control over quality of life and lifestyle, and the regimentation to which participants were subjected. Ray, as other participants, described the heavy regimentation of bedtimes:

> 'Bedtime was very regimented to the extent that you fell into categories so you had "six o'clockers", "half past sixers", "seven o'clockers" and when you got to about 13, the latest you could go was nine o'clock.'

Peter described a similar regimented regime in a school run by nuns:

> 'You weren't allowed to talk at meal times unless they said we could. You had to account for every single thing at St Vincent's, you had to be in a given place, at a given time at all times There was no choice about anything at all. You had to eat what you were given, you weren't allowed to leave food. A lot of people were sick there because they were made to eat things that didn't agree with them.'

This regimentation reverberated through these young people's lives and relationships, including their relationships with other pupils. Mary, Jane's twin sister, told us:

> 'Jane and I had each other but the time we were put on silence I wasn't even allowed to speak to her. I think Jane's depression started from those days, she'd vomit for no apparent reason.'

Jane takes up the story:

> 'The adults resented the relationship I had with Mary, they didn't like us being affectionate. Even if one of us was ill they wouldn't let us

comfort each other. I can remember when I first started the depression I was really ill and Mary was cuddling me and this teacher came up and said "Let go of each other, go up to the surgery Jane." It was awful. We weren't allowed to see each other if we were in sickbay. We hated not being together.'

Mary also recalled the denial of privacy, another common abusive experience in these participants' stories:

'We could have our own radio but I had mine taken away from me for a week because I played it somewhere where I shouldn't have done. It was so stupid, it really was. Another rule was that we weren't allowed to go upstairs into the dormitory during the day. When I got to a certain age, and was allowed to wash my own hair, I would always ask permission to wash my hair on a Wednesday evening so I could listen to a certain programme that was on. It was as silly as that. There was nowhere private, you had no privacy whatsoever, privacy was nil.'

Even letters to parents were censored. Carol's letters home were read and censored and her personal possessions checked:

'I hated having things like drawer check. I don't see why you can't keep your things in a mess in your drawer. In those days you didn't you just did what they said and you were in big trouble if you didn't. You had loss of privileges which meant you couldn't go out so it was a big drawback if you didn't do as you were told.'

In Peter's school, run by Catholic nuns, the scrutiny of every aspect of day-to-day life seemed to know no bounds:

'They were very, very strict about modesty and that sort of thing. For instance as soon as you stood up from the bath you were expected to wrap a towel round your waist so that you couldn't look at yourself while you were drying yourself. Even the totally blind kids had to do all this. There were also very strict routines about cleanliness and so on. Not in the sense of having baths every day, we only had a bath once a week and we only changed our socks and underwear once a week, but they were obsessed with our hair being clean. We used to have our hair fine combed with one of those metal combs twice a term and they used to use this horrible, green liquid stuff. The nuns were quite vicious, I can remember my scalp being quite badly scraped and scratched by those combs. With regard to the underwear they would come round every Saturday to collect your dirty laundry and they would inspect your underpants and if there were any 'skid marks' you were made to go off and wash them under the supervision of one of the nuns, even quite small boys had to do that. It was really horrible especially for the blind kids because they didn't always realise.'

The punishments at Beryl's school involved restriction of activity and isolation:

'They used to stand you out in the corridor. Once I had to stand out in the corridor for two hours, I can't think what I'd done. Another time I had to stand with my hands on my head for two hours. It made my arms ache.'

Enforced silence was another form of punishment inflicted on young visually impaired people. Mary recalled:

'When we were eight because we had talked a lot we were put on silence for a week, the whole dormitory. We were also slapped fairly frequently for talking, or for anything, often on our bare bottoms, I think it was like going into a children's prison. It felt like that.'

In these stories, basic 'care' was often experienced as abusive. Being bullied into eating was, for example, repeatedly talked about. Beryl said:

'Every morning when we went down to breakfast, we had senapods and you had to drink it because if you didn't they used to put your drinking chocolate in the same cup so you had to drink it or you wouldn't have a drink at breakfast time. Awful it was. At teatime they used to give you bread and jam, fish paste or marmite or Bovril. We used to have three halves of bread and butter with marmite or Bovril spread on it. Horrible really.'

Neglect characterized Mike's school experiences:

'In those days you weren't allowed your own clothes. The idea then was that everyone needed to be equal and it was thought to be unfair on those children whose families couldn't buy nice clothes if other people had them. The school provided a jacket, grey trousers and hideous shoes. Basically you were depersonalised in terms of that whole ethos. Even then I think I was aware of the Oliver Twist and the Poor Law ethos ... We had to make our beds in a regimented way, the bed had to be inspected in the morning to make sure that the counterpane was straight ... All we had was a chair and an old-fashioned medical-type locker. That was it. No carpets on the floor, no television. They didn't feel that visually impaired children should watch television. All the things you started watching in the holidays you could no longer see. There was no lounge.'

A second major theme was friendships. The importance of friendship is repeatedly emphasized as the best and most enduring experience from school. For Mary, friendships were the best thing to come out of schooling, and the results of constant abuse the worst:

'The bonding, the friendships we made … In a way we were closer to some of our friends than our own sister because we only saw Sue in the holidays really. Our friends were more like our sisters you know. There's lifelong friendships, strong, strong bonding. We supported each other a lot.'

This was also true for Andrew, who attended a day special school and found himself isolated from his brothers and sisters and other children in the community:

'The best thing about school was the friends I made. I've made some very firm friends. I got very cut off from the other children around me at home when I was at the blind school.'

In Jean's account, friendship took on a quality of resistance and collective survival. Here is the source of positive identity countering the identity imposed by the perpetrators of abuse:

'Friendships were very important. I couldn't have gone on without my friendships. It didn't replace parental care but it kept me going. We all valued our friends at school. They did not like close friendships. They didn't like you putting your arm round somebody. And that was something else they didn't understand, how else can we make contact with each other? We haven't got any eye contact. Why not hold somebody's hand or touch their arm? They regarded it all as soppy, silly and childish.'

Ray's experiences typify those of many other participants who were removed from their families:

'The worst thing about the school was being separated from my family because I ended up with no relationships of significance in my home village. It probably caused loss of family awareness. I knew all my family but as time went by, and also for other reasons like my parents dying when I was 12, it made it even more disruptive. I had brothers and sisters but they were all older than me and they were wanting to spread their wings.'

For some participants, like Beryl, the dislocation from the family was fairly complete:

'I never went home much. I lived in Birmingham and the school was in Birmingham but we had such a big family, lots of little ones, and

I was the eldest. It was difficult for my parents even to come to see me. They had day pupils at the school but I didn't really want to be at home because I didn't get on very well there. I got cut off from my family and I felt I didn't know them any more.'

In residential settings, isolation was again enforced by institutional rules and practices. Edris's experiences were widely shared by the participants:

'We weren't allowed to go out alone at all. We got marched to church on a Sunday if you weren't a "weekender", that's what we used to call them. We went in twos in our brown gabardines, a big line, a blind person with a partially sighted one. It was awful. We used to go once a year to the Delever Road School harvest festival and we went to the seaside once a year. We weren't allowed out often and never on our own.'

Many participants spoke of the 'crocodile walks':

'On Saturdays there were junior trails and senior trails. Juniors went in the morning and the seniors went in the afternoon. They were crocodile walks – sighted/blind, sighted/blind – that sort of thing. Blind and partially sighted people had to walk together.' (Ray)

Participants repeatedly spoke about the influences that schools had had on themselves and their lives. This was particularly highlighted for young people leaving residential settings. As Ray pointed out, school experiences could have dire consequences:

'The drawbacks come when you leave, it's another world altogether, and whether I've actually learned it, or whether the social isolation of those days still holds on, I do wonder. It's hard to know what I would have been like. It's like putting somebody in prison for ten years ... At 18 when I came out of the college I knew I had to learn everything again, it was a new world to me, I only knew how to respond to blind people. I didn't know how to behave. The learning process went on over many, many years and at times I think I'm still having to learn it. I didn't know how to make relationships with people, I didn't know how to go to a club, I didn't know how to ask a girl out, I had no idea so basically I stayed at home for ages. I'd never stayed in another person's house. If I met a girl I didn't know what to do, or where to go together.'

Edris, along with others, felt education had held her back from reaching her full potential in later life:

'In a way I've been disappointed in my working life. I'm sure I could have done more if I'd had the encouragement.'

Others spoke of the low expectations they faced:

'The worst thing was the low expectations, the fact that they didn't put any worth on us at all. They didn't respect us as people, the way we were spoken to, it just wouldn't be tolerated today. The teacher we had at 11+ used to say I was lazy. I wasn't lazy, I was scared. To be continually denigrated and told that you're no good, you begin to believe it. If I have a knock of any sort my confidence still goes very quickly. It still lingers, you never completely lose it.' (Mary)

Jane, Mary's twin sister, talks of the lasting psychological effects of the abuse she experienced:

'I've never had a real boy friend, I don't know really. I think my schooling made me very nervous, very timid. It's still there. If somebody praises me I think "Do I deserve that, I'm not that good". It's affected my self-esteem. If you couldn't do something you were stupid, they wouldn't show you again, you were just stupid.'

Although such experiences clearly generate passivity and feelings of exclusion, the development of the Disabled People's Movement within the UK can in part be traced to disabled people's experiences of residential care. These stories are about survival and, with survival, collective empowerment and resistance. Here we believe is a particular example of contexts from which the Disabled People's Movement grew. The movement came, at least in part, from people's impetus to demand and take control over their own lives – having lived through the denial of their rights and choices.

Living in residential care: more recent experiences

We now turn to a research project that we undertook, with Carole Thirlaway, for and within Leonard Cheshire, one of the largest traditional charities within the UK and, indeed, internationally (Swain et al., 2005). The focus of the research was user involvement within the management of Leonard Cheshire. The research was conducted by interviews and focus groups and included 113 participants, service providers and services users. Officially the focus of the research was user involvement, in formal decision making, management and policymaking within Leonard Cheshire. The data collection, however, led us well beyond this. Although involvement in formal decision making held some importance for service user participants, they were far more concerned about their daily lives, choice, opportunities and control over day-to-day living (see Chapter 7 for a full discussion of user involvement). Below, then, we draw on what became a fairly substantial report to present just a little of participants' experiences. In doing so, we wish to make it clear that though the experiences were predominantly negative, this is not an indictment against the specific services provided by Leonard Cheshire. It is the experiences of disabled residents that are the key and, from our reading of other relevant literature, we would suggest that it is representative of disabled residents' experiences, whoever the provider, whether other charities or local authority services. For instance, Cole, McIntosh and Whittaker (2000) report on the experiences of people with learning difficulties in residential care.

A clear major theme within the data was the experiences and consequences of a lack of 'ground level' staff. This reverberated through many aspects of the experiences of the participants. Most of the residents who were interviewed commented on the lack of 'ground level' staff and how this affected their ability to make choices in their daily lives. This is a major issue that affects all aspects of service users' lives and is probably the pivotal influence in the development of service user involvement. Time and again the reason for lack of choice, not being listened to, lack of dignity and lack of control over lives is given as a staffing problem. This lack of choice could reach a very basic level as is evident in the following quotations:

'We have one bath a week, that's on a specific day.'

'We have two (baths) a week ... we'd like more but they can't do it.'

'The toilet. That to me is basic. I was desperate and I rang the bell and at last they came. There are bells everywhere but the only time you don't have to wait is in the night. I just dread it every day and I think "Oh god, here we go again!"'

There was a clear association between day-to-day user control over their lives and the level of support:

'I don't feel all the time that I'm fully in control of what I do and don't do. For instance, I can't prepare myself a meal and I can't move my chair without the assistance of a carer. If I want to go anywhere quickly, go to the toilet or something like that, and don't get there in time, they say "You should have asked" but if there's not enough staff about it's literally impossible to get there, you have to wait for someone to take you.'

'The other night for what I wanted it was no good ringing because there was no night staff who could get into the dispensary. It wasn't worth ringing and I just laid in pain all night.'

Other people spoke of the lack of personal contact with staff that could affect their well-being, quality of life and their ability to make their views heard:

'Sorry to be negative but I find that if you go out you need a carer to come with you and there aren't always carers around that will come with you. They're always tied up.'

'If you ask them a question they won't answer it. They say "I can't answer it at the moment but I'll look into it".'

'They can't do much for us. All right they do what is necessary but if we want that little bit of extra help, like D might or I might need a bit of help with the computer, it just isn't available.'

'You ask someone something and they say "I'll talk to you later" but it takes a while before they see you.'

'I wait, I can't keep asking because it tires me out to keep asking.'

'By the time you've waited for them to come back you've forgotten what you wanted to say.'

This lack of staff contact and attention to their needs led some residents to feel less than human:

'You're more of a number than a person. You're a commodity. You're just a commodity, nothing else. I mean you're put to bed, you get fed, you get up in the morning and that's it. You can book up to go out but that depends on whether the driver's here or you can get a volunteer which we're very short of.'

In these circumstances, empowerment and user involvement in the day-to-day decisions over their own lives can be seen as a problem:

'One of the problems it [user involvement] causes is when residents become more empowered and aware of the opportunities of life they're likely to ask for more. In asking for more, it usually involves staff, and resources are already very scarce and limited, and centred mainly in providing basic daily care in washing, dressing, eating and they occupy an awful lot of time. Empowerment creates problems of staff support. And if the choice of empowerment involves travel then that's a further added burden. Not necessarily to pay the cost of travelling but to have the opportunity with limited transport or escort.'

The idea that the situation was deteriorating, rather than improving, was a recurring theme with participants:

'Too many regulations, like we should be able to go out, to a degree, if there is no driver and we want to go out, we just have to wait until someone comes. When I first started the key workers would take us out on one-to-one trips. We have more people with higher care needs and it is not possible to go out on one-to-one very much any more.'

'Each one of us has a key worker but they have less and less time to spend on us. There's less and less "one-to-one" going on.'

Staff turnover was repeatedly referred to as a central part of the picture:

'Trouble is when people leave they don't replace them in the proper way, they get agency in and if somebody leaves full-time they get somebody part-time.'

For many service users, staffing levels needed to be seen within a broader context. Some of the residents were convinced that too much money was spent at the top of the organization:

'The organisation is too top heavy. When I came here six and a half years ago, there were forty staff up at head office and now they have ninety. At the same time they reduce the staff here. They take the money away from where it's needed.'

'What I feel is that if head office want extra staff, for anything in particular, they get them but if we want more staff we're told we can't have them. I think there should be a lot of job cutting up there. It's far too big.'

Many residents perceived that their own needs were regarded as less important than issues such as paperwork and staff training:

'I'd like to spend more "one-to-one" with people but they don't have the time. It's simple things like communicating. Most of what they go for training for is common sense.'

'Staff have been given more paperwork and if that paperwork needs to be done then things can't be done for the residents.'

'It all boils down to not enough staff. There isn't always the time, they get so much more paperwork with these new Care Standards.'

'There's so much training going on, training for anything and everything, and it takes staff off the floor while they go for training.'

Some of the residents offered interpretations of the lack of staffing which made basic user involvement impossible. The increasing care needs of residents, together with lack of staff to cope with this, was put forward as a major explanation:

'They seem to be taking more nursing cases which accounts for the lack of staff. They're having to do too much. Then they move on. We had three people who all left at once.'

'They go for more (severely) disabled people to get a higher fee and they aren't increasing the care staff to match.'

'There are a lot of highly dependent people now because of this "care in the community" thing and there just aren't enough carers for the amount of people.'

In the past residents had a say in who was accepted to live in the home but this choice has now been eroded:

'When I first came here six years ago the residents could have a say in who lived here, whether a new person was accepted or whether they were refused. The head of home and the head nurse would be there, there would be a volunteer from the outside world and one or more resident. People had a four-week assessment and not everybody got in on that assessment. Then it got changed and nobody gets refused now. So we have no say in who's coming into the home, therefore each one of the care staff has to do two feeds at mealtimes. All the people who come in are highly, highly dependent now. They haven't got the nursing staff or the care staff to be able to cope with it.'

For many participants, then, the notion of developing user involvement begins with increased levels of staffing:

'We've having less and less control over our lives now to what we had a few years ago. It's government legislation, and policy coming from Leonard Cheshire. We haven't got the staff to enable us to do what we want to do anyway.'

'You have a key worker and she says "Are you happy Lynn? Are you doing this?" But nothing happens, she's just one of the carers. She's too busy. They're all too busy.'

'We want more staff, that's what we want.'

Lack of 'ground level' staff also had a serious impact on the ability of the residents to enjoy life outside the home and to exercise choice in their leisure pursuits. A constant theme was lack of transport and drivers. Clearly transport is fundamental to service users in determining their quality of life:

'The transport is very nice but we don't get out enough. There's a shortage of drivers.'

'Recently we had what is known as "Pop in the Park" and we couldn't get volunteer drivers or escorts for that. Since I've been here I've never known us miss that. Also I think they missed "Proms in the Park" as well. They couldn't get any drivers that was the trouble.'

'They often phone up and cancel because they haven't got a driver.'

As with the transport policy, policies and legislation concerning health and safety were reported by the residents as having an impact on their ability to control their lives. The introduction of an excessively overprotective health and safety policy has been responsible for the erosion of basic human rights throughout the organization. This is a huge barrier to the development of service user involvement or having control over their own lives:

> 'There was an instance a couple of months ago where residents were suddenly told by nursing staff one evening that we had to be checked every hour throughout the night every night on the grounds that it was health and safety requirements. That was a gross infringement. There were objections from many residents and I know that it was not fully implemented in that manner.'

Specific examples were given:

> 'When I first went over there [to a bungalow in the grounds of a residential home] my chair was put on charge in the bungalow and they stopped that because of a fire hazard they reckon, dangerous. I've now been told it's all right to do it but I haven't got it back in the bungalow yet to charge.'

They saw assessment as part of the control that others had over their lives:

> 'You've got to be assessed to go out, assessed to use the microwave.'

> 'You can't go out on your own unless you have an assessment. I find it insulting, very insulting! C said I've got another one today. Then you get frustrated. People think we're imbeciles.'

Service users saw the necessity of health and safety concerns, but also thought their lives were unnecessarily restricted, as the following specific examples illustrate. Part of the problem for service users is the application of blanket and universal rules and procedures that take no account of the individual or the local circumstances:

> 'As an organisation they need to think about our right to take risks because sometimes that's what you want to do. A couple of times I've been advised that I shouldn't do something because they don't feel I'm safe enough. One was standing up to go to the loo. They insisted that I had to be hoisted. I can see the logic of that but I felt I could stand. You've got to accept that they are right at some point but they have got to accept your right to take risks for as long as you feel you can. It keeps coming up, health and safety.'

The picture painted, then, is clearly one of lack of quality of life, lack of choice and support, and associated feelings of denial of self and self-respect. It can be argued that such experiences are generally representative, particularly if compared to an earlier period (Humphries and Gordon, 1992). Returning to where we began this section, it is quite easy to see how such experiences could generate the resistance of disabled people and play a role in the growth of the Disabled People's Movement.

Nevertheless, this is not the whole story. Given the size of Leonard Cheshire and the extent of services provided, perhaps it is not surprising that there are clear differences in service users' experiences. At this point we shall include quotations that express satisfaction with the care provided by Leonard Cheshire. It is notable, too, that some service users in expressing such satisfaction also showed little concern about user involvement in the sense of a more formal influence over decision making.

'The thing I appreciate most here is the privacy. You are entirely private in your own room with en suite and it really is a treat.'

'As far as I'm concerned, I mean I can't do anything for myself, I can't get out of bed, feed myself or do anything, I can't do anything to do with cleanliness, and I do find that they do it very well. They take care of you and do everything. And then we have lots of things to do, a lot of entertainment and we're taken out. It takes your mind off how you are really. In that respect I find it's very good. I've only been here a year and a half, but I find that they have been very good to me.'

Conclusion

As throughout this book, we have prioritized the views and experiences of disabled people within this chapter, focusing on those of people who have experienced residential care. These stories convey, by and large, a negative view of residential care, to the extent that they can be called experiences of abuse. Nevertheless, these stories are about survival and, with survival, collective empowerment and resistance. Here we believe is a particular example of contexts from which the Disabled People's Movement grew. The movement came, at least in part, from people's impetus to demand and take control over their own lives – having lived through the denial of their rights and choices. We are not suggesting this was the sole context, but it is a crucial reflection of the discrimination and oppression that disabled people collectively face and challenge. It is from this point that we can now turn to disabled people's experiences within the community and in particular the growth of the Independent Living Movement.

Reflection exercise

This is a good point at which to think about the role of traditional large-scale charities in disabled people's lives. Examine the following questions in relation to your reading of the discussions in this chapter:

1. Why are disabled people absent from powerful positions in traditional charities and why do agencies controlled by disabled people command fewer resources?
2. Why can the charity model and the civil rights model be said to be 'on a collision course'?
3. Why was one of the first slogans of the Disabled People's Movement 'Rights Not Charity'?

Suggestions for further reading

1. Borsay, A. (2005) *Disability and Social Policy in Britain since 1750.* Basingstoke, Palgrave Macmillan

   Explores experiences of physical and mental impairment in Britain since the start of the Industrial Revolution. Its starting point is the exclusion of disabled people from the full rights of citizenship because of their marginality to the labour market. Institutional living and community care are then examined with reference to the changing mixed economy of health and social care.

2. Humphries, S. and Gordon, P. (1992) *Out of Sight: The experience of disability 1900–1950.* Plymouth, Northcote House

   Focuses on the experience of disability for the (mainly) young in the period before the emergence of the welfare state. In the first part of the 20th century more than half a million children, often from poor backgrounds, had some form of physical impairment and grew up in an age not especially sympathetic to their condition nor understanding of their needs.

3. French, S., Swain, J., Atkinson, D. and Moore, M. (2006) *An Oral History of the Education of Visually Impaired People: Telling stories for inclusive futures.* Lampeter, Edwin Mellen Press

   By means of 61 open-ended interviews with visually impaired people (written as stories) and an analysis of documentary evidence, this book explores the history of education, including residential care, for visually impaired children in Britain since the 18th century.

Control of Health and Social Care Services by Disabled People

In this chapter, we will be looking at innovative services that disabled people have developed themselves, or have brought about through prolonged campaigns and political pressure. We will also discuss how these services relate to, and integrate with, statutory and voluntary services. Although some disabled people have found the interventions of professionals and professional services helpful, others have been critical of the control professionals have over their lives and the restrictive nature of the services they provide (French, 2004a; French and Swain, 2008). This situation has led disabled people to create their own innovative services and to press for legislation that gives them greater control over the services they receive (Barnes and Mercer, 2006). We will start this chapter by discussing Centres for Independent (or integrated) Living (CILs) and will then go on to examine the policies of direct payment and individual budgets. We will end the chapter with a discussion of advocacy, with an emphasis on self-advocacy and peer advocacy.

Centres for Independent (Integrated) Living (CILs)

Hasler defines a CIL as, 'an organisation controlled by disabled people, providing support for independent living' (2006, p. 286). It is important to emphasize at this point, as we mentioned briefly in Chapter 1, that when disabled people talk of 'independence' they are not referring to the ability to care for themselves in a narrow, physical sense but the ability to take control of their lives. As Micheline Mason states:

> We know that we have to gain control over our lives even when we need help from others to function. Unless we do this, we can never

make a real contribution to society because our own thoughts will never be expressed through our actions only those of other people, our 'carers' ... Therefore we redefine 'independence' to mean having control over your life, not 'doing things without help'. (2000, p. 66)

There is a large psychological literature which shows that control over one's life is essential for well-being, health, morale and self-confidence (Glasby and Littlechild, 2009).

Our aim in this section of the chapter is to highlight the ways in which services run by disabled people differ from those of traditional statutory and voluntary services in what they offer, how the service is delivered and the underlying ethos and philosophy. We hope that this will provide a concrete example of how the social model of disability (discussed in Chapter 1) can be put into practice in the context of services.

Centres for Independent Living in Britain took their inspiration and impetus from CILs in the USA. The first CIL was opened in Berkeley, California in 1973 and by 2000 there were approximately 300 similar centres throughout the USA (Charlton, 2000). CILs have now been established in most countries of the Western world and in some countries of the majority world, for example Brazil and Zimbabwe (Oliver and Barnes, 1998). Barnes and Mercer outline the history of CILs in Britain:

Initially, in the early 1980s, user-controlled organisations were developed by groups of disabled people leaving residential care who were seeking practical solutions to overcome the absence of statutory or voluntary agency support for independent living in the community. These included Britain's first two Centres for Independent/Integrated Living (CILs) in Hampshire and Derbyshire. (2006, p. 77)

In Britain, most CILs rely on local government for a substantial part of their funding.

Centres for Independent Living are run *by* disabled people *for* disabled people, although non-disabled allies and supporters are usually welcome. The centres provide many services including peer counselling, advocacy, maintenance and provision of equipment, transport, training in independent living skills, housing, mentoring, attendant services and disability equality training including training of the trainers. Some provide extensive databases on issues relevant to disabled people, such as accessible holiday venues, and undertake research. They also lobby members of parliament and help other groups of disabled people to organize democratically.

Their premises and information are as accessible to disabled people as possible with, for example, induction loops and information in Braille. However, accessibility is sometimes compromised by lack of funding: for example, it may be difficult to obtain fully accessible premises in a convenient central location (Barnes and Mercer, 2006).

Box 5.1	**Southampton Centre for Independent Living (SCIL)**

The SCIL was founded in 1984 by a group of disabled people. In the early days of the organization it was run by volunteers, but by 2004 it had 14 full- and part-time employees and an annual income of £565,000 (SCIL Annual Report 2004–2005). The organization has a large group of volunteers and an active management committee. Its main sources of funding are from local authorities and the National Lottery Charities Board. For the year 2007–2008, 63% of the funding came from Hampshire County Council and 18% from Southampton City Council. The CIL does, however, struggle with funding. Ian Loynes, the chief executive, states: 'Nationally SCIL has a very high profile. Locally we have never enjoyed wholehearted support (or funding) from our Local Authorities … I hope that in the next year we will convince Local Authorities about just how important we and other user-led organisations are in their personalisation agendas' (SCIL Annual Report 20007–2008, p. 11). CILs are in a particularly precarious position in the present financial climate of severe cuts.

The organization is also dependent on raising funds from its own projects. Such money is raised from various activities including disability equality training and consultancy, which in 2007–2008 comprised one tenth of the budget (SCIL Annual Report, 2007–2008).

The aims of the organization are to:

- provide a means by which disabled people may take control of their own lives, achieve full participation in all spheres of society, and effect change in how they are viewed and treated
- provide encouragement, assistance, advice, support and facilities to individuals and groups wishing to live independently
- raise the expectations of disabled people, individually and collectively, and ensure their voice is heard (SCIL Annual Report 2007–2008, p. 13).

The work of the SCIL is based around twelve basic needs which have been identified by disabled people (SCIL, 2005). These are for:

- an accessible environment
- aids and equipment
- personal assistance
- an adequate income
- advocacy and self-advocacy
- counselling
- accessible public transport
- accessible/adapted housing
- inclusive education and training opportunities
- equal opportunities for employment
- appropriate and accessible information
- appropriate and accessible health care

The SCIL works in all of these areas, either directly or by collaborating with other organizations such as the Eastleigh Advocacy Service which works with people with learning difficulties. The SCIL shares premises with the Disability Advice and

Information Network, which enables easy communication and collaboration between them. In 2007–2008 its funded projects were to:

- supply information and support to disabled people receiving direct payments
- provide disability equality training in a wide range of organizations
- assist disabled people in recruiting and employing their own personal assistants
- train disabled people to undertake consumer audit in local authorities and other organizations
- reach out to disabled people, particularly young people and those who are most disadvantaged, to help them take control of their lives
- provide personal development courses, a mentoring service and a peer advocacy service, for instance to help disabled people to make formal complaints against their local authorities.

The SCIL also has an extensive database of information produced in accessible formats. It is a member of the British Council of Disabled People and actively campaigns on issues of concern to disabled people. The organization has been active in campaigning for comprehensive disability discrimination legislation and in a campaign against disabled people being charged for essential community care services. The SCIL is also involved in research, for instance that undertaken by the National Centre for Independent Living (an independent organization run by disabled people) which aims to identify disabled people's support needs.

It is clear from this account that the services offered by this and other CILs differ from those of traditional statutory and voluntary services by taking a broader view of the meaning of disability and acting upon it. The emphasis is not just on health and social care, although this is viewed as very important, but on broader issues such as employment, education, leisure and all aspects of independent living. The SCIL and many other CILs are overtly political and actively involved in campaigning and research to better the lives of disabled people.

From their research, Barnes and Mercer (2006) found user-controlled organizations, including CILs, to be more accountable to disabled people than statutory and voluntary organizations, and more responsive to their needs both in terms of what is offered and how it is offered. User-controlled organizations are more likely to enhance user choice and control and are more aware and sensitive to the impact of physical and social barriers. Barnes and Mercer state that, 'Although lacking the resources to provide a fully comprehensive service, CIL-type services are regarded as substantially more receptive to disabled people's needs' (2006, p. 135).

Local authorities have been reluctant to invest in CILs, which struggle with inadequate and insecure funding (Hasler, 2006). Compared with statutory services, their funding is low, making it difficult for them to fulfil all their objectives and to be competitive (Barnes and Mercer, 2006). Furthermore, if self-funding is increased, by providing disability equality training for example, local authorities are liable to cut the financial contribution they make. User-controlled organizations are also relatively few in number and there is no formal system of referral from other organizations. Barnes and Mercer (2006) found 84 user-controlled organizations in their research, of which 22 were CILs. They state:

> Most disabled people across Britain remain reliant upon a bewildering array of services delivered by a variety of statutory and voluntary agencies generally, but not exclusively, controlled and run by non-disabled professionals and dominated by a culture of 'social care' rather than social right. (2006, p. 121)

Although a good collaborative relationship can be developed between statutory services and CILs, the reliance of CILs on statutory funding can cause problems. Local authorities may, for example, insist that CILs define the people they work with in terms of impairment, which is anathema to those working within a social model philosophy. Local authorities may also monitor performance in terms of quantitative criteria that may not be appropriate for the type of work CILs are engaged in – a problem that health and social care workers working in fields such as mental health may also experience. It has also been argued that professionals working within statutory services, such as social workers, 'colonize' the ideas and initiatives of disabled people, modifying them and taking them over as their own. Centres for Independent Living may, for example, provide statutory and voluntary services with experience, about employing personal assistants for instance, which these services can then use to undercut CILs when competing for contracts (Barnes and Mercer, 2006). Ian Loynes, the chief executive of SCIL, states, 'There are many traditional charities circling like vultures and therefore we all have to work hard to stop our revolution from dying' (SCIL, 2000, p. 15). It should be kept in mind that CILs, and independent living generally, have been achieved in the face of considerable opposition and scepticism by professionals of statutory and voluntary services.

Political campaigning, particularly if it involves direct action, can also be problematic for organizations which are dependent on statutory bodies for some of their funding. Once the ideas and policies of statutory bodies are incorporated into the mainstream political agenda of user-led organizations, their radical edge may be lost (Barnes and Mercer, 2006). This may also be the case if they collaborate with traditional charities. Some user-led groups, for example Disability Action North East, avoided statutory funding in order to remain autonomous although this left them vulnerable – indeed the organization is now moribund through lack of funds.

Equally as important as the many practical services CILs provide, is the challenge they pose to traditional services. Drake states that CILs 'have proved a cogent and powerful alternative to the traditional gamut of projects like day centres and social clubs' (1999, p. 190), and Oliver and Zarb believe that CILs represent, 'an explicit critique of prevailing social structures and the position of disabled people within them' (1997, p. 206). Centres for Independent Living also show that disabled people, rather than being passive victims, are capable of running their own affairs. As Finkelstein states:

> The fact that the centres and the services they provide have been devised and delivered by disabled people ... presents a positive and rigorous public image contradicting the general depiction of disabled people as a burden on the state and an appropriate focus for the attention of charity. (1991, p. 34)

Centres for Independent Living have arisen from the personal and political struggles of disabled people and have engaged statutory authorities in a social model approach. They have also blurred the distinction between users and providers (Priestley, 1998). Barnes states that CILs 'represent a unique attempt to achieve self-empowerment as well as being a form of direct action aimed at creating new solutions to problems defined by disabled people themselves' (1991, p. 223). Despite potential conflict, the New Labour government was in favour of the expansion of CILs and wanted every local authority to have a user-led organization, such as a CIL, in place by 2010 (Prime Minister's Strategy Unit, 2005). Furthermore, in the government paper *Putting People First* (DH, 2007b) it is contended that collective influence, for instance by Centres of Integrated Living, can be important in helping people make individual choices – a view that is supported by Brooks (2007) from the Institute of Public Policy Research.

Direct payment

One way in which disabled people have sought to take control of their lives is through the system of 'direct payment' whereby they receive a cash payment instead of, or additional to, the provision of direct social services.

Box 5.2	**The history of direct payment**

The 1948 National Assistance Act made it illegal for local authorities in England and Wales to provide funding directly to disabled people, or for disabled people to employ their own personal assistants, although by the 1980s some local authorities had found loopholes in the law (Glasby and Littlechild, 2006). Indirect payment, whereby money for personal assistance is administered to disabled people via a third party, was, however, legal and various trusts were set up for this purpose. Such schemes could also be administered by institutions such as voluntary organizations (Pearson, 2006a). In a study by Browne (1990) it was found that by 1990 59% of the 69 local authorities that participated in the study made direct or indirect payments to disabled people.

The first indirect payment scheme in Britain was developed in the 1960s by a small group of disabled people in Hampshire. They persuaded their local authority to re-house them in the community and to use the money saved in doing so to pay for personal assistants. The payments were administered by the residential institution, *Le Court* Cheshire Home in Hampshire, where the disabled people had been living (Barnes and Mercer, 2006).

A major advance in independent living was the Independent Living Fund, which was instigated in 1988 following years of pressure from disabled people (Glasby and Littlechild, 2006). Funding was from central government and went directly to disabled people of working age to purchase personal and domestic services. Applicants were means tested and assessment of need was undertaken by social workers. The scheme was very popular and far outstripped estimated demand, which led to its closure to new applicants in 1993. Existing members continued to receive money from the Independent Living (Extension) Fund but new applicants were only accepted if they were already receiving at least £200 worth of services form the local authority per week. The maximum direct payment they could receive was £375 and applicants had to be under 67.

Following years of intensive campaigning and research by the Disabled People's Movement (led by the British Council of Disabled People's Independent Living Committee) the Community Care (Direct Payments) Act 1996 was passed, and was implemented in 1997. Throughout the campaign, support had gradually been gained from MPs and professional bodies, including the Association of Directors of Social Services (Hasler, 2004) and the British Association of Social Workers (Glasby and Littlechild, 2009).

The Community Care (Direct Payments) Act 1996 was a major break-through in the lives of disabled people, which was achieved through their own persistence, ingenuity and imagination. As Glasby et al. state, 'the campaign for direct payments was initiated, led and brought to successful fruition by disabled people' (2006, p. 25). Zarb and Nadash (1994), for instance, undertook research for the British Council of Disabled People to demonstrate that direct payment was cost effective. This was very important in gaining government support (Barnes and Mercer, 2006; Glasby and Littlechild, 2009). Pearson and Riddell state that:

> Central to these changes were the roles of small groups of disabled
> people demanding a more flexible alternative to rigid and paternalistic
> modes of service provision offered to them by local authorities ...
> implementation of the 1996 Act represented a significant victory for
> the disability movement. (2006, p. 4)

This Act gave local authorities the power, but not the duty, to make cash payments directly to disabled individuals in lieu of social services. In 2001, after further campaigning, direct payment became mandatory. At first, direct payment was restricted to people under 65 but this was lifted in 2000 following campaigns by organizations such as Age Concern and the National

Centre for Independent Living. Direct payments were extended in 2001 to include the carers and parents of disabled children and 16- and 17-year-olds.

Direct payment cannot be used for permanent residential accommodation, and relatives and people living within the same dwelling as the disabled person cannot usually be employed as personal assistants (Hasler, 2004). In some areas, however, it is difficult to recruit suitable personal assistants, which has led to some relaxation of this rule (Prime Minister's Strategy Unit, 2005). Williams (2006) notes, for instance, that in rural areas direct payment may be the only option available. The employment of family members as personal assistants is particularly beneficial to people from ethnic minorities, who may have difficulty finding culturally sensitive services, and some older people. People with dementia, for instance, may only accept care from a close family member (Glasby and Littlechild, 2009). By allowing family members to become personal assistants in some situations, the government is partially absolved of the criticism that it contributes to the exploitation of carers, who are typically women.

Although direct payment is now mandatory, the amount of money allocated to service users is discretionary, which has tended towards a 'post code lottery' and lack of transparency (Glasby and Littlechild, 2009). It can be difficult for local authorities to release money for direct payments as it is often tied up in block contracts. Furthermore, the numbers of clients tend to increase when direct payment is offered (Pearson, 2006b). The assessment of need remains with the local authority and the financial circumstances of the disabled person are taken into account when calculating the amount to be paid. Likewise, the direct payment can only be used to buy what the disabled person has been assessed as needing which is almost always perceived to be basic day-to-day care such as dressing, bathing and preparing food. As Hasler states, 'Although direct payments arose from a disability rights perspective, in legislative terms they fit within community care law. This has been a constraint on how they have developed' (2004, p. 221).

Some local authorities do, however, take a relaxed approach to how direct payments are used. Hasler et al. (1999), for instance, quote a local authority manager as saying, 'Mowing the grass may not be in your assessment but once the resources have been allocated it should be up to you how you deploy them' (p. 54). Local authorities do, however, monitor how the money is spent and whether there is a surplus and the lack of clarity about the rules can cause confusion and anxiety to the people receiving payments (Pearson, 2006c).

The implementation of direct payment has been slow for all disabled people, but people with learning difficulties and users of mental health services have been particularly disadvantaged (Glasby et al., 2006). This has not been helped by the reluctance of some social workers to inform themselves about direct payment and to facilitate its use (Pearson, 2006d). Indeed, Glasby and Littlechild (2009) believe that the attitude of social workers is the most important determinant of whether or not somebody receives a direct payment. The legislation states that recipients of community care must consent to receiving direct payments. Thus the payment cannot be imposed on people and they must be able to manage the payment, although help is now provided if required. This 'willing and able' rule posed difficulties, especially in the early days, for some client groups in obtaining direct payments. Those with learning difficulties and severe mental health problems are particularly affected, although ways can be found to obtain consent by, for example, using alternative communication systems such as Makaton (a sign language), giving sufficient time, and ensuring that information is made as accessible as possible. Hasler believes that, 'Stereotyped ideas about the capacity of mental health service users or people with learning difficulties to manage their own support has limited the spread of direct payments to these user groups' (2004, p. 223), although the passing of the Mental Capacity Act in 2005, and the implementation of the Independent Mental Capacity Advocacy Service, may have helped to resolve this issue. On the other hand, the requirement that disabled people are willing to receive a direct payment may serve to protect those who are considered 'difficult' who may otherwise be 'off loaded' by statutory service providers by providing them with a direct payment against their wishes (Glasby and Littlechild, 2009).

For disabled people who cannot give consent because of profound impairments, 'evidence of consent' is now accepted where the disabled person indicates to others what he or she likes and dislikes by, for example, showing signs of happiness or distress (Williams and Holman, 2006). Direct payments may also be provided through someone with power of attorney for the user (Hasler, 2004) and, since the Health and Social Care Act 2008, the direct payment can be made to a 'suitable person' acting on the disabled person's behalf (Glasby and Littlechild, 2009). Talking of the benefits of direct payment to people with learning difficulties, Williams and Holman state:

> [P]eople with learning difficulties often need considerable and on-going support to manage direct payment ... but with the right support their lives can be turned around. Where previously they felt controlled entirely by others expectations and demands, direct payments give them a unique chance to gain some real autonomy by controlling their own service. (2006, p. 74)

Ryan and Holman tell of the transformed life of a man with learning difficulties who received direct payments:

> Peter has a hectic life now. He does the things that he wants to do. He really enjoys swimming, bowling and visiting museums. His itinerary is decided by Peter himself and his personal assistants explore new ideas with him. Peter indicates what he likes to do and when he wants to do it. (1998, p. 22)

Despite these benefits, Hasler (2004) states that by the end of 2001 only a minority of people using direct payment had learning difficulties and an even smaller number had mental health problems. Similarly, Glasby and Littlechild (2002) state that in 2000 only 6% of people receiving direct payments had a learning disability and that 20% of local authorities had not implemented a direct payment scheme. Some local authorities were innovative, while others withheld payments to all but a tiny minority of disabled people until direct payments became mandatory in 2001. Local authorities are, however, now assessed by the number of clients receiving a direct payment. As Riddell states, 'In England the Department of Health has used the proportion of direct payment users among community care users as a key indicator contributing to local authority star ratings' (2006, p. 40). Although this may be beneficial to those disabled people who want a direct payment, it also has the potential to push direct payments on to people who may not want it.

Although the benefits of direct payment to people with learning difficulties and mental health problems are clear, Williams points out the considerable difficulties that can arise when somebody else, a parent for example, is managing the direct payment. In this situation there are questions over ownership of the payment, the purpose of which may be as much about fulfilling the needs of the family as about the independence of the disabled person. Thus conflict between disabled people and 'carers' is not necessarily reduced, and could be made worse, by receiving a direct payment.

The uptake of direct payments has also been slow among disabled people from ethnic minorities. Various barriers have been identified by Butt et al. (2000) and Glasby and Littlechild (2009) that mirror problems of access to health and social services among ethnic minorities generally (see Chapter 8). This includes lack of accessible information, lack of outreach services, lack of involvement of people from ethnic minorities in policy, practice and research, poor recruitment of health and social care staff from ethnic minorities, cultural insensitivity and racism. Although the use of direct payments among all groups is rising, people with physical impairments still make up the majority of users and there are great regional variations, with those in London and the southeast of England being the best served (Glasby and Littlechild, 2006).

As noted above, the struggle for direct payments was part of a wider, and ongoing, campaign among disabled people for independent living. This reflects the dissatisfaction disabled people feel with the support offered by statutory services, which are often inflexible and unreliable (Riddell, 2006; Glasby and Littlechild, 2009). Disabled people are, for instance, frequently kept waiting for long periods of time or are forced to go to bed and get up at times that are not of their choosing. Barnes and Mercer report from their research that 'Several people talked about the frustration of not knowing when, or sometimes whether, staff would turn up' (2006, p. 118). High staff turnover and inexperienced or unknown staff performing intimate tasks was also a major concern yet complaining was problematic because of the fear of being labelled a 'trouble maker' and the impact this may have on future care.

Disabled people's experience of direct payment

Many disabled people find that the services they receive when controlling the resources themselves through having a direct payment are superior to those provided by statutory services even though the cost is the same or less (Holman and Bewley, 1999; Williams, 2006). Dawson found that disabled people value the greater flexibility that direct payment provides as well as the decrease in involvement with professionals and professional agencies. She quotes many people whose lives have been transformed by the policy. Below is an example:

'With Social Service home care I feel that they came in, "did me" and then went off and "did" someone else, I was beholden to them. With Direct Payment I'm the boss and the employee has a different approach to me as I'm paying them rather than someone sending them to help a hopeless person.'
(Dawson, 2000, p. 19)

Jackie Gelling, a service user, says that 'direct payments have revolutionised my life' (2006, p. 129) and Simone Baker states 'I am less tired, experience less pain ... I am left with enough energy at the end of the day to do things with my daughter that she wants me to do' (2006, p. 133). Campbell believes that: 'what is probably common to all direct payment users is that they start us on the road to participating in society as equal citizens' (2006b, p. 131). Angie Stewart makes a similar strong personal statement 'having direct payments to employ personal assistants has increased my confidence, enhanced my management skills and for the first time ever put me in control of my life and my future' (2006, p. 128). Hasler states that:

'The flexibility offered by the system allows people to work, to travel, to be active parents, in short to do the range of things that non disabled people expect to do. The denial of opportunity to do these things is a denial of basic freedoms.' (2004, p. 221)

Many disabled people contend that those who have never worked within health and social care make the best personal assistants because they come to the job with few preconceived ideas about what disabled people need and what they can and cannot do (Smyth, 2006). Morris, talking of his experience of employing a personal assistant, states:

'I'd never done it before. I was used to being told what to do, when to do it, where it should be done and how it should be done. The PA had never really seen a crip before and also didn't know what to do thank god. So we actually learnt together.' (2000, p. 17)

Talking of older people who are receiving direct payments, Clark states 'generally speaking most wanted someone they could get on with, who was trustworthy and who would respect them, their homes and belongings' (2006, pp. 33–4). Part of the benefit for the older people was to be able to laugh and chat with the personal assistant and to go shopping.

At the present time, an individual's health needs cannot be met by a direct payment despite joint funding between health and social care agencies (Glendinning, 2006). This is so even though the divide between health needs and social needs has always been blurred. Glendinning (2006) found, however, that the health care needs of disabled people were frequently met by their personal assistants, who undertook physiotherapy, stoma care and general nursing during periods of illness. Personal assistants are relatively flexible whereas health professionals are often unavailable or will deal with only part of a task. Glasby and Littlechild (2002) claim that some disabled people who receive direct payments purchase the services of health professionals. They believe that this is unjust both in terms of having to spend money that has been designated for social needs on health care needs and for creating a two-tier system where those who receive a direct payment can purchase health care services more readily than others. Government has also acknowledged this to be a problem (Prime Minister's Strategy Unit, 2005).

Williams (2006) found that one of the biggest benefits of direct payment was being able to choose personal assistants. Stevens agrees that 'Employing staff can be one of the most empowering things when it works' (2006, p. 134), but he also relates various problems he has had with personal assistants including robbery. A number of concerns have also been raised by service users and professionals about the employment of personal assistants including the possibility of fraud, robbery, abuse and exploitation. However, it is also emphasized by disabled people that taking risks is an important part of full citizenship and that, historically, disabled people have always been at risk of abuse. As Vasey states:

> Disabled people are forever being cast as vulnerable, hence the
> services that support us tend to be overprotective. Direct Payments
> are about the right to take risks to learn, like everybody else does,
> from our mistakes and to develop into wiser, stronger people. That is
> independent living … Having PAs enabled me to find out who I am
> and now enables me to be who I am. (2000, pp. 129–30)

Glasby and Littlechild, while believing that safety issues need attention, conclude that 'provided that sensible precautions are taken, it is difficult to see how receiving direct payments could be any more risky than receiving indirect services' (2002, p. 119).

Supportive organizations are available to people who choose to have a direct payment but do not wish to take on the full role of employer. These organizations may, for instance, help with contracts, the payroll and the recruitment of personal assistants. Many of these organizations are independent of social services and are user-led, for instance CILs frequently undertake this work. Pearson (2006c) found that support organizations can greatly encourage uptake of direct payment, particularly in the case of user-led organizations where peer support networks are frequently developed. However, as noted above, user-led organizations have problems with securing funding from local authorities because of their campaigning role and broad interest in all facets of independent living rather than a narrow focus on 'care'. For this reason, non-user-led organizations may sometimes win contracts over those that are user-led. As Pearson states, 'local authorities are more comfortable in funding a designated service with a set number of roles ... rather than user-led organisations with a wider remit' (2006c, p. 32). Ian Loynes, the chief executive of the Southampton CIL, is critical of the way in which contracts for work with disabled people sometimes go to non-user-led charities. He states:

> Non-user-led charities continue to steal peer support services from groups of disabled people and I feel we should start calling these organisations to account – How can they claim to be committed to the empowerment of disabled people on the one hand and then, on the other hand, take work away from us? Charitable hypocrisy is unending and we should highlight it for what it is. (SCIL Annual Report 2007– 2008, p. 13)

Williams (2006) found that users welcome organizations that are independent of social services.

| Box 5.4 | Observing care by direct payment |

From September 2007 until November 2008, I, Sally, had the opportunity to observe the working and personal relationship between a close friend, Sue, and Sandra her personal assistant. Sue, who died of breast cancer in November 2008, received personal care for the last eighteen months of her life. She was assessed by social services as needing one hour of care each day to help with personal tasks such as bathing and preparing meals. At first, the service was provided by a local care agency and many different people came to help Sue. They were mostly kind and willing but time-keeping was erratic and Sue found some people more capable than others. She would, for instance, only allow specific people to help her with bathing which involved the use of a hoist. There were also many rules about what help they could provide. They were not, for instance, permitted to do shopping or cleaning.

After a few months Sue initiated a direct payment on the advice of a social worker. She chose to employ Sandra, who had worked for the care agency but had since become self-employed, as her personal assistant. Sue did not want to cope with the administrative side of being an employer so this was fully managed by a local disabled people's organization.

Sandra stayed with Sue until the last week of her life when she was transferred to hospital. She visited Sue's home at specific times of Sue's choosing for half an hour in the morning and half an hour in the evening. She was always on time and was prepared to do a wide variety of tasks. As well as assisting with personal care, she did the shopping and cleaning, sorted out technical problems with Sue's computer and mobile phone, put some 'flat-packs' together, looked after the cat, watered the garden and helped with the mail. When I stayed with Sue, Sandra liked to look after us both – bringing us cups of tea in bed and preparing breakfast. At first I felt guilty and embarrassed about this but soon realized that she was trying to make our time together as happy as possible. Many of the tasks Sandra performed were not, I am sure, in Sue's care plan – but, happily, nobody checked.

Probably the most important of Sandra's attributes was her ability to allow Sue full control of her life and not to impose her own values. Sue was a self-contained, disorganized, untidy and somewhat eccentric person. Sandra was willing to help with any task but never attempted to cajole or persuade Sue that the room needed tidying, that the bed needed changing or that she ought to get up. She did what Sue wanted her to do and, with just one hour each day, contributed positively and significantly to Sue's life practically, socially and emotionally, and enabled her to keep her identity and maintain her chosen lifestyle until the end.

Criticisms of direct payment

Despite the benefits of direct payments, there have been some criticisms. Disabled people are still assessed on the basis of need by health and social care professionals, which, as Waters and Duffy (2007) point out, is perceived as a gift rather than a right. As noted above, there is lack of transparency regarding finance and an uneven distribution of people who receive a direct payment in terms of both impairment and geographical location (Barnes and Mercer, 2006). The payment disabled people receive varies and can be inadequate, leading to poor working conditions for personal assistants. Although direct payment may be cheaper than traditional services, there are hidden costs in setting it up, for instance the expense of advertising for personal assistants. Recruiting staff can be difficult and disabled people do not always receive adequate support – CILs, for instance, which provide peer support, information, training, advice and advocacy, are often struggling for survival due to inadequate funding. Glasby and Littlechild (2009) contend that the policy of direct payment has not fundamentally changed the underlying system of health and social care but has rather been an important 'bolt on' to the existing system. Furthermore, disabled commentators have criticized the policy of direct payment on ideological grounds. Priestley points out that taken as an isolated policy, without social and environmental change, direct payment reinforces the idea that disability is an individual problem. He states that, 'direct payment legislation is being played out within a needs–based system of distributive welfare rather than within a rights–based framework for inclusive citizenship' (1998, p. 205).

Shakespeare (2000) also sees the contradiction between the individualism of direct payment and the collectivism of the Disabled People's Movement. He believes that the overall philosophy of individualism, as well as barrier removal and the need for personal assistance, must be addressed if the aspirations of disabled people are to be realized. The Community Care (Direct Payments) Act 1996, which was brought in by a Conservative government, fitted the philosophy of 'marketization of care' and, as noted above, was found to be cost effective. This neoliberal agenda sits uncomfortably with a human rights approach and has been regarded by some as 'back door privatization' (Williams, 2006).

Whatever the limitations, Priestley believes that, 'Direct payment legislation is an important policy development for the Disabled People's Movement. It challenges and undermines cultural associations between disability and dependence' (1998, p. 204). Bornat goes further in believing that, 'the very nature of direct payment raises questions about the future direction of health and social care in the 21st century' (2006, pp. 2–3).

Individual budgets

In recent times, government thinking has turned towards the policy of individual budgets (also known as personal budgets). Individual budgets can be a mixture of statutory, private and voluntary services as well as cash, including direct payment, which can be spent on anything that meets the person's needs or desires, provided they are legal and viewed as legitimate by the local authority.

Individual budgets promote financial transparency and fairness in a way that direct payment, with its postcode lottery, does not. With individual budgets, people are placed in a funding bracket according to their needs and are told how much money has been allocated to them. The policy also promotes self-assessment and flexibility over how budgets are spent and how much control people have over them (Prime Minister's Strategy Unit, 2005). Glasby and Littlechild (2009) believe that the policy of individual budgets is attempting to transform the culture and practice of the social care system as a whole and that, in time, they may simply be used as an income adjustment.

An individual budget may comprise funding from many different agencies, including health, education, social care, employment and equipment grants, as a way of providing greater flexibility and individuality. In *Improving the Life Chances of Disabled People* it is stated that, 'The budget should be used to get whatever type of support the individual needs, personal assistance, housing adaptations, help with transport to work or something else entirely' (Prime Minister's Strategy Unit, 2005, p. 13). Assessments from different funding organizations, and crucially disabled people themselves, are, therefore, pooled to meet the needs of individual disabled people. Services may be provided by community groups, the voluntary sector, the private sector, social services and family and friends. In this way it is hoped that disabled people will gain greater control of their lives than direct payment allows (Carr, 2008). The popularity and success of direct payments has stimulated much of the thinking about individual budgets. As Carr states, 'Personalisation has some of its roots in the disability, mental health survivor and service user movements' (2008, p. 10). Inter-agency working among professionals is essential for this policy to be implemented successfully.

The implementation of this policy involves the following steps as explained by Glasby and Littlechild (2009). It can be seen that the focus has moved away from assessment and towards support.

- Set the personal budget
- Plan support with help if needed. Some people may manage their own support entirely while others may want a care manager. Although support may come from CILs, it will be individual rather than block purchased and of the individual's choosing
- Control budget according to the individual's wishes. Disabled people may choose to control the budget themselves or may welcome help
- Organize support – with or without help
- Live life
- Review and learn – in collaboration with the local authority

These steps are underpinned by the following key principles (adapted from Glasby and Littlechild, 2009), which are markedly similar to those of the Southampton CIL that we discussed above:

- The right to independent living
- The right to an individual budget
- The right to self-determination
- The right to accessibility
- The right to flexibility in using the budget
- Accountability – the government and the person using the budget have a responsibility to each other to share learning and explain decisions
- The right of the disabled person, their families and communities to be considered capable of managing support

The results of small-scale studies that have been conducted with disabled people receiving a personal budget show that satisfaction is high, with people reporting a greater quality of life, the ability to leave institutions, greater control and more use of community facilities rather than 'special' facilities such as day centres (Poll et al. 2006, cited in Glasby and Littlechild, 2009).

Individual personal health budgets are now being piloted in various parts of the country following the 2009 Health Act. Health care trusts have, for some time, offered personal budgets but have not been permitted to give money directly to individuals. When this policy is fully implemented, people will be assessed to establish their health care needs and will then have the freedom to spend their health budgets to meet those needs. For instance, a person with chronic back pain may choose to pay for regular massage.

Possible problems with individual budgets

The policy of individual budgets is part of a wider vision of personalization in services. As discussed above, it involves innovative partnerships and collaborative ways of working in order to provide tailor-made support for individual people. Such full inclusion has always been the aspiration of the Disabled People's Movement but there is scepticism of its realization without a substantial increase in funding (Barnes and Mercer, 2006). Indeed, in *Improving the Life Chances of Disabled People* it is stated that individual budgets will only be implemented 'subject to the availability of appropriate resources to initiate change' (Prime Minister's Strategy Unit, 2005, p. 93) and that pilot studies need to address whether individual budgets are cost effective. Williams (2006) voices a note of caution concerning the underlying ethos of individual budgets, which we discussed in relation to direct payment, as to whether the agenda of the government concerns the broad notion of citizenship or simply the marketization of care.

Another concern is the attitudes and knowledge of frontline staff and whether the success of individual budgets will depend on this. There is a risk that the lack of understanding of the philosophy of individual budgets could limit their effectiveness. Furthermore, staff may obstruct individual budgets, including direct payment, because of fear of loss of control, lack of training and information, perceived expenditure, workload implications, lack of a 'champion' to promote the policy, vested interests (for instance threats to services such as day centres) and lack of trust that the money will be spent appropriately. As Glasby and Littlechild state:

> [S]ocial workers have been shown to use their professional discretion in order to balance competing priorities and to protect themselves against the overwhelming pressures that they face ... Often they will seek to manage their work loads by making assumptions about their service users, categorising them and forming stereotyped responses to their needs, thereby adding a degree of stability and predictability to their work. (Glasby and Littlechild, 2009, p. 141)

Other possible problems, which have been voiced in relation to direct payments and personalized services, include risk to disabled people who may be vulnerable to abuse, and exploitation of personal assistants due to inadequate finance, their isolation and lack of a career structure. However, despite these problems, research indicates that job satisfaction among personal assistants is very high (IFF Research 2008, cited in Glasby and Littlechild, 2009).

Despite possible problems, Bewley believes that social workers are crucial to the success of direct payment schemes and that the sharing of power 'is a fantastic opportunity for care managers to be inspired by their job' (2000, pp. 14–15). Glasby and Littlechild (2002) agree that direct payments offer an exciting role for social workers, although they recognize that, for direct payments to be successful, social service provision, policy and practice need to be 'consistent with the goals of the Independent Living Movement and be guided by the considerable expertise of disabled people' (2002, p. 139). They go on to state that:

[D]irect payment and personal budgets have the potential to free social workers up to focus on people who most need their support and to reconnect with the value base and core principles of the profession. (Glasby and Littlechild, 2009, p. 175)

Advocacy

In this section of the chapter we will examine different types of advocacy. We will discuss the possible advantages and limitations of each, from the perspective of disabled people, and whether it is possible or desirable to mix the different approaches. We will then conclude by considering how relevant advocacy is for health and social care workers who work with disabled people.

Box 5.5	What is advocacy?

Advocacy is essentially about speaking up for oneself or for others. Atkinson defines advocacy in the following way:

'Advocacy takes very many forms but it is essentially about speaking up – wherever possible for oneself (self-advocacy) but sometimes with others (group or collective advocacy) and where necessary through others.' (1999, p. 5)

Advocacy is particularly relevant to groups who have been oppressed and abused and whose wishes, needs and rights have been disregarded. As Gray and Jackson explain:

'[G]roups who are portrayed as "less than human" ... have suffered throughout history from society's tendency to question their essential humanity and, therefore, their right to a voice.' (2002, p. 7)

Citizen advocacy

Citizen advocacy was promoted by Wolfensberger and others in the 1970s and originated in the context of normalization and social role valorization for people with learning difficulties, which was a philosophy aimed at assisting people with learning difficulties to lead socially valued lives. Citizen advocacy has also been practised with older people by groups such as Age Concern (Atkinson, 1999). It involves an advocate working alongside a disabled person and speaking up to ensure that that person's needs and rights are addressed. A key feature of citizen advocacy is that the advocate should be independent of services. Citizen advocacy was defined by Wolfensberger as:

[A] one-to-one relationship by which a competent citizen volunteer, free from built-in conflicts of interest, advances the welfare and interests of an impaired or limited person, as if that person's interests are the advocate's own. (1977, p. 31)

A major justification for citizen advocacy is that those with severe impairments may be unable to speak up for themselves. Walmsley states that, 'Arguably people with learning difficulties are one of very few groups in society who continue to rely heavily on others to do their advocating for them' (2002, p. 26). Rooney agrees that:

There are ... many people with complex needs who do not have anyone to speak for them. As a consequence they are often overlooked ... Opportunities for citizen advocacy could make a significant difference to the way people with complex disabilities are helped to have their opinions heard. (2002, pp. 165–6)

An interesting offshoot of citizen advocacy are Circles of Support, which have developed in relation to people with learning difficulties, where the disabled person is supported by a group of people, rather than one person, on a long-term basis (Atkinson, 1999).

Various problems have been discussed in relation to citizen advocacy. It has often been rejected by disabled people (in favour of peer advocacy), as the role of citizen advocate and disabled person are inherently unequal. There is also the danger, as Lewis and Phillips (1997) point out, of citizen advocates internalizing professional discourses, thereby remaining in control. Simons (1992) believes that, in the context of service provision, disabled people may be reluctant to raise issues for fear that intervention by the advocate will make matters worse within the context of services, and Boxall et al. (2002) state that citizen advocates tend to leave when issues become too difficult. Citizen advocacy may also be used by organizations to obscure serious organizational and structural problems, as described by Hunter and Tyne in their study of long-stay hospital closure. They state:

It was clear in our evaluation that advocacy schemes were under pressure to provide what we termed the 'ferry-man' model of advocacy, in which volunteers were recruited to provide a shuttle service for residents across the big divide between hospital and community. (2001, p. 560)

A recent type of citizen advocate, the independent mental capacity advocate (IMCA) arose in 2007 in relation to the Mental Capacity Act of 2005. These advocates work with people who lack the capacity to make important decisions, such as housing and medical care, and have no family member or friend to support them. Such people may include those with severe learning difficulties, brain injury, mental health problems, dementia, or autism, or people who are unconscious. In this situation, the NHS and local authorities have a duty to consult an IMCA (DH, 2007a, 2009b).

IMCAs are independent of the NHS and local authority and anyone caring for the disabled person. They are experienced in working with people with communication difficulties and are obliged to undergo specific training. Their role is to ascertain the feelings and views of the disabled person if this is possible. Otherwise they must represent the person and ensure that their rights are upheld – this is termed 'non-instructional advocacy'. They must also investigate the circumstances surrounding the case and check that decisions made are in the best interests of the disabled person, challenging them if necessary. Advocates are expected to be knowledgeable about health and social care systems and community care law (DH, 2007a, 2009b). They are drawn from many organizations such as MIND, Age Concern, Skills for People, Leeds Advocacy and POhWER.

Professional advocacy

Professional advocacy is paid and is found most commonly within children's services (Walmsley et al., 2002). The salaried nature of the work and the fact that the roles and identities of professionals are embedded in the institutions providing the service can be viewed as a serious problem as it goes against the tenet of independence from services. The advocacy provided is also likely to be narrow in focus and the concept of advocacy may be distorted to simply mean 'meeting clinical needs' (Pilgrim and Rogers, 1999). As Goble states:

> [I]t can be strongly contended that the capacity of professionals and service workers to advocate for people with learning difficulties is severely restricted, and some would say fatally compromised by the fact that they are salaried by agencies which are often the major sources of oppression ... Nurses may well be able to function as advocates within health and social care systems ... but these are actually very narrow and service orientated contexts in which to work. (2002, pp. 74–5)

Read presents a similar case for independent advocacy from the perspective of service users:

> Generally service users are scared of mental health workers ...
> Obviously the powers under the Mental Health Act have a lot to do with this. It is not easy for us to say, or even think, what we want in a situation such as a ward round or a review, especially if we fear that what we want to say is not what the mental health workers want to hear. Service users need access to independent funded advocacy services, to support them to put their views across. (1996, pp. 176–7)

Goble (2002) believes that advocacy needs to challenge power structures and that it is a political rather than a therapeutic activity. Atkinson agrees and states that, 'Social workers are not advocates (although they may have an advocacy role)' (1999, p. 34). Similarly Pochin (2002) warns that advocacy should not be viewed as a service but rather as community development. Pound, on the other hand, views advocacy as a political activity but does not discount its use by knowledgeable and politicized professionals. She states, 'No reflective therapist can be neutral politically, and advocacy is a political skill to learn given the profound impact that the social, economic and political context has for those with illness' (2004, p. 36). Brandon (2000, p. 7) lists the following skills that social work advocates need when working with clients:

- Careful listening
- Accurate note taking
- Explaining the process
- Taking instructions from clients
- Gathering relevant information
- Feeding back lucidly
- Negotiating for improvements

Brandon believes that, as well as engendering trust and confidence in the client, advocates in social work should endeavour to bring about practical change. He admits, however, that. 'Social work advocates are often torn between their responsibility to agency and to service users' (2000, p. 7). Similarly, Mello-Baron states that, 'Mental health social work encompasses what appears to be a conflicting function of advocacy on behalf of mental health service users with legal powers to remove their liberty' (2003, p. 124).

Rather than suggesting that advocacy is part of health and social care work, other writers believe that health and social care workers should be skilled in supporting groups and enabling individuals to access training, support and advocacy services (Stalker and Robinson, 2008). Dowson and Whittaker (1993) believe that advisors should aim to work themselves out of a job although, as Goodley (2000, p. 21) points out, this may be difficult when, 'support is part of the working week' and when 'the general principle of "letting go" directly opposes the philosophy of professional intervention'.

Self-advocacy

Swain et al. define self-advocacy as a means to 'speak out either individually or collectively and with or without support. It involves being assertive, standing up for one's rights, expressing one's needs and getting things done' (2003, p. 148). According to Goodley, self-advocacy is a 'counter-movement to state paternalism' which 'captures resilience in the face of adversity' (2000, p. 3).

Box 5.6	The history of self-advocacy

Self-advocacy is mostly associated with disabled people, including those with learning difficulties and survivors of the mental health system. It has evolved from disabled people themselves and has its roots in organizations such as the British Deaf Association (founded in 1890), the National League of the Blind (founded in 1898), the Union of the Physically Impaired Against Segregation (founded in 1974) and The National Council for Civil Liberties (now Liberty), which campaigned against compulsory detention in mental handicap hospitals in the 1950s (Walmsley, 2002). Gray and Jackson believe that, 'It is likely that advocacy behaviours have been a constituent part of the human repertoire since the earliest times' (2002, p. 9). Talking of people with mental health problems, for instance, Campbell states that, 'there has always been protest by mad persons at their negative designation in the eyes of society and at the systems societies have set up to deal with them' (1996, p. 218). Organizations such as the Alleged Lunatic Friends Society (founded in 1845) and the Lunacy Reform Association (founded in 1873) also make it clear that people labelled mad had allies who were fighting for their cause.

More recent groups include Survivors Speak Out, a self-advocacy group of survivors of the mental health system, which was founded at a Mind conference in 1985, and People First, a self-advocacy group of people with learning difficulties which was founded in 1984. The first conference of Survivors Speak Out was held in 1987 where a charter of needs and demands was forged. There are also larger umbrella groups such as the United Kingdom Advocacy Network (UKAN), founded in 1990, which links user groups and promotes user-led independent advocacy and user involvement in all aspects of mental health, and Values Into Action, a national campaigning organization, founded in 1971 as the Campaign for People with Mental Handicaps, which runs conferences and undertakes research, consultation and training. Another umbrella group that potentially covers all types of advocacy, but is likely to compete with self-advocacy, is Advocacy Alliance which was founded in 1981. It is a coalition of five major charities – Mencap, Leonard Cheshire, Mind, Scope and One-to-One – and is mainly involved in research and consultation (Gray and Jackson, 2002).

The Campaign for the Mentally Handicapped held participatory events in the early 1970s where people with learning difficulties had a chance to express their views and concerns for the first time. Prior to that there is no formal history of advocacy among people with learning difficulties (Walmsley, 2002). Advocacy among this group is, however, now prominent in policy especially since the publication in 2001 of the white paper (Cm 5086) *Valuing People* (Walmsley et al., 2002). Advocacy for people with learning difficulties, and for all other groups, is also linked to user involvement and the NHS and Community Care Act 1990 and has been boosted by the Human Rights Act 1998, especially the right to a fair hearing and the right to self-expression.

Collective self-advocacy is regarded by some as being a new social movement where disabled people are influencing policy and practice and where their aims are more in tune with civil rights and changing society rather than merely changing services (Atkinson, 1999; Goodley, 2000). The organizations People First and Survivors Speak Out are examples of self-advocacy collectives. Talking of survivors, Wallcraft states that, 'The self-advocacy movement, at its best, represents a flowering of the potential of a group of people whose humanity has been denied for centuries' (1996, p. 192). Walmsley et al. believe that self-advocacy has special importance when compared with other types of advocacy because, 'Self-advocacy is not just one of many equally valid forms. It is about self-empowerment and as such deserves a special place in the pantheon of types of advocacy' (2002, p. 90).

Walmsley and Johnson view self-advocacy as being beneficial to people at both an individual and a group level. They state:

Self-advocacy is both an individual and a group activity. At the individual level it promotes having a voice, an identity and a sense of rights and responsibilities. At a group level it represents the collective voice of people with learning difficulties, people joining together to thrash out political positions and to fight for their interests. (2003, p. 55)

Spedding et al., a group of people with learning difficulties, give voice to the positive effect that self-advocacy can have:

'Since I joined People First I speak out for myself – I'm not afraid to speak my mind now.' (2002, p. 146)

'People know I won't let them get away with things; I used to let people walk all over me but I won't let them now. I don't get treated badly now.' (2002, p. 148)

Goodley believes that, 'The move from parent and professional advocacy to self-advocacy mirrors the developmental task of growing up and marks the recognition that people with learning difficulties are adults with their own agendas' (2000, p. 13).

Self-advocacy can be linked to research, which, in turn, can enable disabled people to represent themselves. Research, for instance, has been developed by some self-advocacy organizations (Walmsely and Johnson, 2003) and, likewise, the way into research may be through self-advocacy. As Atkinson explains, 'There is a two way link between advocacy and research. Self-advocacy makes research possible – but at the same time research supports self-advocacy' (2002, p. 131).

An example of a self-advocacy group that undertook research is the Bristol Self-Advocacy Research Group (Palmer et al., 1999) where people with learning difficulties interviewed their peers and gathered information on a wide range of topics including work, being labelled, transport, support from staff and advocacy itself. Conferences on learning difficulties now almost always include people with learning difficulties (Atkinson, 2002) and various chapters and books have been written and co-authored by people with learning difficulties and their allies (see, for instance, Atkinson and Williams, 1990; Cooper, 1997; French and Swain, 1999; Atkinson, 2002).

Various problems have been raised in relation to self-advocacy, mainly concerning its dilution or corruption when practised within professional services. As Chappell explains:

> [I]n some self-advocacy groups attached to day centres, staff may begin as facilitators with the intention of supporting the self-advocates. Yet they end up domineering proceedings so that meetings become an opportunity for staff to justify the operation of the service and pay lip service to the principles of self-advocacy. (1997, p. 57)

Boxall et al. agree that:

> [P]eople with learning difficulties are speaking out about their experiences and are doing this with strength and conviction. But the self-advocacy that many people with learning difficulties are being sold amounts to an abbreviated version of the political face of the disabled people's movement. (2002, p. 183)

People with learning difficulties have been critical of the way in which they are controlled by professionals: As Spedding et al. state, 'a facilitator who didn't like you having a giggle ran the workshop I was in. She used to tell you that there was time for that after sessions. A lot of us think that people with learning difficulties should run the workshops' (2002, p. 141).

A further concern for some people has been the lack of representation within collective self-advocacy. Walmsley (2002), for instance, believes that those who represent disabled people are not always representative, and McCarthy and Thompson (1995) note that self-advocacy groups tend to be dominated by men. However, Ward warns that, 'If self-advocates are articulate, they are dismissed as "unrepresentative". If they are not articulate then it is difficult for them to put their case and bring about change. An impressive catch 22' (1995, p. 15). There is also concern that the skills gained in self-advocacy groups may not be readily transferable. Simons (1992) suggests, for instance, that people who can be assertive in self-advocacy groups cannot always be assertive in family settings.

Peer advocacy

Peer advocacy is similar to citizen advocacy but with the very important difference that the advocate is an 'insider' (Walmsley et al., 2002). For instance, Gloria Ferris, a woman with learning difficulties, talks about how she befriended another patient, Muriel, in a mental handicap hospital and how this evolved into the formal role of advocate when the hospital was closed:

> 'I've known Muriel for over 40 years, since 1956, when we were both in St Lawrence Hospital. Of course she was quite young when I took

her on, nine or ten ... In 1994 I became an advocate for Muriel. And that was the year she left St Lawrence and went to Whitchill House to live ... I go to see Muriel two days a week.' (Cooper et al., 2000, pp. 188, 192)

As noted in the first section of this chapter, peer advocates also work within organizations of disabled people, such as Centres for Independent Living, where they may be paid.

Parents and carers may also take on the role of advocate. Organizations such as Mencap and Scope, for instance, which would claim to advocate for disabled people, were started by parents soon after the Second World War when very few facilities were available. As Lillian Fisher, recalling the early days of Mencap, states:

'Suddenly we realised we weren't on our own ... it was a great relief ... The society helped to get rid of embarrassment and stigma because it was talked about, it was in the open. It did seem really miraculous that we were going to these little functions where we were all acceptable, and our daughter Wendy was particularly welcome ... we made things happen ... We could use all sorts of talents that had laid dormant for years.' (Rolph, 2002, p. 45)

The ideas and interests of parents and their disabled children may, however, be very different. Garth and Aroni (2003) found that parents and their children with cerebral palsy had very different perceptions and experiences of medical consultations and Mitchell (1997) found that adults with learning difficulties could not always translate ideas from self-advocacy groups into the family home because of resistance by parents. The philosophy and practice of *Shared Action Planning*, formulated by Brechin and Swain (1986), is worth mentioning here as it demonstrates an early attempt to promote self-advocacy among people with learning difficulties. However, as the views of 'significant others' (such as the parents of adults with learning difficulties) are given equal weight in decision making, and given the likely inequalities in relationships between parents and children and disabled and non-disabled people, it is unlikely that full empowerment would have been gained. It did, however, challenge the control of professionals in decision making and the marginalization of disabled people and their parents.

Box 5.7	**Can different types of advocacy be mixed?**

As noted above, many disabled people have rejected citizen and professional advocacy and have founded their own self-advocacy groups and organizations such as People First, Survivors Speak Out and Centres for Independent Living. McNally (1997) believes, however, that citizen advocacy and self-advocacy are not mutually exclusive and Boxall et al. (2002) contend that citizen advocacy has gained from the insights of self-advocacy and that they should go 'hand in hand'. However, Clements feels that mixing the two types of advocacy has led to confusion:

> '[C]itizen advocacy organisations have reacted to the challenge of self-advocacy and assimilated the currency of empowerment into their own values, and in doing so have muddied the notion of what citizen advocacy actually is.' (2002, p. 62)

Walmsley et al. (2002) agree that there is a place for both types of advocacy: and that the same person may benefit from different types in different situations. Atkinson (1999) is largely in agreement but believes that the tension between citizen advocacy and self-advocacy is, at present, more destructive than helpful.

Despite the many types of advocacy, it is important to realize that most advocacy groups struggle to remain financially viable, which makes it difficult for them to remain independent. Most exist precariously on short-term funding, which makes future planning difficult or impossible. Self-advocacy groups are particularly vulnerable as they tend to receive less funding from government than other types of advocacy (Atkinson, 1999). Atkinson concludes from her research that:

> Advocacy is fragile and fragmented. It needs to be coherent and co-ordinated otherwise there will always be schemes that fold, gaps and shortfall in provision and people who happen to be in the wrong place when they most need advocacy. (1999, p. 41)

She also makes a plea that, despite the funding problems and the scarcity of advocacy, people who are hard to reach, for instance those from ethnic minorities, are not overlooked. A similar argument applies to people with specific impairments. Townson et al., for instance, document the exclusion of people with autism and Asperger's syndrome from self-advocacy. They state that, 'the exact characteristics of people who live with autism and Asperger's syndrome need to be taken into account in terms of developing advocacy' (2007, p. 533).

Conclusion

Disabled people value the skills and expertise that health and social care workers have to offer but they need to be in an equal partnership where their knowledge, skills and experience are equally valid and where disability is viewed as a social and political phenomenon. The philosophy and practice of CILs and the policy of direct payment and individual budgets show how different services become when disabled people take control and when the complexities of disability are fully acknowledged. Such a change of orientation may, however, be difficult for professionals to accept and implement without support, especially in an inter-agency context.

It is not easy for individual practitioners to change practice in substantial ways as change depends on the ability to exercise power as well as the historical and social context in which the worker is placed. As Welshman states, 'There is a long time lag between ideas and implementation' (2006, p. 18). To give an example, the National Council for Civil Liberties exposed exploitation of people with learning difficulties within institutions in their book *50,000 Outside the Law* in 1951, but the number of people in mental handicap hospitals rose well into the 1970s. However, Walmsley, talking of these institutions, states, 'Although it is important to stress that ideas alone did not drive change, they did create mental frameworks within which change was conceptualised' (2006, p. 55).

Health and social care practitioners may feel challenged by self-assessment, self-directed support and working with a wide variety of unfamiliar agencies. However, Leadbeater et al. suggest that individual budgets and self-assessment may mean more creative and enjoyable work for practitioners as role boundaries are likely to blur with more scope for counselling, advocacy, community development and other innovative practices. They suggests that professionals will need to become 'advisors, advocates, solution assemblers, brokers' (2008, p. 60) and that the role of professionals 'will be vital to mediate the individual's relationship with the service he or she needs' (2008, p. 77).

Reflective exercises

1. How does the philosophy and practice of CILs differ from that of statutory and voluntary services? How far can the principles of CILs be applied in inter-agency settings?
2. How far do you agree that the advantages of direct payment and individual budgets outweigh possible disadvantages? How may any disadvantages be resolved?
3. What types of advocacy do you feel would be appropriate to use in a multi-agency setting? How far should different approaches be mixed?

Suggestions for further reading

1. Barnes, C. and Mercer, G. (2006) *Independent Futures: Creating user-led disability services in a disabling society*. Bristol, Policy Press

   Draws on extensive evidence to analyse user involvement and user-led organizations in health and social care. Considers the factors that inhibit these developments and discusses future policy implications. Chapter 3 explores the struggle for independent living, Chapter 5 examines the growth of user-led services and Chapter 7 explores service users' views and experiences.

2. Glasby, J. and Littlechild, R. (2009) *Direct Payment and Personal Budgets: Putting personalisation into practice*. Bristol, Policy Press

   Written with frontline practitioners in mind, this book explores the development of direct payment and individual budgets, placing these policies in context and linking them with relevant legislation. Chapter 2 explores the history of direct payment and personal budgets and Chapters 6 and 7 examine their advantages and possible barriers.

3. Gray, B. and Jackson, R. (eds) (2002) *Advocacy and Learning Disability*. London, Jessica Kingsley

   Gives a full account of the history and current policy and practice of advocacy for people with learning difficulties. Chapter 1 explores different types of advocacy, Chapter 5 considers conflict in advocacy, Chapter 9 examines the experiences of a self-advocacy group and Chapter 10 gives an overview of formal advocacy for people with learning difficulties.

4. Prime Minister's Strategy Unit (2005) *Improving the Life Chances of Disabled People*. London, TSO

   This government document gives a detailed account of the New Labour government's long-term plans for the policy and implementation of individual budgets.

5. Leece, J. and Bornat, J. (eds) (2006) *Developments in Direct Payments*. Bristol, Policy Press

   Gives a full account of the policy of direct payment including its development and current practice. It covers different user groups and focuses on the direct experiences of disabled people using direct payment. Chapter 5 focuses on people with learning difficulties, Chapter 6 old people, Chapter 7 people with mental health problems and Chapter 8 children. Chapter 9 explores the experiences of disabled users and Sections 4 and 5 of the book examine the experiences of employees.

6. Welshman, J. and Walmsley, J. (eds) (2006) *Community Care in Perspective: Care, control and citizenship*. Basingstoke, Palgrave Macmillan

   Provides a historical context to understanding community care policy from 1948. It includes the experiences of different user groups as well as practitioners and informal carers (Chapters 10–14). The emphasis is on people with learning difficulties. It also has a section that explores the development of community services overseas (Chapters 6–9).

6 Towards a Social Model of Inter-agency Working

In this chapter we discuss:

- What is inter-agency working? Forms of partnership
- What are the barriers to inter-agency working? Views of service users and providers
- How are the barriers to be overcome? Inclusive communication, disability equality training, participatory research

This chapter focuses specifically on the notion of inter-agency working and the possibility of this being grounded in a social model. So a starting question is the meaning of the notion of inter-agency working. There are closely related terms, particularly multidisciplinary working and inter-professional working, which you might like to follow up. These terms seem to us similar enough to focus on inter-agency working as an umbrella for the key issues.

Schalick (2006) tells us that 'interdisciplinary team', one of the terms related to inter-agency working, is 'a managerial concept that has as its goal the efficient execution of care by team members through cooperation, communication, and identity as a unit within a larger structure' (p. 964). Cohen (2005), using the term 'inter-agency collaboration', goes down similar lines: 'a relationship between agencies and services which may involve collaboration in planning, working together on specific issues or projects, or the sharing of posts' (p. 2). This notion of inter-agency working is, then, centrally a service providers' agenda, which at heart concerns closer and more effective working between services. As throughout this text, we broach this topic by prioritizing the viewpoint of service users and the questions this raises. What is a social model of inter-agency working? Where are the voices of disabled service users in inter-agency working and what are the implications for the power relations between service users and service providers?

We explore, first, the meaning of inter-agency working by putting this within the broader context of partnership – inter-agency working being one form of partnership. We then turn to the barriers of changing practice, changing power relations, and looking towards the social model of disability as the generator of policy and practice. Finally, the focus turns to possible processes of changing policy and practice, effective communication, participatory research and training.

What is inter-agency working?

In recent policy developments, partnership has been a dominant concept signifying the attainment of greater equality in professional–client relations generally. At a policy level, partnership and collaborative working are considered to be a 'good' thing. Governments of all persuasions have placed emphasis on the need for different agencies to work together to provide more 'seamless' service provision by moving towards more integrated health and social care provision (for instance, DH and DOE, 1992; DH, 2000; and the *Health, Social Care and Well-being Strategies (Wales) Regulations 2003*, which required local authorities and local health boards to formulate and implement a local health, social care and well-being strategy).

Defining the concept of partnership, however, is difficult because partnership means different things to different groups of people. Looked at broadly, it refers to organizations or individuals working together or acting jointly (Ovretveit, 1997). It is associated with numerous other terms such as participation and empowerment.

Box 6.1	The different forms of partnership

- Partnership refers to the relationship between professionals and professional organizations, and associated terms include 'inter-agency collaboration', 'joint working' and 'multi-professional practice'.
- It refers to the relationship between disabled people, or more particularly service users, and the service system. A key term here is 'service user involvement'. This is again mandated within policy. For instance, one of the Department of Health's six medium-term priorities was that health authorities should:

  'give greater voice and emphasis to users of NHS services and their carers in their own care, the development and definition of standards set for NHS services locally and the development of NHS policy both locally and nationally.' (NHS Executive, 1997, p. 9)

- Although much less recognized, the term can be applied to relationships between disabled people, to include partnerships within and between organizations of disabled people. Barnes and Mercer state:

  'The gap between disabled people's expectations and their actual involvement in the statutory and voluntary sectors has reinforced claims from disabled people's organisations that the move to a more equal and democratic society demands a bottom-up approach to politics and policy making. Its potential is realised by the emergence of active user-led organisations.' (2006, pp. 91–92)

- The term also refers to the more immediate relationship between a professional and a service user. This again can encompass different terms such as 'client-centred practice'. Sumsion defines this as follows:

  'In the UK client centred occupational therapy is a partnership between the client and the therapist that empowers the client to engage in functional performance and fulfil their occupational roles in a variety of environments. The client participates actively in negotiating goals that are given priority and are at the centre of assessment, intervention and evaluation.' (2005, p. 100)

In examining the more specific concept of inter-agency working, it can help to put it under this broader umbrella of partnership. Although the notion of inter-agency working is clearly an important one, it can be seen as more of a concern for professionals and service providers, than disabled people as service users. There is, however, much within the literature documenting the views and experiences of disabled service users that is pertinent to inter-agency work, including dealing with the sheer numbers of professionals who provide 'treatment', and the levels of communication between them.

What are the barriers to inter-agency working?

We turn, then, to the documented experiences of disabled service users. What are the barriers for them?

Box 6.2	Disabled people's views of service provision

The following draws on a report summarizing some of the views expressed in a focus group of disabled people at Derbyshire Centre for Integrated Living (Swain, 2005). They were discussing the barriers they face in their daily lives.

Disabled participants repeatedly referred to the attitudes of those with power over their lives and, associated with this, the presumptions that are made about themselves and their lifestyles. Relations with professionals who profess the expertise to define disabled people's needs together with being providers of the solutions, which they also control, are key to the barriers to independent living. Participants spoke of their power struggle in everyday interactions with health and social care professionals.

'It's the professionals ... they do what they consider a care package but it's not a lifestyle package ... they just put what they see your needs ... they don't see transport, they don't see social, they just see fed and watered and go to bed ... you are socially excluded because of what they perceive.'

'Life's a constant battle ... they just don't see you the way they see themselves.'

'Most OTs have genuinely impressive knowledge of the muscular-skeletal system, but the system they work then supposes on that basis they can determine the physical, emotional, intellectual, social and spiritual needs and requirements of any person with any kind of impairment.'

'They purport to have the expertise.'

The report by Shaping Our Lives National User Network (Beresford, 2003) offers some comparable findings. This project focused on service users' perspectives of social care services, though took a holistic approach to include issues such as housing transport, employment, income and benefits and broader issues around discrimination and equality. Common themes that were reported to emerge included the following, each of which is pertinent to the barriers to the development of inter-agency working.

1. Respect for service users: as in the above research, participants gave examples of their experiences of being treated without respect by service providers.
2. Domiciliary care and having a clean and tidy home environment was important to the majority of service users, and associated with quality of life.
3. Direct payments: participants were interested in direct payments but had some reservations about how they would work in practice.
4. Mobility and access: perhaps not surprisingly, participants placed considerable importance on being able to get around and to access facilities.
5. Information: another key theme was the difficulties of getting information about services and the inevitable difficulties that this led to in obtaining services.

(You might compare these with the 12 basic needs developed by the Southampton Centre for Independent Living, see Chapter 5.)

As you may have found evident, there are a number of underlying messages within the quotes in Box 6.2. The first, for us, is the unequal power relations between disabled service users and (predominately non-disabled) service providers and, by implication, the supposed lack of expertise on the part of service users. The second is the individual and, particularly, medical model perceived as underpinning practice. Disabled people, as with non-disabled people, take a holistic perspective of themselves and their lives, whereas service providers focus on their particular area of expertise. Taking this a step further, a question arises about the whole notion of inter-agency working with regard to power relations. Given the experience of service users with individual professionals, what implications does this have for a disabled person facing a team of professionals, armed with their agreed assessments and in agreement about the needs of the disabled person?

Box 6.3	**Models of inter-agency working**

Schalick's (2006, p. 964) four models of inter-agency working are:

- The strict medical model, with the physician controlling communication and referrals in a vertical hierarchy
- The multidisciplinary model, in which the physician coordinates communication between services
- The interdisciplinary model, in which communication takes place laterally between services as well as vertically through the physician
- And finally, the transdisciplinary model in which, according to Schalick, professionals are trained in several disciplines

It is difficult to see the possibilities of a social model of inter-agency working in these models, with disabled people remaining on the bottom rung of the vertical hierarchy of power relations. It can be argued, however, that the transdisciplinary model might provide professionals with a more holistic perspective than a focus solely on a particular arena of expertise, with the possibility of moving towards a more social model perspective. Nevertheless, this needs to be looked at critically, as sometimes a particular expertise is just what a disabled client is looking for.

Turning to the literature from the service providers' perspective, the most radical criticisms centre on the loss of power by professionals. Coming from this direction, for instance, the introduction of multidisciplinary agencies and partnerships (with the voluntary and community sectors) has marginalized and reduced social work to crisis management (Jordan, 2001). There are a number of recurring themes coming largely from service providers themselves, academics and research with providers.

Rivalry between professionals

Waterfield argues that shared skills and knowledge may be problematic for professional groups as they challenge the uniqueness of professionals. She writes, 'There has always been a certain rivalry between physiotherapy and other practitioners such as osteopaths, nurses and occupational therapists' (2004, p. 200).

She suggests too that there are hierarchies and factions within professions that certainly complicate relations between them. Hierarchical structures have been an important barrier to the effective functioning of multi-professional teams (French, 1999). Different professional agencies may 'fear that someone else may be after their money or taking their job, do not understand or respect the other agency and see them in stereotyped ways' (Heywood, 2006, p. 37). When the roles of other professions are poorly understood, rivalry and miscommunication become extremely likely.

The socialization of professionals

A substantial barrier to the creation of genuinely collaborative relationships with clients is created by the very lengthy professional socialization of all health and social care professionals. This, in part, is the inculcation of the individual model, and the associated expertise grounded in objective scientific knowledge. Hafferty argues that this has created dilemmas for professionals in relation to partnership:

> Recent calls for a 'patient-centered' medicine rooted in egalitarian
> notions of a 'partnership among equals' have served to heighten
> this tension between traditional medical authority (for example the
> physician as expert – the patient as the object of that expertise) and the
> physician–patient relationship as a partnership of authoritative equals.
> (2006, p. 1298)

Relevant here, too, is the separation of professionals in their education courses – social work education for social workers, nurse education for nurses and so on. You might reflect on how many different professionals you came across in your education and how many sessions you attended that could have been called multi-professional. Taking this a step further and moving towards the more general notion of partnership, what part did disabled people play in your education? Were disabled people present as students and/or tutors? It can also be argued that lengthy socialization of professionals may enhance inter-agency working as it strengthens professional identities. The idea being that collaboration is improved when each agency has full knowledge of its arena. Please reflect on this from your experiences of inter-agency working, from both your own profession and from the viewpoint of professionals you work with. Does strength of professional identity enhance or hinder inter-agency working?

The complexity of the professional system

The organizational context, particularly within the NHS, is highly complex. The notion of partnership relies on the coordination of effort among many different professional groups, each with rather different priorities, conceptual frameworks, jargons, cultures and ways of working. Mello-Baron (2003) argues that in the movement towards Trust status there was a lack of resources and attention to partnership. He states:

> The professional domains remain focused upon 'how we can work
> together' rather than addressing common skills and values, which may
> lead to a 'generic', 'hybrid' or 'doubly qualified' worker ... The new
> welfare picture leaves users in a position of initiating, developing and
> maintaining links across many specialist areas. (2003, p. 129)

Limited resources

It is also a markedly resource-limited environment, so it is not surprising that professional groups sometimes perceive competition with each other for the resources to do their jobs effectively. Each professional agency advocating for ostensible scarce resources for their role does not present an easy context for establishing effective partnership.

Professionals as gatekeepers

The organizational context can also impede effective relationships between service providers and users through setting up health professionals as 'gate-keepers'. This again is a resources issue, as service providers are placed in a role of rationing limited resources to clients. Inadequate budgets, for instance, may force occupational therapists to limit the provision of aids and adaptations that they know would make a great deal of difference to a client's quality of life. Arguments about ostensible lack of resources can be and are seriously questioned, however, and priorities challenged. Such questioning is fuelled by considerable regional differences and the proportion of budgets taken up by staff and management costs.

Government targets and deadlines

Government targets and deadlines (for example to reduce waiting lists) inevitably impact not only on the wider organization but also on individual encounters between health and social care service providers and a client. For example, pressures on appointment times may encourage therapists to focus narrowly on biomedical or functional issues and to ignore the wider psychosocial problems that the client is experiencing.

The powerlessness of service users

People who are powerless and marginalized within society may not be able readily to express themselves, to make complaints or to effect change. O'Sullivan states that:

> A principle of sound decision-making practice is for clients to have the highest feasible level of involvement, but they may not always feel sufficiently empowered to make decisions ... Stakeholders need to consult with each other to share information but the presence of clients at these meetings is not sufficient in itself to ensure their involvement. Active steps may be required to prevent them being excluded from meaningful participation. (2000, p. 86)

Although there are some parallels between the perspectives of professions and service users, there are also clear differences. The starting point for professionals is the provision of services and the relationship between services, whereas for service users it is their lives and their struggle to get the services they need.

Box 6.4	Disadvantages of inter-agency working

Glasby and Dickinson (2008, p. 63) list the following:

- Scope for the medical model to dominate other perspectives
- Potential for more social alternatives to be overshadowed by psychiatric approaches
- Less chance of one partner to advocate on behalf of users with the other partner
- Possible loss of local services as the partnership rationalizes its provision
- Having one point of contact can give users nowhere else to go if this attempt to contact services does not work as well as it should
- Concerns about a loss of key relationships with staff and about potential change in use of local buildings

The challenge to practitioners, managers, professions and organizations is that of being more responsive to the needs and desires of service users. It is to this challenge that we shall now turn.

How can we overcome the barriers?

The challenge, then, is for the development of effective inter-agency working which is built upon and is geared towards the social model of disability and the voices of disabled service users. Tope and Thomas (2007) argue that that 'for decades the UK government has given directives for an inter-professional, interagency workforce'. There are clear examples of policy such as the white paper *Our Health, Our Care, Our Say* (DH, 2006), in which the government sets out a clear vision for the development of integrated services, which offer personalized care where people are empowered to exercise personal choice and control over services.

In 2005, the DH published *Supporting People with Long Term Conditions* (DH, 2005b) which outlined a new NHS and social care model as a framework to care for individuals living with long-term conditions. The model was regarded as an aid to 'ensure effective joint working between all those involved in delivering care – including secondary care, ambulance trusts, social care and voluntary and community organisations – so patients experience a seamless journey through the health and social care systems' (p. 12).

The gap between policy and practice, however, has long been a central topic within the literature relating to service provision. We focus here on three possible generators of change: inclusive communication, inclusion in education, particularly disability equality training, and participatory or user-led research. Our prime concern throughout is the voices of disabled service users in instigating, furthering and reviewing processes of change.

Towards inclusive communication

First, then, we look at the notion of inclusive communication, and tentatively offer some general principles. 'Inclusion' has been seen by many as a process of social change, rather than a particular state (Oliver, 1996a) and this can be seen to apply equally to communication and relationships.

> But without a vision of how things should and ought to be, it is easy to lose your way and give up in the face of adversity and opposition ... we all need a world where impairment is valued and celebrated and all disabling barriers are eradicated. Such a world would be inclusionary for all. (Oliver and Barnes, 1998, p. 102)

Participation

Priority needs to be given to the participation of disabled people in the planning and evaluation of changing policy, provision and practice in developing inclusive communication. The onus is on service providers to face the challenges of enabling true participation of disabled people in decision-making processes, recognizing that disabled people wish to participate in different ways. These include the democratic representation of the views of organizations of disabled people. Participation also includes as wide a consultation process as possible. Disabled people often continue to be treated as passively dependent on the expertise of others yet control seems to have become increasingly central to social change for disabled people. As a disabled man states:

> 'Users should have more power. Until you give users real power, real control we'll get nowhere ... there's an awful lot of people with a lot of vested interests. The more we shout about rights the more people get afraid. I'd like to see therapy training following the social model rather than the medical model. The only way to do it is to get much more input from disabled people into the training.' (French, 2004b, p. 102)

Accessible communication

Much is known about the accessibility of information based on the views expressed by disabled people. Clark (2002) offers wide-ranging recommendations which cover such things as: alternative formats (for example, 'the following formats should be available – large print, large print with pictures and symbols, Braille, computerdisc containing the file in plain text format, accessible website, audio CD, DVD with plain, spoken language, audio description and British Sign Language' (2002, p. 62)); suggestions for plain written language; typeface and font size; signage; layout; and websites.

For some people, particularly with communication disabilities, the issue of time can be crucial to an inclusive communication environment. For people with communication disabilities, a slower tempo can be the only accessible pace to ensure understanding. A participant within research by Knight et al. explains:

'I prefer to speak for myself and I would rather repeat myself several times than have someone say they understood me when they did not.' (2002, p. 17)

Diversity and flexibility

The recommendations for communication access, as produced by Clark (2002) and others, clearly challenge the imperatives of normality and emphasize the diversity of communication styles and formats. Nevertheless, there are diverse needs even within specific groups of people with impairments, which again puts the emphasis on listening to and control by individual people. I (Sally), as a person with a visual impairment, have found, for example, that I am often presented with large print even though it is the depth, font and colour contrast that is more important to me and am usually quite happy using a magnifying glass (of which I have several of different powers) to read print that is too small.

There are, of course, many social factors within the diversity of the needs of disabled people. As Dominelli argues, for instance, 'translation services should be publicly funded and provide interpreters matched to clients' ethnic grouping, language, religion, class and gender' (1997, p. 107). (Chapter 8 focuses specifically on questions of difference and diversity.)

Human relations

Communication is constructed and embedded in relationships between people. The notion of personal relationships can be seen as irrevocably intertwined with communication. Communication is a means of expressing a relationship; it constitutes the initiation, maintenance and ending of a relationship; and it is the medium and substance through which the relationship is defined and given meaning. A disabled client offered advice to therapists on the basis of her experience:

'Forget you're a therapist – just be yourself. I don't mean forget all your training – but be yourself. Don't be afraid of showing the real you because that's what makes people respond, when they're ill they respond more easily if the therapist is being real.' (French, 2004b, p. 103)

Use of inclusive language

In part, this reflects the idea that language controls or constructs thinking. Sexism, ageism, homophobia, racism and disablism are framed within the very language we use. This has been characterized and degraded by some people as 'political correctness' (PC), often with reference to examples seen as trivial or fatuous (for example being criticized for offering black or white coffee). Use of language, however, is not simply about the legitimacy of words or phrases – what we are allowed to say or not say. As Thompson (1998) explains, language is a powerful vehicle within interactions between health and social care professionals and clients. He identifies a number of key issues:

- Jargon – the use of specialized language, creating barriers and mystification and reinforcing power differences
- Stereotypes – terms used to refer to people that reinforce presumptions, for example disabled people as 'sufferers'
- Stigma – terms that are derogatory and insulting, for example 'mentally handicapped'
- Exclusion – terms that exclude, overlook or marginalize certain groups, for example the term 'Christian name'
- Depersonalization – terms that are reductionist and dehumanizing, for example 'the elderly', 'the disabled' and even 'CPs' (to denote people with cerebral palsy)

In this light, questions of the use of language go well beyond listing acceptable and unacceptable words to examining ways of thinking that rationalize, legitimize and underline unequal therapist–client power relations.

Training/Education

Professional training/education clearly plays an important role in generating change. In their review of inter-agency working, Tope and Thomas state:

> The Government has also signalled its intention that 'wherever practical, learning should be shared by different staff groups and professions' and that this should be as close to the workplace as possible. Just how much learning and working together happens in practice has been afforded much greater credence recently. (2007, p. 27)

The key to our analysis, however, is the role of disabled service users within training.

A major strategy to changing disabling behaviours and practices is through the development of 'disability equality training' (DET). DET was originally devised by disabled people themselves and pioneered by a small group of disabled women in London (particularly by Jane Campbell, Micheline Mason and Kath Gillespie-Sells). In its strict sense, DET originally referred to courses delivered only by tutors who had been trained by organizations of disabled people (Swain et al., 1998). These organizations train disabled people themselves to be trainers. DET courses are not about changing emotional responses to disabled people but about challenging people's whole understanding of the meaning of 'disability'. They provide a basic introduction to the social model of disability and, in particular, the attitudinal, environmental and language barriers that deny disabled people equal access to institutions and organizations. The following are the stated aims of courses run by disabled trainers who have themselves been trained through the work of the disability resource team:

> A DET course will enable participants to identify and address discriminatory forms of practice towards disabled people. Through

training they will find ways to challenge the organisational behaviour which reinforces negatives myths and values and which prevents disabled people from gaining equality and achieving full participation in society. (Gillespie-Sells and Campbell, 1991, p. 9)

Micheline Mason explains:

It was designed to give service-providers the means to 'deconstruct' the medical model, understand the social model, and apply this new viewpoint to their particular area of influence or expertise … It is an attempt to help people realise how their perceptions of disability have become distorted, and to give them a brief insight into our own viewpoint on our situation. The goal is structural change. Through this training we have succeeded in creating a growing awareness amongst professionals that disability is a human rights issue. (2000, p. 109)

There are predominantly two types of disability training in practice. Disability Awareness and Disability Equality. The differences between the two are as follows:

- Awareness tends to focus on individual impairment and will often involve simulation exercises (simulation being the pretence of impairment, such as the wearing of a blindfold to simulate blindness).
- Equality on the other hand explores the concept of the social model of disability and would be carried out by a disabled person well versed in the social model.

Organizations may be becoming increasingly aware of their role in providing customer care for all their customers and clients. As Priestley (1998) points out, DET is now an established (albeit small) part of social work training courses in Britain. The United Nations Standard Rules on the Equalization of Opportunities for Persons with Disabilities stipulate that disabled people's organizations should be involved in training development and that disabled people 'should be involved as teachers, instructors or advisers' (UN, 1993, Rule 19.3). Awareness in Britain has been increased, in part, due to the high profile of the Disability Discrimination Act and also to the awareness-raising initiatives being put in place by leading and local disabled individuals and disability groups. Oliver and Barnes (1998) argue that the widespread use of DET as a radical new method of consciousness-raising has played a role in intensifying 'the pressure for nothing less than the full inclusion of disabled people with comprehensive civil rights legislation as the main vehicle for its achievement' (p. 90).

There was evidence to suggest that DET was not widely offered to professionals on an in-service basis (Swain et al., 1998). A more recent picture is even less easy to discern. There has been a broadening of access to

DET, particularly through the Internet (see, for instance, Scope's Interactive Disability Equality Training Toolkit (scope.org.uk/work/det). However, there is no available evidence about the use or effectiveness of this or other sites. Furthermore, experience suggests that courses offered under the umbrella of DET differ quite widely in terms of their aims, who delivers them and how they are delivered. DET is not necessarily delivered by trainers who have been trained by organizations of disabled people. Also, some distance learning packages that claim to offer DET, for instance, are designed to raise awareness of impairment, though this strategy has been rejected by organizations of disabled people and research evidence has repeatedly shown that such a strategy is ineffective in challenging social barriers.

Taking a more general stance, but focusing specifically on social work training, Levin (2004) has looked at the involvement of service users and carers. She suggests along the following lines:

- The involvement of service users and carers in the design and delivery of the social work degree offers a major opportunity for a new generation of social workers to gain a thorough grounding in service users' and carers' experiences and expectations from the very start of their training and careers.
- Many universities and colleges that are offering the degree programme in England in 2003, together with their allies in service user and carer organizations, have made a good start at working together but progress is uneven across the country and the specific aspects of the programmes.

There are a number of issues, as Levin makes clear, including the payment of service users for their time and expertise.

Participatory and user-led research

So far we have looked at the communication environment and training, knowledge and skills building. We turn next to evidence-building and the involvement of disabled service users in research. We are turning then to the possibilities of a knowledge base, generated by disabled people, their views and their experiences, in promoting inter-agency working grounded in a social model of disability. The first focus is on the general concept of participatory or user-led research. Second, we look at a specific approach, narrative research, drawing on one illustrative example. Finally, we summarize a number of projects that could be said to take a participatory approach.

So, what is participatory research? It has its roots in a number of developments including the development of service user involvement generally and developments in qualitative research, such as participatory action research (French and Swain, 2008). It has fed into research literature with the term 'participants' ousting the term 'subjects'. It is about a shift in the management, control and processes of research about disabled people.

Box 6.5	**Benefits of user-led research**

Turner and Beresford (2005) see the benefits it offers to service users as follows:

- Strong commitment to and particular capacity to make change in line with what service users want
- Emphasis on supporting more equal research relationships
- Rationale of making involvement in research a more positive experience for participants

Service users talk about the particular capacity of user-controlled research to:

- Be useful, because it starts from service users' shared experience and understanding
- Identify and develop new issues of importance to service users
- Be more inclusive than traditional research approaches, for example, because it generates trust among potential research participants
- Offer personal benefits to research participants (through its concern with equality and empowerment), as well as having particular contributions to make to research

One approach that is closely associated with participatory ideals is narrative research. This covers a broad range of approaches, including autobiography, oral history and life story. Cotterill and Letherby (1993) propose that the research narrative is, in fact, an amalgam of two narratives – that of the researched and that of the researcher. They suggest that the researcher needs first to give consideration to their own autobiography and then 'place herself in relation to the issues she is researching' (p. 72). Higgins and Swain (2009) suggest that although reciprocity is vital for relationship building, this approach is not without its own set of problems. The sharing of autobiographical detail considered to be largely unproblematic, for example, can sometimes subtly interfere with the research process. Higgins found that identifying herself, as a parent of a disabled child, affected how freely one participant in this study was able to verbalize her opinions on how disabled children can be problematically perceived by their parents. The reality of this situation reflects the fact that when researching the experiences of oppression, there is no neutral position for the researcher.

Examination of the role that reciprocity plays in facilitating a positive research relationship has been a concern of feminism for some time. Oakley (1981), for example, challenges the traditional research model and questions the presumption that research could be a non-reciprocal process. In other words, she would question whether is it possible for the researcher to be a recipient of information, yet resist any wish to share their own views, feelings and experiences. She would perhaps be the first to question a researcher's reluctance to offer any personal involvement, or self-exposure, when engaging in research that expects participants to share intensely personal information.

The practicalities of facilitating a life story interview have been considered by a number of authors. It is probably fair to say that once volunteers have got to the point of agreeing to be involved in research they are generally keen to tell their story, but often need to prepare and get their thoughts together beforehand (Atkinson, 1998). Other writers' work indicates that asking a generative narrative question can be helpful in terms of preparation and stimulating narrative (Flick, 1998). The use of a 'time line' or 'life map' (Walmsley, 1998) is also used as an aid to narration. This involves the breaking down of their life story into more manageable chunks, so that the recounting of information might be made easier. This approach is consistent with the writings of Flick (1998) who suggests that our experiences are 'stored and remembered in forms of narrative-episodic and semantic-knowledge' (p. 106). Episodic knowledge is associated with concrete situations or events. The process of choosing what to share in the interview is not a random choice for the participant, but the result of the ever-changing meaning attached to the narrative. It is a snapshot of a person's interpretation of events at a particular moment in time and further influenced, to a lesser degree, by the research dynamic.

Higgins and Swain (2009) collected the stories of seven disabled adults who had been sexually abused as children (see Chapter 3 for further information about this project). It was clear that volunteering to be involved in a research project was a significant event in each individual's own personal journey. For these survivors, it marked the fact that they had reached a particular benchmark in their recovery process where they felt confident enough to allow their narrative into the public domain. Undoubtedly, the research narrative has a political function, with an intention to raise public awareness of disability and child sexual abuse. Participation, however, was a hugely personal matter, as can be observed in the following different viewpoints:

'Being involved in research is an experiment for me in that I haven't had this sort of conversation in a non-therapeutic context before except with my partner. Talking about it to an almost stranger is different, but I do feel that the reason that I have gone through all of this in the past couple of years has been to sort out my life and try to be happier.'

Lyn

'The final thing I wanted to say is that my process of recovery has been about looking at the story of my life, so it's something that I'm continually working with in a therapeutic way and in my visual arts work. It feels good to be reflective about my past, to be able to see it all in context.'

Jean

'Having it (the narrative) all in one place is useful because when you have counselling you deal with separate bits at a time. I know people say that (by breaking it down) you can see how that relates to that, but I don't think that it sinks in the same as having it in front of you.'

May

The process of narrative production, the telling of stories of abuse, can itself promote healing and encourage the development of an authentic sense of self. This process is neither easy nor linear.

Finally, we shall look at some projects with disabled people that involve them and give their perspectives. These projects have been selected to reflect a range of topics and participant groups relevant to health and social care.

Closs (1998) explored the views of children and young people with life-threatening or life-shortening medical conditions. Six young people participated in the study by reflecting on their childhoods, responding to key issues in the literature and criticizing the researchers' drafts. A number of themes were extracted from the data which were considered critical to the quality of the young people's lives including: the individual's understanding of his or her condition, feelings of sameness/difference, educational experiences and attainments, friendships, family, and experience of the medical and paramedical services and hospital life. In relation to the last of these themes, comments from the young people illustrated some distressing experiences, such as, 'If they didn't call it treatment you could call it torture', 'I could write a book about doctors, good, bad and unspeakable', and 'I realised I had nothing on under the sheet. Maybe it was easier for them to put in tubes ... but I felt really embarrassed' (Closs, 1998, p. 121).

Fifty people with aphasia were involved in a study by Parr et al. (1997). In-depth interviews were adopted to allow important topics and issues to be raised by the participants, in addition to those on the researchers' agenda. One topic was people's experiences of services. From participants' detailed accounts, attributes of successful services included: availability and accessibility, appropriateness and adequacy, flexibility and responsiveness, integration, reliability and consistency, respectfulness, ability to support communication, and ability to provide relevant and accessible information (1997, p. 66). The experiences of individual participants varied greatly. Madge felt that she had been supported and that the care she had received had been satisfactory. Rebecca's views were, however, very different:

'When you can't communicate they treat you like a kid and that is just so frustrating. A handful of doctors were just awful. You just wanted to say, "Do you know what this is like?"' (Parr et al., 1997, p. 74)

This research was the first extensive study of aphasia from the perspective of people with aphasia themselves. It demonstrates that people with impaired language can, under the right conditions, be interviewed and that their views can be used to inform professionals and improve services.

The next example comes from research with people with learning difficulties. Atkinson, along with others, has been developing an auto/biographical approach that:

> has the capacity to combine the political document with the
> historical – to reflect the lives which have been lived, but to see beyond
> the individuals to a wider view of learning disability. Auto/biography
> contains many voices and tells stories at different levels. (Atkinson,
> 1998, p. 22)

Individual life stories were recounted and shared in a group context. Nine participants with an age-range of 57 to 77 years met on 30 occasions. One of the themes was 'tales of hospital life' and the following is a short extract in which Margaret tells her story of running away from a mental handicap hospital:

> 'The sister would keep on at me, saying my work wasn't done properly.
> She was being horrible. I'd scrubbed the ward and she said I had to do
> it over again. I said, "Well I ain't going to do it over again!" I told the
> doctor. He come round and he wanted to know what I was doing on
> the stairs again. I said, "I've been told I've got to do it again, it wasn't
> done properly."

> I planned it with the other girl, we planned it together. She was fed up.
> She was doing the dayroom and dining room, cleaning and polishing.
> Then I was put on it, as well as scrubbing. We planned to get into
> Bedford, walk across the fields.' (Atkinson, 1998, p. 91)

We finish with an example of research in which the participants were involved in the decision-making process throughout. The project, which we mentioned briefly in Chapter 5, was controlled, conducted and reported, with support, by the Bristol Self-Advocacy Research Group, a group of four people with learning difficulties, and was funded by the National Lottery Fund (Palmer et al., 1999). The research involved interviewing other people with learning difficulties about their experiences. The response of the researchers was positive:

> 'We've all really enjoyed the research visits, meeting new people and
> making new friends.'

> 'I was looking at my photographs yesterday when I was at home, and
> all the different places I've been. And I've got the photographs in
> my photograph album at home. I'm quite proud of what I did. And
> you feel very important. People say: "You do do a lot." They're quite
> impressed with what I do. I've achieved a lot – too much.' (1999, p. 34)

Under the theme of support, for example, the research participants speak about being forced to be independent:

> 'Staff people always think that we all want to be more and more independent. This can be wrong, because they expect us to do too many things ourselves. It should be our choice, not theirs.' (1999, p. 42)

We hope that these examples give an indication of how the principles of participatory research, to a greater or lesser extent, can be applied to research in order to gain a better understanding of issues from the viewpoint of disabled people.

Conclusion

It is clear that the notion of inter-agency working is a major driver in the policy and practice of health and social care. It is less clear whether it is being realized in actual practice and whether the barriers to development are being addressed and overcome. And it is even less clear whether it is realized through service user control. From our analysis, the review of inter-agency working must come from service users, whether their needs, desires and aspirations are being met. There are possible generators of change including inclusive communication, service user involvement in training, and user-led research. Nevertheless, we are some way from realizing a social model of inter-agency working to support independent living and the full participatory citizenship of disabled people.

Reflection exercises

1. Consider your experiences of inter-agency working within your training/ education and practice. Reflect on the relationships between professionals; what have been the barriers and what strategies are in place to address them?
2. In your experience, what have been the implications of inter-agency working for service users?
3. What evidence is there of service users' views and experiences being taken account of in the development of inter-agency professional practice?
4. Finally, think from the viewpoint of other professionals you have worked with. What from their viewpoint have been the main barriers to inter-agency working and what approaches have come from them for developing strategies for overcoming the barriers?

Suggestions for further reading

1. Glasby, J. and Dickinson, H. (2008) *Partnership Working in Health and Social Care*. Bristol, Policy Press

   Provides a 'warts and all' introduction to partnership working, summarizing current policy and research, setting out useful frameworks and approaches, and helping policymakers and practitioners to work more effectively together. Short, accessible and practical, the book is aimed at students, practitioners, managers and policymakers in health and social care.

2. Tope, R. and Thomas, E. (2007) *Health and Social Care Policy and the Interprofessional Agenda*. London, Health Economics Research Centre

   Discusses with detailed evidence the following: partnerships are not a soft option but hard work; partnerships take time to develop; partnerships must be realistic and aim for what can be achieved, not be set up to fail by being too ambitious; partnerships can, if successful, achieve more than individual agencies working alone.

3. Turner, M. and Beresford, P. (2005) *User Controlled Research: Its meaning and potential*, Bristol: Shaping Our Lives and the Centre for Citizen Participation, Bristol University

   The aim of this project is to find out more about the definition, nature and operation of user-controlled research.

4. Higgins, M. and Swain, J. (2009) *Disability and Child Sexual Abuse: Lessons from survivors' narratives for effective protection, prevention and treatment*. London, Jessica Kingsley

   Examines the ways in which society marginalizes, institutionalizes and places disabled children in situations of unacceptable risk, and how, as evidenced in the survivors' narratives, patterns of service delivery can contribute to the problem.

7 User Involvement in Services for Disabled People

In this chapter we discuss:

- Why user involvement is necessary
- User involvement in user-led and statutory services
- The development of user involvement
- Methods of user involvement
- Dismantling barriers to enable good practice
- User involvement in social work
- Principles of good practice

Robson et al. define user involvement as 'the participation of users of services in decisions that affect their lives' (2003, p. 2) and Croft and Beresford believe that 'speaking and acting for yourself and being part of mainstream society, lies at the heart of ... service user involvement' (2002, p. 389). The concept of 'user involvement' is now well established within professional and managerial practice, in both health and social care, and enshrined within legislation and policy such as the NHS and Community Care Act 1990 and the NHS Constitution (DH, 2009a). It is no longer the case that managers and professionals can or should make decisions on behalf of those they serve. When considering how disabled people can influence health and social services, the term 'user' is preferred to 'patient' or 'client' which both have connotations of passivity.

In this chapter, user involvement in the health and social services will be discussed focusing on disabled people. We will first ask why user involvement is so important and the chapter will then continue with a brief historical overview of user involvement in health and social care services to the present day. Some methods of user involvement will be described and the chapter will conclude with an examination of the various barriers that impede user involvement by disabled people and how these may be removed or minimized to enable good practice. The discussion throughout will explore the implications for the management and delivery of health and social care services.

Why is user involvement necessary?

There are many reasons why the involvement of disabled service users in health and social care services is not only necessary but essential. Disabled people are experts when it comes to understanding disability and what they need to achieve a full and happy life (Lester and Glasby, 2006). As Dow states, 'our views are valuable, they are necessary and are based on real experience, real hurt and sometimes real anger' (2006, p. 52). Nancarrow et al. (2004) believe that the involvement of users may force professionals and managers to be more accountable to disabled people and provides a way for services to be monitored and evaluated. Carr points out that user involvement can be tremendously beneficial as it provides 'a unique opportunity for organisations to develop and transform through critical enquiry with service users' (2004, p. 28). At the present time, however, evidence that user involvement improves services remains unconfirmed (Bradshaw, 2008).

The experience of being involved in decision making in health and social care may also empower service users and narrow the power imbalance between them and those who provide and manage the services. Lester and Glasby (2006) believe that users of services bring to the fore different perspectives and approaches which have the potential to provide greater social inclusion and 'joined up' services. At its best, user involvement is a way of increasing the rights and dignity of disabled people.

Box 7.1	User involvement in a user-led organization

The Herefordshire Centre of Independent Living is a user-led organization that is very careful to involve all the users of its services in decision making:

'Our service user involvement project offers service users the opportunity to be involved in many different aspects of the organisation and its services. Regular feedback from service users helps us to make changes to the organisation, our services and to ensure we are meeting service users' needs. The project also enables service users to be involved in staff recruitment, ensures the information that we provide is user friendly and accessible via a reading panel of service users, and offers service users the support they need to become involved in external consultations and forums.' (2009, p. 1)

Other activities that service users engage in include peer mentoring and the delivery of disability equality training. You may have noted similarities with the Southampton Centre of Independent Living which we discussed in Chapter 5.

User involvement in health and social care organizations generally falls short of that in user-led organizations. A service user interviewed by Branfield states, 'The government is driving for user involvement, but a lot of it is not real ... They want passive user involvement' (2007, p. 11). Dow, another service user, is also sceptical. He states:

> They only need to show to their political and financial masters that
> they are doing the job within their job description. And unfortunately
> ... that job description doesn't ask them to demonstrate that they
> know how to work alongside us. It doesn't ask them to show how
> they have given power to us, or to show how we can trust them.
> (2008, p. 52)

Bradshaw agrees that, despite policy and legislation that makes user involvement mandatory, 'the service as a whole is still far from patient centred' (2008, p. 679).

Drake (1996) believes that consultation can be used as a sop to offset political protest and Mercer states that 'Too often user participation in public service provision has turned out to be little more than cosmetic' (2004, pp. 177–8). An institution or organization can, in the present cultural climate, be given enhanced credibility through its public face of user involvement (Robson et al., 2003). Branfield and Beresford (2006) note that the benefits of user involvement, if there is no real commitment to it, have been questioned by providers and researchers as well as disabled people themselves. For instance, Duffy (2008) reports the results of a questionnaire on user involvement in health and social care where 127 respondents out of 143 (89%) reported dissatisfaction. Perez and Flynn state that:

> We know that consultation processes are underdeveloped and little
> used. Research practice and our experience confirm that consulting
> with and involving people are long distance goals rather than realities.
> (2009, p. 34)

It remains to be seen whether the new coalition government will help or hinder user involvement in health and social care.

The development of user involvement

The development of user involvement in services for disabled people arose in Britain in two main ways. Following the election of Margaret Thatcher as Conservative prime minister in 1979, there was a shift towards a market ideology in health and social care. A quasi-market was introduced into health and social services to allow some degree of choice for patients and clients, who were now regarded as consumers. The idea was that services would be 'needs led' rather than 'service led' and that disabled people and other service users would be assessed for individual 'packages of care' within a 'mixed economy of welfare' including private, voluntary and statutory services (McPhail and Ager, 2008).

These changes were backed by legislation and various policy documents from the Department of Health, including the Children Act 1989, the NHS and Community Care Act 1990, *The Patient's Charter* (DH, 1991) and the Carers (Recognition and Services) Act 1995. User consultation and collaboration in service planning and delivery were made mandatory in these Acts. This reflected the consumerist ideology of the political right and was viewed as a way of cutting costs, providing more flexible services and reducing state involvement and the power of professionals (Beresford and Croft, 2000). See Chapter 2 for more details of these policies.

Box 7.2	New Labour's modernization agenda

In 1997 these policies were, in essence, continued in New Labour's modernization agenda for health and social care where user involvement was central to NHS reform. The need for user involvement was laid out in the policy document *The NHS Modern, Dependable* (DH, 1997), which included notions of citizenship, rights and responsibilities and stated that in order for the NHS to be accountable to people it must be shaped by the public (Mercer 2004; Carr 2004). The Health and Social Care Act 2001 put a duty on all Trusts to consult with patients and the public about the planning and development of health and social care and the Department of Health Priorities Framework 2003–2006 (DH, 2003) emphasized the need to defer to patient and public knowledge. The white paper *Our Health, Our Care, Our Say* (DH, 2006) stipulates that users should have a stronger voice and be the main drivers of services, and the government report *Improving the Life Chances of Disabled People* states that 'New arrangements should be established for securing participation of disabled people in policy design and delivery at all levels' (Prime Minister's Strategy Unit, 2005, p. 195). Similarly the National Health Service Act (England) 2006 requires patient forums to be established in every NHS Trust. Scandals, such as that which led to the Bristol Royal Infirmary Inquiry (2001) into the treatment of children undergoing complex heart surgery, have hastened such reforms in an attempt to create a more open and accountable health service.

In 2009 the NHS Constitution came into force. This lays out the principles, values and pledges of the NHS in England as well as the rights and responsibilities of both NHS staff and patients. According to the *NHS Constitution*, it is the duty and responsibility of the NHS and social care providers to take into account the views of those they serve. It is stated that:

'You have the right to be involved, directly or through representatives, in the planning of healthcare services, the development and consideration of proposals for changes in the way these services are provided, and in decisions to be made affecting the operation of these services.' (DH, 2009a, p. 7)

Patients also have the right to be involved and consulted on all aspects of their care and treatment.

As a result of these changes in ideology, policy and legislation, there has been a considerable growth in user involvement initiatives where thousands of disabled people now participate in a range of activities (Carmichael, 2004). Few initiatives, however, have been thoroughly evaluated and many have proved ineffective (Beresford et al., 1997; Carr, 2004) and Robson et al. (2003) note the lack of research, monitoring and evaluation with regard to the impact and outcome of user participation. Carr states:

> There is a general lack of research and evaluation on the impact and outcomes of service user participation. Little seems to be formally recorded at local, regional or national levels and the influence of user participation on transforming services has not been the subject of any major UK research studies. (2004, p. vi)

Agencies tend to focus on the benefits of participation itself rather than on the outcomes achieved, sometimes even viewing participation as a form of 'therapy' to improve the skills, competence and self-esteem of disabled people (Braye, 2000; Carr, 2004). Beresford et al. (1997) and Priestley (1998) emphasize that user involvement is merely a vehicle for effective change in terms of the services delivered and the behaviour of those who deliver them. Similarly, Carmichael stresses that 'user involvement is a means to an end and not an end in itself' (2004, p. 201) and Gee and McPhail (2008) point out that user involvement is a process not an event.

Box 7.3	User involvement initiatives in the NHS

The Expert Patient Programme

In 2002 the Expert Patient Programme was launched by the NHS. This initiative involves patients with chronic illness engaging in a highly structured course, run by trained volunteers with chronic illnesses themselves, to help them manage their illness. It is recognized that people with chronic illness are experts in their own right but that they need to develop skills to manage their condition and their lives effectively. It is stated by the Department of Health that:

> 'The knowledge and expertise held by the patient has for too long been an untapped resource. It is something that could greatly benefit the quality of the patients' care and ultimately their quality of life, but which has been largely ignored in the past.' (DH, 2001a, p. 5)

The course is highly structured and detailed and involves confidence building, skills in communicating with health professionals, exercise and dietary advice, problem solving, 'developing strategies to deal with the psychological consequences of the illness' and 'learning to cope with other people's response to their chronic illness' (DH, 2001a, p. 17).

Furthermore, NHS Direct Wales suggests that patients undergoing these programmes are taught anger management skills and how to cope with daily activities.

Although some people may be helped by this programme, it does nothing to address the disabling environment but, instead, requires disabled people to 'accept' and 'manage' their situation. Encouraging disabled people to deny their anger and develop individual coping strategies by using their own resources, rather than demanding political and social change, constitutes what Sutherland (1981) termed 'the disabled role'. It is disheartening that, despite progress in some areas, these ideas persist and have been given new impetus. The fact that the disabled people running the training are unpaid volunteers also gives rise for concern.

LINks (Local Involvement Networks)

The LINks project was developed in 2008 and is financed by local councils at a projected cost of £84 million between 2008 and 2011 (www.nhs.uk/NHSEngland/links). The aim is for individual and community groups, from all sectors of the community, to work together to improve health and social services. The networks consist of individuals, community groups and professionals who provide feedback from the local community to health and social care providers. They, in turn, are required to respond to suggestions and to outline what actions they will take. LINks can refer issues direct to the local council, and health and social care establishments are obliged to allow LINks representatives access to their premises. As Bradshaw states, LINks 'provide a one-stop stop for the community to engage with care professionals and vice versa' (2008, p. 678). It is questionable why, when large sums of money are put into projects such as this by the government, that user-led organizations are struggling to survive financially through lack of government support.

It is interesting to speculate whether initiatives such as these will be continued or cut by the new coalition government. Programmes such as LINks may conceivably fit in with David Cameron's notion of the 'Big Society'.

Despite all the legislation that pertains to user involvement in health and social care, it would be a mistake to imagine that government is entirely behind the need for strong user involvement. In a recent report by the Public Administration Select Committee of the previous Labour government, for instance, it is stated:

Involving service users is not always appropriate. In some circumstances it could create inequalities in services, as well as being risky and expensive. In other situations people may simply be unwilling or unable to engage in this way. A key challenge for the government and public service providers will therefore be to establish where user involvement is desirable and in what form. Service providers also need to ensure that user involvement complements – rather than conflicts with – the contribution made by public service workers. (2008, p. 8)

A second development during the 1970s and 1980s was the emergence of well-organized and strengthening user movements, including the Disabled

People's Movement, which demanded involvement in health and social care planning and delivery (McPhail and Ager, 2008). The agenda of the Disabled People's Movement, however, goes far beyond the issue of services (however important they may be) to full democratic citizenship and the dismantling of a disabling environment in terms of physical and social barriers (Barton, 2004). Whereas service providers in health and social care are concerned with budgets, policy and the smooth running of organizations, the concerns of disabled people are to fundamentally change, not only the services they receive, but society itself. Other social movements, such as Survivors Speak Out, Gay Pride, and the Self Advocacy Movement, have similar agendas. This leads to conflict because, whereas the professional approach starts with 'the system' and how it can be adjusted, the approach of disabled people is concerned with changing the reality of their lives. Beresford and Croft note the tension between the ideologies of the government and those of the Disabled People's Movement. They state:

> These two approaches to participation, the consumerist and democratic approaches, do not sit comfortably. One is managerial and instrumental in purpose, without any commitment to the redistribution of power or control, the other liberational with a commitment to empowerment. (2000, p. 356)

Brown emphasizes the depth of this conflict:

> Service users have not only focused on the way they want services delivered but also challenged the relevance and appropriateness of the knowledge base upon which professionals traditionally draw. User movements have increasingly been involved in generating theory about their position in the world – theory which rests on the analysis and lived experience of people who use health and social care services. (2000, p. 99)

Beresford (2007) notes that the tension between these two approaches also causes problems for professionals and managers when trying to implement user involvement.

In terms of legislation, it can be argued that a framework for change in user involvement is being established. As well as the various Acts and policy documents outlined above, the Disability Discrimination Acts of 1995 and 2005, the Human Rights Act 1998, the Mental Capacity Act 2005 and the Equality Act 2010 have gone some way in assisting disabled people in their struggle for full participative citizenship. Article 10 of the European Convention on Human Rights, for instance, established the right to self-expression and article 6 established the right to a fair hearing. The Mental Capacity Act 2005 stipulates that people must be assumed to have capacity to make up their own minds, unless proved otherwise, and that they have the right to support when making decisions and the right to make what others may consider to be eccentric or unwise decisions. The power of legislation to bring about change is, however, frequently exaggerated as is apparent in the continuing discrimination against ethnic minorities and women despite the passing of anti-discrimination Acts to safeguard the rights of these groups over thirty years ago.

Box 7.4	**User voices**

We turn now to the views expressed by disabled people in focus groups within two organizations of disabled people, DANE (Disability Action North East) and DCIL (Derbyshire Coalition of Inclusive Living) (Swain, 2005). The two groups also discussed the general processes of policymaking. The overall consensus among participants was that disabled people are the experts on disability issues and their participation must be central to the decision-making processes and structures. Participants stated:

'Service user involvement at the earliest possible time, not some consultation exercise further down the line.'

'Enforcement of genuine user involvement.'

Their exclusion from policymaking is in part due to poor physical and communication access, the attitudinal and economic barriers they experience on a daily basis, and the failure to develop processes and strategies of involvement:

'If I had a quid for every consultation I have been to I'd be a rich woman ... disabled people have been used as a cheap source of information for many years.'

'The area where most problems come from it's not European policy, it's not government policy, it's not even council policy, it's policy made up in offices to suit expediency made up without consultation.'

There are possibilities for improvement, however, one being the opening up of communication:

'Sometimes I think technology is a good thing ... to be able to email is to be able to get everybody's attention, whether they choose to do anything about it is another thing ... you can get your word out better.'

There were examples too of disabled people being influential in developing policy, though the ability to influence policy is, like policy itself, a postcode lottery:

'Disabled People's Advisory Committee, this is where disabled people meet with (the) Council ... in some places it is just an exercise ... but (in X) we have proved that they do take notice of us ... we have been able to influence that they put in an accessible fire exit ... we were in on the planning stage on the transport scheme ... we have worked very very hard.'

Methods of user involvement

Methods of involving users in health and social care can take many forms. Brown's (2000) list of methods is shown in Box 7.5.

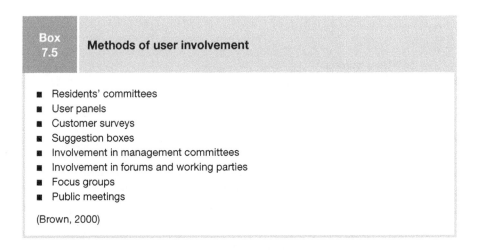

Box 7.5	Methods of user involvement

- Residents' committees
- User panels
- Customer surveys
- Suggestion boxes
- Involvement in management committees
- Involvement in forums and working parties
- Focus groups
- Public meetings

(Brown, 2000)

Goss and Miller (1995) depict user involvement as a ladder with the top rung giving total control to users and the bottom rung giving no control at all (see Box 7.6).

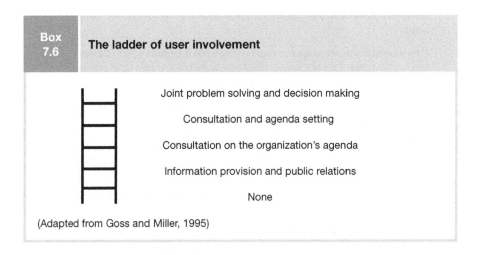

Box 7.6	The ladder of user involvement

Joint problem solving and decision making

Consultation and agenda setting

Consultation on the organization's agenda

Information provision and public relations

None

(Adapted from Goss and Miller, 1995)

Bewley and Glendinning (1994) warn against relying heavily on any one method or model, as none are perfect and a variety are needed to reach all disabled people. They note a heavy reliance on formal meetings in user involvement, which, according to Duffy (2008), can reinforce power inequalities. Evans, Carmichael et al. are particularly critical of the widespread use of public meetings in user involvement initiatives. They state:

> To engage in public meetings ... demands, on the whole, familiarity and confidence with the normal style, format and language of these meetings. In addition very practical issues of physical access, transport, interpreters, signers, personal assistance and so on must be addressed by social and health services if disabled people are to be enabled to take part in consultation meetings. (2002, p. 20)

Bewley and Glendenning (1994) point out that in order to reach black disabled people, people living in rural areas and other marginalized groups, such as travellers, people with mental health problems and people with learning difficulties, a community development approach, working with local networks, needs to be adopted on a sustained basis. Fergusson and Ager believe that social workers have, in recent years, become deskilled in this important area of work. They state:

> There is a long tradition within social work of community development and social networking approaches which have been eclipsed in recent years by the dominance of care management and individual approaches. (2008, p. 71)

Carr (2004), in her review of the literature, found that little attention was paid to the diversity of users even though those from ethnic minorities were often in most need of services. She also found that the belief that disabled people from ethnic minorities 'look after their own' (and therefore do not need services) is still prevalent, as will be discussed in Chapter 8. Connelly and Seden advise that 'When planning the structure of services to be delivered to a diverse range of people, it is important to find service users who represent that range of diversity' (2003, p. 38).

Branfield, in her work on user involvement in social work education, promotes advocacy, outreach work and partnerships with service user groups but recognizes that user-led organizations are rarely secure financially and have little capacity or infrastructure to become involved in assisting other organizations. One of the people she interviewed said, 'How do you make the time to keep up to date with all the things you are asked to be involved in?' (2007, p. 14) and another said, 'If your group has two users and a volunteer what will you offer the university? Who has even got the time to contact the university?' (2007, p. 14). Duffy (2008) advocates a pool of users to avoid 'consultation fatigue' and undue pressure on any one organization.

Box 7.7	User involvement in a traditional charity

In 2004 we (Swain et al., 2005) undertook a study on user involvement for a large charity which provides residential care for disabled people. Although it had in place various formal mechanisms for user involvement, for instance committees and a Disabled People's Forum with paid disabled staff (including a member on the senior management team), most residents viewed user involvement in terms of their day-to-day lives with such things as availability of transport, staffing levels, ability to go out and continuity of staff as most important. This seemed to be because user involvement was defined in informal, rather than formal, terms and that formal involvement was viewed as ineffective within existing power relations and management structures. (See Chapter 4 for more details of this research.)

Although formal methods and structures are necessary, Finlay et al. (2008) warn against the tendency to regard user involvement only in these terms. They state:

'Empowerment is not just about choosing to take this kind of support rather than that or providing input into the evaluation and process of a service in structured situations, but is about what happens between people moment by moment, the mundane details of everyday interaction. Power permeates everyday life – it is exercised in the way people talk to each other, in what utterances are taken up and what are ignored, in how and what options are offered, in how information is presented, how spaces are opened up for people to express preferences and in how spaces are shut down.' (2008, p. 350)

They believe that monitoring, such as inspections, can lead to defensive practice where, for instance, health and safety legislation is followed even if disabled people find it disempowering. One of the residents we interviewed said:

'When I came here with my husband we lived in the annexe and we didn't have to have any assessments. I'm now in a double room on my own and before I can use my microwave I've got to have an assessment on it, the same for boiling the kettle. What an insult! I did it in the community but I couldn't do it here until I'd had an assessment.' (Swain et al., 2005, p. 26)

Finley et al. (2008) also found that user meetings could be very disempowering when facilitated by a staff member, although evidence of such meetings is often produced to show that user involvement is taking place.

Leadbeater agrees that there is a need to improve services to disabled people rather than focusing on user involvement in policy. He states, 'Treating people as citizens who can re-shape services through formal political debate, is worthy but abstract ... Users want direct attention to their needs' (2004, p. 32).

Service user involvement, as generated within the development of the Disabled People's Movement and other user movements, needs to be understood within a wide range of strategies for social change and the management of changing power relations between service providers and service users. Such strategies go beyond 'methods' of user involvement and include direct action, lobbying and the provision of disability equality training, controlled and delivered by disabled people themselves.

Research also has an important role in user involvement but it is essential that disabled people are centrally involved, not just to give their responses to questions, but to decide on the research agenda, the methodology and how the research will be used and disseminated. Talking of medical research, Swain and French state:

> Many disabled people are of the opinion that medically orientated research has not fundamentally altered their position within society ... the way in which disability has been researched has become a major issue for disabled people and their organisations in recent times. (2004, p. 322)

Participatory or user-led research has increasingly come to the fore over the past twenty years (see Chapter 6).

Dismantling barriers to enable good practice

Many practical, organizational and cultural barriers need to be addressed if the involvement of disabled people in the management, planning and delivery of health and social care services is to become a reality. A central issue is the unequal power relationship between service users and professionals and managers (French and Swain, 2001). Priestley states that:

> It is impossible to discuss user participation without reference to power. If providers are committed to increasing user power then they must contemplate a corresponding reduction of their own power. (1998, p. 158)

Similarly Dow, a service user, states:

> Power issues underlie the majority of identified difficulties with effective service led change. The message is that any service user participation initiative requires continual awareness of the context of power relations in which it is being conducted. (2008, p. 14)

One clear strategy in the face of barriers to service user involvement has been the alignment of people with power to those who are powerless, in order to help them express their needs and concerns and to bring about change. It follows from this that independent advocacy is an essential service when considering user involvement, as discussed in Chapter 5. Training may be useful, to both disabled people and professionals and managers, when involving users in decision making (Branfield, 2007; Duffy, 2008).

Box 7.8	The power of words

The power imbalance between disabled people on the one hand and professionals and managers on the other extends to the meaning of important concepts that affect disabled people's lives. Disabled people and professionals tend, for example, to have a different definition of 'care' with the view of professionals and managers predominating and being translated into policy and practice (Goble, 2004; Finkelstein, 2004). Disabled people prefer the notion of 'support' or 'assistance' rather than 'care', where they are in control of the help provided. Beeton (2008) believes that users of services need to be involved in defining important words and terms such as 'care' and 'quality of life' as their definitions are frequently fundamentally different from those of service professionals and agencies.

People with learning difficulties have, for instance, frequently been denied treatment because their quality of life is assumed to be poor. Mencap state that:

'[H]ealth professionals often make personal assessments of a patient's quality of life and view this as a caring step to take in their decision making process. This is despite good quality evidence demonstrating the very poor correlation between a professional's opinion of a patient's quality of life and a patient's opinion of their own quality of life.' (2007, p. 22)

A further way in which inequality of power is apparent in health and social care services is in the setting of agendas for the planning of those services. These are usually set by professionals and managers rather than disabled people themselves (Carr, 2004). Therapists, doctors and nurses may, for example, decide how to organize their work in the community without consulting with those they will serve. Ager and McPhail state:

Power dynamics are frequently acknowledged in the literature of service user and carer involvement. However, from our experience, this is the 'elephant' in the middle of the room, rarely discussed explicitly at government, policy, senior management or institutional level. (2008, p. 14)

This is confirmed by Dow, a service user, who states:

The people who use services and who have been on this journey to influence how those services are designed and delivered see the power differences between them and the professionals, and the unfairness this causes, as being the single most important issue to contend with. (2008, p. 55)

Fergusson (2008) points out that simply asking for power will not be effective, as power is always won through struggle.

Priestley (1998) believes that true user involvement means equal partnership at the management level of organizations and Rice and Robson (2006) agree that membership by users within governing bodies in health and social care is key to successful user involvement, although there is sometimes a level of seniority above which service users are not permitted to go. Robson et al. (2003) note that a controlling style of management can be a strong and destructive barrier to user involvement and, conversely, a facilitatory style can be beneficial. Influential allies within the power structure can enhance the potential of users to influence decisions, as can external groups such as researchers and disabled people's organizations.

Box 7.9	The danger of tokenism

A common complaint that disabled people have when they take part in user involvement initiatives is the lack of feedback they receive from researchers or managers about the impact of consultation (Bewley and Glendinning, 1994; Duffy, 2008). Carr states that: 'lack of feedback can result in frustration and cynicism about the practice of service user participation as well as potential disengagement from the process altogether' (2004, p. 9). Duffy (2008) believes that user involvement must be related to tangible outcomes, and Perez and Flynn state that:

'users respond poorly to tokenism, oppressive practice and manipulation ... if the project of realising improvements in service delivery is perceived to be small then people's desire for involvement is unlikely to be sustained.' (2009, p. 1)

Users need a high level of involvement at all levels of the organization in order to influence services. Evans (1999) describes this as 'riddling the system' with user involvement. It is often the case that insights from users are not translated into practice by professionals and managers. Motivation can be quickly lost if their input has no effect (Beresford et al., 1997; Duffy, 2008). As McSloy, a user, points out: 'Any involvement that does not value the use of people's time and wastes that time by not using the outcome to influence change should be questioned' (2008, p. 44). Beresford et al. urge professionals to take disabled people seriously in order to move forward. They state:

'Until service users have a sense of and confidence in the validity of the contribution they have to make, it will be difficult to establish relationships of trust with professionals and to work together on a basis of mutual respect.' (1997, p. 69)

Disabled people are becoming more selective in deciding when, how and to whom they will give their time, effort and views and are formulating 'rules of engagement' to be followed when their opinions are sought (Carmichael, 2004).

Robson et al. (2003) point out the need for a stable and committed staff who will assist in taking user involvement initiatives forward They note that user involvement initiatives can be slowed down or stopped if the turnover of staff in organizations is high. The amount of time and support managers and professionals can give will, in turn, depend on how well they are supported. Priestley states that, 'Effective user involvement requires a strong political commitment at the "top" of the provider or purchaser organisation. The commitment needs to be a contractual requirement for staff at all levels' (1998, p. 163). Duffy contends that 'Effective user involvement and partnership working must be based on values such as respect, humanity, partnership, inclusion and a commitment to respecting the right to consultation and involvement' (2008, p. vii). Fergusson (2008) believes that building trusting relationships takes time and, that if time is not made available, users are likely to 'vote with their feet'. User involvement is both costly and time consuming. The issue of cost and funding is prominent in the literature and organizations are under increasing pressure to provide evidence that user involvement is effective. This is illustrated in the following quotation from a government paper:

> It is still early days for many of the stronger forms of user involvement
> … Initial evidence about such initiatives seem promising, but there is
> still a need for comprehensive and rigorous monitoring and evaluation,
> particularly regarding the cost effectiveness. (Public Administration
> Select Committee, 2008, p. 3)

The involvement of disabled people is dependent upon resources and adequate funding, for example accessible and affordable transport, physical access to premises and payment for their services. As noted above, the poor funding of user organizations is also a problem as it dictates how much time they have to become involved with organizations which seek their help. It seems likely, in the current economic climate, that, despite the importance of user involvement in health and social care, its cost will become an even larger issue.

'Knowledge is power' but all too often accessible information is lacking. Information needs to be accessible to all disabled people, regardless of impairment, if user involvement is to succeed. This may include information in Braille, in pictorial form, or on audio CD. Disabled people, like all people, also need background information in order to participate meaningfully (Evans, 1996). Disabled people, however, face numerous barriers to accessing information, and are consequently marginalized unless this issue is resolved. Being unable to access information is, for instance, a problem faced in all areas of life by visually impaired people. Stereotypical responses to what people need, for instance assuming that all blind people read Braille, are also common.

Pound points out the ways in which people with language impairments have been excluded from having an influence in health and social care services. She states:

> It is easy to take for granted the power of language. Language is not
> just the means of communicating with each other, it is the means

of forming and refining ideas. It is the medium of understanding, questioning and developing thoughts and discussion. It is the means of being included, having a voice and exercising influence. (2004, p. 163)

She goes on to say:

Communication access is a poorly understood concept that offers intriguing challenges to all concerned with inclusionary practice. Moving beyond tokenism places significant resource and training demands on people and environments. (2004, p. 167)

The pace of work can be exclusionary to many disabled people (Carr, 2004, p. 20). Visually impaired people, for example, may need more time to read documents and people with learning difficulties may need help in understanding concepts.

Services to people with learning difficulties have a record of being extremely poor. It is very important that the views of people with learning difficulties and their allies are heard and that they are part of the user involvement movement in health and social care. This may take time and imagination but without it services are likely to be poor. As Mencap states:

[T]he NHS has a poor track record in dealing effectively with people with a learning disability. As a result people with a learning disability have poorer health, greater health needs and shorter lives. There is a real concern that negative, discriminatory attitudes and poor communication skills among healthcare staff contribute to this unfortunate state of affairs. (2004, p. 31)

One of the problems that is frequently mentioned in relation to the poor health status of people with learning difficulties is 'diagnostic overshadowing', where any problems or symptoms the person may have are viewed in terms of their learning difficulty (Mencap, 2004; DRC, 2006). This makes it difficult for people with learning difficulties, and those trying to assist them, to be taken seriously by health care professionals. An example of this is given by the mother of James, a man with learning difficulties:

'James kept telling me that he could see a "funny black thing". I took him along to see the optometrist, but he didn't seem to take us seriously. I knew that there was something wrong, so I kept taking him back. On our fourth visit James said: "Black blob bigger". This finally prompted the optometrist to have a look at the back of James' eyes. He found two detached retinas, which it has so far not been possible to repair. James has now been registered blind.' (Mencap, 2004)

Disabled people have frequently been disempowered by previous experiences, for example time spent in institutions, and need time, support and resources to build up sufficient confidence to participate fully (Evans, 1999). In her study, Carmichael (2004) found that consciousness-raising and empowerment were very important to disabled people when seeking to influence services, and Bewley and Glendinning (1994) found that preliminary work with service users is frequently required before consultation can begin. Carr concludes from her review of the literature on user involvement that 'if organisations are serious about listening to users, they also need to be prepared to make radical changes of approach in order to take into consideration what ... people are saying and address this in mainstream services' (2004, p. 14).

Box 7.10   **User involvement in social work education**

The Carers and Users Group of the Department of Social Work at the University of Dundee define themselves as a 'group of influence' not an advisory group. Their aim is to impact their views on social work education. They are supported by a network of forty users and carers. The carers and users group contribute to:

- Lecturing
- Innovative teaching such as role play and inviting students to their homes
- Developing social work programmes
- The selection of students
- Involvement in course development, for instance in the development of an MSc in Social Work module entitled 'Making Sense of the Caring Experience'
- Involvement in the formation of a users' and carers' network
- Assisting students with assignments

Formal assessment is, however, still undertaken by university staff. Fergusson and Ager state that:

> 'The quest to further integrate learning and assessment based on service user and carer knowledge and expertise will inevitably challenge institutional academic practice.' (2008, p. 65)

Disabled people are constantly accused of being unrepresentative when they express their views or when they attempt to speak on behalf of other disabled people (Lester and Glasby, 2006). Evans, Carmichael et al. state that:

> Representatives from organisations of disabled people, including self-advocacy groups, were sometimes dismissed by social and health service officers as being unrepresentative of users because they appeared to be too articulate to be 'real' users. (2002, p. 22)

Similarly Brown notes that, 'Users who represent the movement may not be representative in the sense of being "typical" ... this may be used to challenge the legitimacy of their position in speaking for others' (2000, p. 105). Lindow (1999) contends, however, that users are more likely to be representative than professionals and asks whether professionals would choose to send their least confident and articulate members to speak for them.

Beresford and Campbell (1994) believe that the emphasis by health and social care workers on the representativeness of disabled people is a way of maintaining their power base. Furthermore, disabled people are often used in a tokenistic way, for example having just one disabled person on a committee, where, in effect, they have little or no power although the service may be seen to be 'doing what it has to do' (Evans, Carmichael et al., 2002). Carers are also asked to represent disabled people especially people with learning difficulties or those who cannot speak English even though their views may differ (Bewley and Glendinning, 1994). Duffy (2008) found, for instance, that disabled children sometimes express differing views from their parents. Beresford and Campbell believe that managers and professionals, who follow such practices, are in no position to criticize the representativeness of disabled people. They state:

> Questions about the mandate of disabled people and service users ignore or deny the validity of the large and growing number of democratically constituted and controlled local, regional, national and international disabled people's service users and self-advocacy groups and organisations to which they belong and which they are elected or chosen to represent. (1994, pp. 316–17)

Successful user involvement is not easy, not least because disabled people are a diverse and heterogeneous group and, as Bewley and Glendinning state, 'To expect that consultation will reveal a single common view is an illusion' (1994, p. 38). These tensions can be made worse if more than one group of users are involved who have different ideologies and historical roots, for example disabled people and 'carers' where 'carers' usually have more power.

Box 7.11	**Good practice**

The following list sums up many of the points concerning good practice in user involvement in health and social care that we have raised in this discussion.

- An open, flexible organizational culture
- Shared values underpinned by the social model of disability
- High value on user knowledge
- Employment of disabled people in the organization
- Adequately funded user involvement initiatives with sufficient time and staff for their development
- Networking and community development

- Outside support, for instance consultants and researchers
- Sufficient training for users and staff
- Adequate funding and financial security
- An acknowledged and sincere attempt to reduce power imbalances
- Involvement of users throughout the organization
- Compulsory disability equality training for professionals and managers
- Continuous monitoring and evaluation by service users and professionals
- Partnership with service user groups
- Support for users, including induction to organizations and the provision of documents in advance
- Payment of users
- Accessible information
- Accessible communication
- Adequate feedback

Croft and Beresford (2002) provide six factors that they believe contribute to successful user involvement in health and social care:

- The resourcing of user-led organizations
- Systematic and central involvement of users in professional education
- Self-definition of need and design of services by service users
- Equal access and opportunities for disabled service users
- User-led standard setting and definition of outcomes in policy and practice
- User-led monitoring and evaluation of provision

Evans, however, warns of the danger of being presented with lists such as these. She states that:

> 'it is all too easy to get so overwhelmed by wanting to change the world that one fails to get started. Faced with the conservative nature of social services and health bureaucracies even the small changes user organisations make need to be recognised and celebrated.' (1999, p. 9)

Conclusion

As we have seen, there are many barriers to successful user involvement, which both professionals and disabled people face (Dow, 2008). However, although there are still ideological differences between professionals and disabled people, Drake notes the influence that disabled people have had on both policy and services in health and social care. He states:

> [I]t is important to give due weight to the contribution that the disability movement has made in changing the thinking of governments, bringing injustice to light and forcing a radical alteration of the policy agenda. (1996, p. 187)

Disabled people are becoming empowered within society and are no longer prepared to have decisions made on their behalf. It is the challenge of professionals and managers in health and social care to ensure, not only that the involvement of disabled people is possible, but that it is extensive, meaningful and translated into practice with positive outcomes for disabled people's lives. Robson et al. make the point that 'When user involvement is second nature to enough people in an organisation it becomes "the way we do things round here" and, in a sense, ceases to exist as a separate or optional activity' (2003, p. 23).

Reflection exercises

1. Duffy (2008), from her interviews with service users in Northern Ireland, found the following to be the major themes underpinning successful user involvement in health and social care:
   - Communication
   - Values
   - Training
   - Practicalities
   - Knowledge of organizations
   - Support for a user group network
   - Feedback
   - Resources

Thinking about three different organizations in health and social care, jot down some concrete ways in which each of these important themes may be realized. For instance, under 'communication' you may place 'sign language interpreters'.

2. Using the ladder of user involvement in Box 7.6 as a guide, where do these organizations stand in relation to user involvement? What would need to be done for these organizations to ascend the ladder by one rung?
3. In these organizations, what would the practical implications be of increasing user involvement? How far would this need (a) funding and (b) support from management?

If possible discuss these issues with people who work within or receive services from these organizations.

Suggestions for further reading

1. McPhail, M. (ed.) (2008) *Service User and Carer Involvement: Beyond good intentions*. Edinburgh, Dunedin Academic Press

   Gives a useful overview of user involvement in Scotland, focusing on social work education. It examines issues of power and the vital importance of a grassroots approach. Chapter 2 on issues of power and Chapter 5 on the perspective of service users are of particular relevance.

2. Branfield, F. and Beresford, P. (2006) *Making User Involvement Work: Supporting service user involvement and knowledge*. York, Joseph Rowntree Foundation

   In this national survey of user involvement, a large, diverse group of service users and service user organizations were interviewed. Many barriers to user involvement are highlighted and the central importance of networking among service users and having their perspectives heard are emphasized.

3. Carmichael, A. (2004) The social model, the emancipatory paradigm and user involvement, In C. Barnes and G. Mercer (eds) *Implementing the Social Model of Disability: Theory and research*. Leeds, The Disability Press

   Explains the central importance of the social model of disability as an underlying ideology in successful user involvement.

4. Carr, S. (2004) *Has Service User Participation Made a Difference to Social Care Services?* London, Social Care Institute for Excellence

   Provides a thorough overview of user involvement among disabled people and focuses on the extensive barriers that must be overcome in order to achieve its successful implementation.

5. Duffy, J. (2008) *Looking Out from the Middle: User involvement in health and social care in Northern Ireland*. London, Social Care Institute for Excellence

   Provides a thorough account of user involvement of disabled people in health and social care organizations in Northern Ireland.

6. Finlay, W.M.L., Walton, C. and Antaki, C. (2008) Promoting choice and control in residential services for people with learning disabilities, *Disability and Society* 23(4): 349–60

   Focuses on the possibility for user involvement in the day-to-day lives of people with learning disabilities in residential care. It warns against an overemphasis on formal structures for delivering user involvement.

8 Disability and Diversity

The meaning of diversity

Social divisions within society underpin the notion of diversity. They include social class, ethnicity, age, gender, sexual orientation and disability. Social divisions help us to understand how society functions and our place within it at any particular time. They are associated with hierarchies of power and subsequent access to material and social goods. For instance, people of high socioeconomic status will usually have a high income which will give them access to private education and health care and enable them to go on expensive foreign holidays. These goods are, in contrast, unlikely to be available to people of low socioeconomic status who may struggle to obtain a basic standard of living. Social diversity is often viewed in positive terms, for instance job advertisements may state that diversity is welcomed or that a diverse workforce is needed. However, people who belong to certain social groups, for instance disabled people, old people and people from ethnic minorities, may experience prejudice (hostile attitudes) and discrimination (unfavourable treatment) in many areas of life.

In this chapter, we will consider the situation of disabled people in terms of health and social care. We will do this by examining two major social divisions in relation to disabled people: socioeconomic status (social class) and ethnicity. Disability is an important social division in its own right with disabled people contending with disablism (hostile and unthinking attitudes and behaviour towards disabled people) on a daily basis. They are, however, also disproportionately represented in the lower socioeconomic groups which are associated with low income, poor housing, poor education, limited access to transport and leisure facilities, and ill health. Disabled people from ethnic minorities are in a similar situation to other disabled people with the important and major exception that they also experience racism and racial discrimination. Stuart (1993) contends that black disabled people are on the margins of both disability and ethnic minority groups and experience discrimination from both. This gives rise to a unique form of discrimination which, he believes, is more complex than the sum of disablism and racism. Old age is another important social division in relation to disabled people as the majority of disabled people are over 65.

The experience of oppression (social injustice and lack of power) within different social groups gives rise to many commonalities with the potential to connect people across these social divisions (Vernon and Swain, 2002). For instance, people with young children who use pushchairs may have much in common with physically disabled people as they struggle with physical barriers in the environment such as steps and inaccessible public transport. Similarly, black people and older people may experience prejudice and discrimination when attempting to find employment. The situation is, however, complex, as there are many divisions both between and within social groups. For instance, disabled women may have different concerns from disabled men and deaf people may have different access needs to blind people. A large group of people speaking with one voice, for instance the Disabled People's Movement, can be very powerful in bringing about social and political change but, if the needs of particular sectors are overlooked, this tends to give rise to discontent and possible splintering of the group. Morris (1993b), a disabled feminist, has, for instance, taken issue with the women's movement because of its neglect of disabled women and for viewing disabled people as a burden to carers.

In the next section of this chapter we will consider how disability intersects with socioeconomic status to give rise to inequalities in health and social care.

Disability, socioeconomic status and inequalities in health and social care

A major source of diversity when considering health and social care is the extent to which health and ill health are distributed within the population. In order to examine this, it is first necessary to consider what is meant by 'health'. In 1984, the World Health Organization (WHO) defined health as:

> the extent to which an individual or group is able, on the one hand, to realise aspirations and satisfy needs; and, on the other hand, to change or cope with the environment. Health is, therefore, seen as a resource for everyday life, not the objective of living; it is a positive concept emphasising social and personal resources as well as physical capacities. (WHO 1984, cited in Ewles and Simnett, 2003, p. 7)

It can be argued that unless we feel good about ourselves and have meaning in our lives, such as going to work, raising a family, learning new skills, visiting friends, helping others or pursuing hobbies and interests, we cannot be fully healthy. Having a sense of control over our lives and being connected to the people around us are also important for health and well-being (Wiles, 2008). However, to achieve such goals some degree of physical health may also be necessary – although it is important to realize that ill and disabled people frequently report a good quality of life (Beeton, 2008; Swain and French, 2008). It is clear that this broad definition of health is applicable to both health and social care services.

There are many influences on all aspects of our health. Dahlgren and Whitehouse (1991) depict these as layers piled on top of each other.

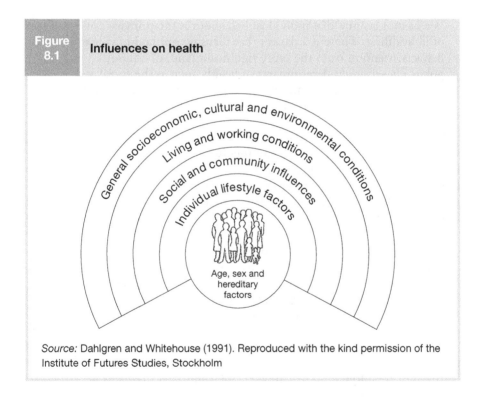

| Figure 8.1 | Influences on health |

Source: Dahlgren and Whitehouse (1991). Reproduced with the kind permission of the Institute of Futures Studies, Stockholm

At the bottom of the pile are biological factors. These include our sex and age and the genes we inherit from our parents. Many diseases become more common as we grow older (for example cancer and cardiovascular disease), some diseases are specific to men or women (for example prostate and ovarian cancer), while others are genetic or congenital in origin (for example cystic fibrosis and haemophilia). Most of these diseases are associated with impairment and disability.

The second layer focuses on our behaviour. This includes whether or not we smoke cigarettes or eat too much, the amount of exercise we take and how much stress we put ourselves under. Most policy initiatives from government have focused on this layer where attempts have been made to change people's behaviour in order to improve their health (L. Jones, 2000). Wiles (2008), for instance, gives examples of community and primary care trust (PCT) partnerships which focus on activities such as walking, cooking, singing, yoga, dancing, craft and improving self-esteem. This emphasis on personal behaviour has, however, been criticized. Asthana and Halliday state that 'the government's strategy suggests an implicit assumption that health inequalities can be reduced without changing overall levels of inequality' (2006, p. 98). There is also a denial of the ways in which the social setting affects our behaviour. Ewles and Simnett believe that:

> We cannot assume that individual behaviour is the primary cause
> of ill health ... There is a danger that focusing on the individual
> detracts attention from the more significant (and, of course,
> politically sensitive) determinants of health, such as the social and
> economic factors of racism, relative deprivation, poverty, housing and
> unemployment. (2003, p. 41)

This emphasis on the individual has implications for disabled people, who are expected to accommodate themselves to existing structures in, for instance, employment, education, leisure and housing, although there has been some improvement in recent years as the social model of disability gains influence (Swain, French, Barnes and Thomas, 2004). Imrie, talking of housing, states:

> Most dwellings are designed and constructed as 'types' that comprise
> standard fixtures and fittings that are not sensitive to variations in body
> form, capabilities and needs ... Builders, building professionals and
> others assume that disabled people will be able to adjust to the pre-
> fixed design of domestic space. (2006, p. 13)

It is notable too that many disabled people would have problems accessing the activities, such as walking, dancing and craft, provided by the PCT partnership mentioned above. Indeed, such initiatives tend to be geared to the 'average' person.

The next layer concerns social and community influences. The people around us, including family members, neighbours, colleagues and friends, can influence our health by giving meaning to our lives and providing assistance and support in times of illness, difficulty and stress. Organizations such as the church, leisure clubs and self-help groups may also be important. Conversely, these people can have a detrimental effect on our health by neglect, abuse, discrimination or failing to take account of our needs.

Feelings of isolation can lead to poor physical and mental health. Eberstadt and Satel (2004) note that people who are socially isolated die at twice the rate of those who are well connected and that they are prone to depression which can lead to poor health habits and risk-taking behaviour. Conversely, positive social relations are linked to good health (Asthana and Halliday, 2006; Wiles, 2008). As Putnam states:

> As a rule of thumb, if you belong to no groups but decide to join one, you cut your risk of dying in the next year in half. If you smoke but belong to no groups, it's a toss up statistically whether you should stop smoking or start joining. (2000, p. 331)

Berkman and Melchior (2006) point out that social networks provide opportunities for support, access, social engagement and social and economic advancement, allowing individuals to participate in work, community and family life. Social networks can, however, also lead to discrimination, hostility and exclusion.

Box 8.1	Social exclusion from the community

As a visually impaired person, I (Sally) have been prevented from joining groups on the grounds of disability on several occasions. In 2009, I was denied access to a ramblers' group (unless I brought somebody along with me on every occasion), although I later found another group that did accept me. In 2000, I was turned down as a volunteer to help teach adult literacy even though I had been involved as a voluntary tutor in the adult literacy movement in its early days and am a qualified and experienced teacher of adults.

Disabled people are likely to experience social isolation and discrimination because the barriers within society (environmental, attitudinal and structural) make it difficult or impossible for them to participate as full citizens. This, in turn, is likely to impact adversely on their physical and mental health. Lester and Glasby (2006) point out that mental and physical ill health frequently co-exist. Needing substantial help from relatives and friends can also lead to resentment and breakdown of relationships as the social rule of reciprocity, which underpins most relationships, may be breached (Wiles, 2008). Social isolation and discrimination are likely to be particularly marked for older disabled people, who may also experience ageism and may become isolated through retirement, widowhood or the death of friends.

Living and working conditions comprise the next layer of influence. It is well known, for example, that the type of house in which we live and our environment at work can affect our health. Work pressure or noisy neighbours may cause depression and anxiety that can lead to physical ill health (Leon and Walt, 2001) and physical hazards such as dampness, poor architectural design and dangerous work practices can cause disease and injury (Siegnal and Theorell, 2006). Living in deprived neighbourhoods also increases the risk of ill health and mortality, despite the individual's personal situation (Steptoe, 2006; Wiles, 2008).

It is well known that unemployment is correlated with poor physical and mental health and high mortality rates (Siegnal and Theorell, 2006) but employment can also have adverse effects on our health. Low-salaried workers have the worst physical and psychosocial environment at work, which, in turn, can lead to poor physical and mental health (Dahl et al., 2006). Siegnal and Theorell (2006) state that people in jobs where there is high demand and low control are particularly likely to experience stress, although low demand and low control is also stressful, particularly if it is linked to low levels of support. High effort and low reward can also lead to ill health because of the lack of reciprocity in the arrangement, which is likely to give rise to damaging negative emotions. Certain people, including disabled people, are more likely to accept work of this type through lack of opportunity and choice (Siegnal and Theorell, 2006).

Even disabled people in professional occupations are likely to experience additional stress, often because it takes more time and effort to succeed in the job. This is explained by a visually impaired physiotherapist who is talking about the administrative aspects of his job:

'Visually impaired people, with the best computerised systems available, are at a disadvantage because of the amount of time and concentration it takes ... I take time at the end of the day ... I nearly always work my lunch hour. It's got worse over the years.' (French 2001, pp. 126–7)

Disabled people are also far more likely than non-disabled people to be unemployed (Stanley, 2005) and unemployment is associated with poor physical and mental health (Reine et al., 2004).

Barnes and Roulstone (2005) believe that disabled people should not be judged in terms of whether or not they are involved in paid employment and that the benefits system should be de-stigmatized and more generous to improve their quality of life. It is, for instance, important that they have sufficient resources and access to engage in purposeful activities of their own choosing. Barnes and Roulstone (2005) also believe that the effort involved in coping as a disabled person in a disabling environment should be regarded as work and that their role as employers of personal assistants and the considerable work opportunities for non-disabled people generated by the 'disability industry' should be recognized.

The outermost layer affecting our health concerns general socioeconomic, cultural and environmental conditions. This includes the economic state of the country, the level of employment, the tax system, the degree of environmental pollution and our attitudes, for example towards ethnic minorities and disabled people. All the major research reports over the years demonstrate that mortality, morbidity and life expectancy are strongly correlated with socioeconomic status, with those of the lowest social status being at a considerable disadvantage (Power and Kuh, 2006; Siegrist and Marmot, 2006; Steptoe, 2006).

Lack of an adequate income can impact on health in many ways. Yeandle et al. (2008) interviewed men and women on low incomes who reported depression, anxiety, high blood pressure and headaches. They had insufficient fruit and vegetables in their diet and little time for exercise. Women were most affected as they usually put their partners and children first. They also suffered feelings of guilt and failure when they could not give their children what they wanted or what other children enjoyed.

Despite the various influences on our health, the evidence overwhelmingly suggests that broad social factors concerning housing, income, educational level, employment and social integration are more important than our individual behaviour or medical practice and advances (Ewles and Simnett, 2003). People of the lowest socioeconomic status are at far higher risk, not only of physical illness and early death, but also of accidents, premature births, mental illness and suicide. Children in the lowest two social classes, for instance, are 16 times more likely to die in fires than children in the highest social class (Office of the Deputy Prime Minister, 2005). Smith and Goldblatt (2004) report that of the 66 major causes of death, 62 are more prevalent in the lowest two social classes. It is also the case that men in professional occupations live, on average, seven years longer than men in manual occupations and that the children of manual workers are twice as likely to die before the age of 15 than the children of professionals workers (Naidoo and Wills, 2008). In addition, Hargreaves (2007) reports that in 2002–2004, infant mortality was 19% higher among manual workers than professional workers and that the gap had steadily widened.

There are also regional differences, for instance in Manchester life expectancy for men is reported to be eight and a half years less than men in Dorset (Social Exclusion Unit, 2004). The Acheson Report (1998), which was based on government-commissioned research into inequalities in health, found evidence that every aspect of health is worse for people living in deprived circumstances. Overall, this situation has not changed. As Wiles notes, 'across the life span there are inequalities in people's health that follow from their economic position. Poor people are more likely to be in poor health and to die at an earlier age' (2008, p. 52).

Box 8.2	The meaning of poverty

Although Britain has, overall, become healthier and wealthier over the years, health inequalities persist, in fact the gap between the richest and poorest sectors of society has widened considerably since 1979 (Asthana and Halliday, 2006; Wiles, 2008). Poverty in Britain is relative rather than absolute, with people being categorized as poor if their income is less than 60% of the national average. This included between one fifth and one quarter of the UK population in 2007 (Palmer et al., 2007). Although people now have the basic necessities for survival, poverty deprives them of many goods which other people enjoy, excluding them from the culture of the community and causing considerable ill health and social isolation There is a danger, in the present economic climate, that this situation will worsen.

It is important to realize, however, that the health of a country does not equate to its wealth but rather to how fairly the wealth is distributed (Eberstadt and Satel, 2004). Asthana and Halliday (2006) note that longevity rises in societies that are more equal and socially cohesive, especially when infectious diseases have been controlled. They contend that psychosocial stress is related to feelings of relative disadvantage and to subordinate status, which, in turn, can lead to mental and physical ill health. Siegrist and Marmot state that:

> 'An exclusive emphasis on the physical life circumstances associated with low income fails to recognise the importance of a broad spectrum of psychosocial influences on health that interact with material conditions and that may be decisive in explaining the social gradient among populations with standards of living above a certain threshold of poverty and deprivation.' (2006, p. 6)

Thompson (1998) agrees that poverty has significant psychological and social implications, in terms of insecurity, social exclusion, self-esteem and access to resources. Dahl et al. (2006) note, however, that health inequalities are not consistently better in social democratic countries than in those with conservative and liberal regimes.

In the government paper *Sustainable Communities: people, places and prosperity,* a commitment is made to 'make sure that mainstream services do at least as well for the worst-off as they do for others' (Office of the Deputy Prime Minister, 2005, p. 35) and to substantially reduce health inequalities by 2010.

The stresses in people's lives tend to be cumulative (Eberstadt and Satel, 2004; Asthana and Halliday, 2006; Power and Kuh, 2006) with adverse physical, social and psychological conditions, which often start in early infancy or before birth, leading to biological, psychological and social disadvantage. Talking of infancy, Power and Kuh (2006) point to insecure attachment, institutionalization and lack of emotional support as being damaging factors. Most disabled people are of lower socioeconomic status and experience disadvantage over a long period of time. They are, therefore, particularly likely to experience ill health in its broadest sense. Furthermore, their impairments, for instance needing to keep warm or reliance on taxis to go out, incur additional cost.

Box
8.3 **The interaction of various influences on health**

The levels of influence on our health that Dahlgren and Whitehouse (1991) describe
all interact and influence each other. House (2001) found that all risk factors for
health (behavioural, social, psychological and environmental) increase with low
socioeconomic status, however it is measured, for instance by income, education,
housing or occupation. If the economic state of the country is favourable, people are
likely to have more disposable income, which may improve their health by allowing
them to buy good quality food and housing of a better standard, engage in leisure
pursuits, give their children more opportunities and enjoy relaxing holidays to reduce
stress. Similarly, if a person is attempting to give up drugs, success is more likely if
community support is strong and if government is willing to act by establishing and
financing supportive policies. Conversely, smoking or excessive alcohol consumption
may serve to reduce stress caused by poor income, discrimination, poor housing
or lack of support (Asthana and Halliday, 2006; Yeandle et al., 2008). It is clear that
people in deprived circumstances have the fewest choices, including those concerning
their health.

Reducing inequalities in health

It is at the macro-sociological level that government can be particularly
influential in reducing inequalities in health by implementing policy and
passing legislation to bring about wide social change, for instance seat belt
legislation, restrictions on cigarette smoking and equality legislation such as
the Disability Discrimination Act 1995. In 1997, the Labour government
set up the Social Exclusion Unit in recognition that some groups, including
disabled people and people from ethnic minorities, have particular problems
accessing goods and services such as health care, housing, employment and
education. In 2006, the Social Exclusion Task Force was formed to coor-
dinate the government's drive against social exclusion in many areas such
as housing, employment and leisure. There is recognition by government
that social exclusion is created by complex interlinking social problems. As
Wiles states:

> Governments have recognised that social exclusion can be addressed
> only by tackling the linked problems of employment, low qualifications,
> educational underachievement, crime, ill health and substandard
> housing in a 'joined up' way. This means ... organisations ... and local
> residents ... working together to alleviate the causes and effects of all the
> problems, rather than working in isolation. A particular advantage of a
> community approach is that it encourages people to work together across
> traditional boundaries. (2008, p. 35)

It is recognized by government that disabled people and people from ethnic minorities are among the groups most likely to be socially excluded and to benefit least from government initiatives (Department of Health, 2004b). It is frequently necessary to develop outreach and advocacy services to help such groups to access health and social services, as we considered in Chapter 5. It should be recognized that social exclusion is not the same as poverty, although the two are frequently linked. A wealthy disabled person, for instance, would still have difficulty accessing many services and leisure activities within a disabling environment and a gay or lesbian disabled person may face discrimination when hiring personal assistants.

In 1999, the government programme *New Deal for Communities* was implemented where time-limited funding was made available to tackle social exclusion within a broad strategy of neighbourhood renewal. Engaging with residents was a requirement of these programmes, which resulted in local people and volunteers working with paid professionals from various agencies in an inter-agency context. Dinhan (2005) notes, however, the tendency for professionals to take over due to unequal power relations and how this can have a detrimental effect.

Despite the individualistic stance of most health policy (Machenbach, 2006), it can be seen that recent governments have taken some heed of the social determinants of health. However, Asthana and Halliday (2006) note a recent shift from a concern with macro-sociological factors, as seen in the Treasury review *Tackling Health Inequalities* (DH and Her Majesty's Treasury, 2002), to a concern with changing behaviour, which is evident in the white paper *Choosing Health: Making health choices easier* (2004b). Asthana and Halliday (2006) point out that structural causes of ill health are difficult to measure, under-researched and poorly understood. It is certainly the case that most research about disabled people has taken an individualistic, rather than a social, stance (Swain and French, 2004).

It can be seen from this account that the health of disabled people is particularly at risk. Most disabled children are born into families of low socio-economic status, for instance low birth weight babies, who are particularly likely to have impairments, are more common in poor families. Disabled people are less likely to gain a good education and are more likely to be unemployed or in low-paid, monotonous work with little disposable income. They must contend with an inaccessible and sometimes hostile environment, in terms for instance of inaccessible transport and buildings, which, in turn, makes the establishment of supportive social networks, including friendships and intimate relationships, more difficult. Furthermore, these factors accumulate over the disabled person's life. A focus on the environment, which, through disabled people's own efforts, has started to take effect, is likely to be the surest way to improve the health of disabled people in the broadest sense and would also have the effect of reducing disease and impairment. Clearly an interdisciplinary approach is needed, with professionals from many fields, including employment, housing, architecture, education, health and social services, working alongside disabled people themselves, to promote change at every level.

Disabled people from ethnic minorities: implications for health and social care

The previous discussion showed that illness and impairment are positively correlated with low socioeconomic status, including poor housing and higher rates of unemployment. The Audit Commission (2004) found that people from ethnic minorities are more likely to be of low socioeconomic status than the white population, and to experience multiple inequalities They note, for instance, that 70% of the ethnic minority population live in the 88 most deprived neighbourhoods. These results are confirmed by Nazroo et al. (2008) in their study of inequalities in England. Bhopal states that 'Socio-economic factors are accepted as profoundly important in explaining and countering health inequalities' (2007, p. 153) and notes that there is more unemployment and low-paid work among ethnic minority groups. He points out, however, that biological and cultural factors are important in the aetiology of some diseases. Bhopal also notes that there is great heterogeneity among ethnic minority groups and states that 'Lumping disparate groups together can mislead policy and planning' (2007, p. 178). It is noted by the Home Office (2005), for instance, that people of Pakistani and Bangladeshi descent are particularly disadvantaged with nearly two thirds of children living in poverty compared with one fifth of children in the population as a whole. Because people from ethnic minority groups are disproportionately represented in the poorest strata of society, they experience a higher level of illness and impairment than the majority population (Atkin et al., 2004). African-Caribbean people, for instance, have a higher incidence of stroke, Asian people have a higher incidence of diabetes; and the babies of women from many ethnic minority groups are smaller than average, which predisposes them to impairment.

Box 8.4	Specific diseases affecting minority ethnic groups

There are a number of diseases and impairments that mainly affect people from specific ethnic minority groups. One of these is sickle cell disorder, which is transmitted genetically and largely affects African and African-Caribbean people in the UK (Anionwu and Atkin, 2001). It is estimated that one in five hundred people in these communities have the condition, which makes it Britain's most common genetic disease. There is also a higher than average incidence of tuberculosis, rickets and osteomalacia among Asian people, and specific eye conditions, which can lead to severe visual impairment, are more common in some ethnic minority groups than others (D. Mason, 2000). Diabetic retinopathy, for example, is particularly common among Jewish people, and cataracts are prevalent among Asian people. White people are, of course, similarly affected with a high incidence of specific conditions, such as cystic fibrosis and breast cancer, so any tendency to view the health needs of people from ethnic minority groups in terms of 'problems' is unjustified (Atkin et al., 2004).

In general, provision for those with sickle cell disorders remains under-resourced and poorly cooordinated, especially when compared with services for those with cystic fibrosis and haemophilia, which mainly affect the majority population (Anionwu and Atkin, 2001). Tuberculosis, which is more common in certain ethnic minority groups, has, in contrast, had a high profile, probably because of its perceived threat to the majority population (Bhopal and White, 1993). As Ahmad and Bradby state:

'Early interest in ethnic minority health came from public health and tropical medicine specialists with an initial focus on protecting the British population from diseases which could be imported from immigrants.' (2008, p. 6)

The lack of knowledge of conditions that specifically affect people from ethnic minority populations can easily interact with racist attitudes concerning illness behaviour, leading to a lack of belief in symptoms such as pain. This is a common experience of people with sickle cell disorders, where they may be stereotyped as drug addicts or as people with a low pain threshold (Anionwu and Atkin, 2001).

It must be emphasized that low socioeconomic status, often resulting from racism, and leading to poor housing, diet, and unemployment, is far more influential than ethnic origin or cultural difference with regard to the incidence of disease and impairment (Nazroo, 1998). For instance, the higher incidence of tuberculosis, rickets and osteomalacia is often the consequence of socioeconomic disadvantage. Bhopal (2007) believes, however, that researchers and policymakers have concentrated on differences and ignored similarities to the detriment of ethnic minority groups. He states, 'Despite all their splendid variety, individual humans and human societies are actually most remarkable for their similarity' (2007, p. 2). The emphasis has been on meeting the specific needs of people from ethnic minorities rather than challenging the whole health care system to include people from ethnic minorities. Bhopal (2007) promotes the mainstreaming of ethnic minority groups within the health and social care system which is now made mandatory by the Race Relations (Amendment) Act 2000. However, the Audit Commission (2004) believes that both specific services and the mainstreaming of services for people from ethnic minorities are necessary.

Barriers to health and social care services for disabled people from minority ethnic groups: ways forward

Box 8.5	Barriers to health and social care services for people from minority ethnic groups

There are many barriers to health and social care for disabled people from ethnic minority groups. These are summarized by Butt (2006):

- Lack of knowledge among black and minority ethnic communities about available support

- Lack of appropriate services
- Poor quality services
- Lack of choice
- Workers lacking effective communication skills
- Workers lacking the skill and experience to work with racially and culturally diverse communities
- Direct and institutional discrimination

The MacPherson Inquiry into the death of Stephen Lawrence (MacPherson, 1999) emphasized the idea that institutional racism was rife in UK organizations. This was followed by an amendment to the Race Relations Act 2000 which requires public services to eliminate racial discrimination, promote race equality and to identify and address inequalities in services, whatever the size of the ethnic population. Indeed, this was one of the key factors in the modernization agenda for health and social care (Audit Commission, 2004). For instance, in the white paper *Our Health, Our Care, Our Say: A new direction for community services* (DH, 2006) there is a commitment to promote diversity.

Institutional racism is embedded in the ideology of organizations and the erroneous assumptions informing organizational practice. It occurs when policies lead to discrimination regardless of the behaviour of individual employees (D. Mason, 2000). This is not to imply that direct racism no longer exists. Direct racism occurs in many ways, for instance when health professionals deny the reality of pain in sickle cell anaemia, when people from minority ethnic groups are portrayed as being demanding or excessively passive (Ahmad and Bradby, 2008) or when they are blamed for failing to adjust to a system that does not meet their needs (Bhopal, 2007). It may also result from a lack of understanding of the behaviour of people from ethnic minority groups, which, in turn, may be a factor in explaining the high number of people from ethnic minority groups in psychiatric hospitals (Watters, 1996; Thompson, 2006). Racism can, however, be a causal factor in mental illness (Bhopal, 2007). Institutional racism is not a new idea and, for some time, it has been helpful in making sense of health inequalities and inappropriate and inaccessible services. Disabled people from ethnic minority groups are, of course, likely to experience both institutional racism and institutional disablism (Vernon and Swain, 2002).

Institutional racism is a major explanation of the barriers people from ethnic minorities face when trying to access appropriate health and social care services. If diversity is not recognized and respected, the service will be geared to a 'white' norm and the specific needs of disabled people from ethnic minorities, for instance their dietary, linguistic and cultural needs, will be ignored (Thompson, 2006). Bhopal states that:

Despite the multi-ethnic and multi-cultural nature of modern Britain, and notwithstanding the enormous efforts of both institutions and individuals, NHS health care and training are still largely based on an understanding of what constitutes illness, disease and health care in terms of so called 'Western medicine' and this is firmly based on the teachings of British medical schools. (2007, p. 98)

This is an example of ethnocentricity, which is defined by Bhopal as 'the inherent tendency to view one's own culture as the standard against which others are judged' (2007, p. 16). Some health and social care workers may be ill-equipped to respond to cultural differences that they may not fully understand (Anionwu and Atkin, 2001). Special bathing aids, for instance, may be completely inappropriate for people whose washing methods are different from those of the indigenous population. Childcare practices may vary, and ways of coping with terminal illness and death may differ. It may be totally unacceptable for people from some ethnic minority groups to be treated by, or in view of, a person of the opposite sex, for instance in a physiotherapy gymnasium or hydrotherapy pool (Atkin et al., 2004). These examples may be due to a lack of cultural competency rather than racism. It is not possible for health and social care workers to understand the culture of every ethnic group but it is important that they are open and willing to learn from disabled people and to adapt to their needs.

The most obvious example of the failure to recognize cultural diversity is the inability of the NHS to provide adequate support for those whose first language is not English (Robinson, 2001; Butt, 2006). Qulsom et al. (2002) found that this had serious implications for Pakistani and Bangladeshi parents of disabled children both in terms of communicating with professionals and finding out about services. They found that some of these parents could not distinguish one professional from another and did not understand their roles. Furthermore, families facing most deprivation were least likely to be receiving services and least likely to speak English. Because of these and other problems, people from ethnic minority groups are more likely than other people to be dissatisfied with public services (Audit Commission, 2002). However, satisfaction should not necessarily be equated with a good service. Lawton et al. (2006), for instance, found that although their sample of diabetic patients from South Asia expressed extreme gratitude for the service they received (which they compared with the service they would have received in their country of origin), their level of knowledge about diabetes was poor and they reported confusion about dietary advice. They also found the advice they were given culturally inappropriate.

Interpreters are often in short supply (Robinson, 2001) so family members are sometimes used as interpreters, which many people dislike (Atkin et al., 1998). In some cases, young children are required to act as interpreters of complex medical information, often about sensitive and embarrassing issues. The problem of providing a good interpreter service is highlighted by Greenhalgh et al. (2008) who report that one of the GPs they interviewed had encountered 27 languages in his practice in the space of a fortnight.

They also found that, whereas medical needs and practice are unpredictable, interpreters frequently worked set hours and were not always available.

In their study of South Asian patients with diabetes, Lawton et al. (2006) reported that patients often felt that information had been lost, even when using a professional interpreter. They also felt under pressure to keep questions short and were often left with unanswered questions and concerns. The parents of severely disabled children interviewed by Chamba and Ahmad (2000) reported inaccuracies, an unsympathetic approach and lack of confidentiality. Interpreters may also fail to interpret medical information and sometimes speak in a different dialect to that of the patient (Atkin et al., 2000). Douglas et al. (2004) found interpreter services to be patchy but also found examples of very good practice.

Accessibility of information is vitally important if services are to be equitable. As well as transcribing information into a variety of languages, a wide variety of alternative formats may be necessary for disabled people including Braille, large print, sign language, DVD, audio CD, pictures and symbols as advocated by Clark (2002). For some people, particularly those with communication disabilities such as aphasia, the issue of time can be crucial to inclusive communication. For instance, a slower tempo may be the only accessible pace to ensure understanding (Pound, 2004). It is also important that written information is translated into minority languages. Kroll (1990) contends, however, that pamphlets should be used only to consolidate information that has been given orally, and Bahl (1993) believes that people from ethnic minority groups should be involved in producing their own health education literature to ensure its accessibility.

Barriers to communication are, however, about far more than language. Douglas et al. state that 'other factors, such as class, region, religion and geography may impinge on the process of interpreting and communication – such that just speaking the same language may not necessarily mean the same understanding will follow' (2004, p. 74). For instance, different cultural groups may differ in their emotional expressiveness, how much they are prepared to disclose and how far they wish to consult with family members (Robinson, 2004). Lawton et al. (2006) found that advising patients from South Asia to exercise posed difficulties because taking exercise without involving the family was viewed as selfish and women were not permitted to expose their bodies or to take sufficient time outside the home.

Stereotypes about people from minority ethnic groups can also undermine communication (Vernon and Swain, 2002). One common stereotype is that people from minority ethnic groups 'look after their own' and, therefore, do not want or need help from statutory or voluntary services (Quershi et al., 2000; Butt, 2006). However, Seymour et al. state that, 'Few older adults of all ethnicities have carers readily available' (2008, p. 88). The idea that people from ethnic minorities 'look after their own' is clearly a dangerous assumption since it can easily be used as an excuse not to plan or provide for the needs of these communities.

There is a history of defining illness and impairment faced by minority ethnic communities in terms of cultural deficits where a shift towards a Western lifestyle is offered as the main solution (Atkin et al., 2004). Impairment among Asian communities, for instance, has often been attributed to consanguineous marriages and therefore considered to result from cultural and biological pathology (Ahmad et al., 2000; Ahmad and Bradby, 2008). Asian people have also been blamed for vitamin D deficiency, because of their diet and the way they dress, even though vitamin D was not initially added to ghee or chapatti flour as it was for the flour consumed by white people. The preoccupation with cultural practices in explaining impairment means that other important explanations, such as the role of poverty or inadequate services, are rarely considered. Such an approach also creates mistrust between health professionals and those they serve (Ahmad et al., 2000). This is not to dismiss the role of cultural identity in informing people's service needs but to challenge accounts that seek to pathologize and simplify cultural practices. Fernando warns that, 'the promotion of cultural sensitivity without challenging racism may result in the reinforcement of racism by masking it and thereby inducing complacency' (1989, p. 187).

Box 8.6	**Access to services for ethnic minority communities: ways forward**

In a qualitative study of 20 Pakistani and Bangladeshi parents of disabled children, Qulsom et al. (2002) found that reluctance to use respite care resulted from concerns over whether their children's cultural needs would be met. Similarly, Flynn (2002) found that lack of information and inappropriate services led to poor service uptake. As Nawaz, talking of fostering, states:

'Ethnicity is not just about skin and hair care. It is about shared history and background including the food eaten, the books read, spirituality and cultural influences. Most parents, not just black parents, are generally happier for their child to go to a carer who shares a similar family environment and values to their own.' (2006, p. 66)

Only one of the 20 families in Qulsom et al.'s study had a social worker and most had no contact with professionals other than their children's teachers and the GP. They were also very unlikely to belong to a support group. Qulsom et al. (2002) found that parents lacked important information, for instance they did not know about the Family Fund that supports parents on low incomes, and those who could not speak English were only half as likely to receive the Disability Living Allowance or the Invalid Care Allowance. Furthermore, no one looked holistically at the situation of the families. As Qulsom et al. state:

'Neither the health or education systems offered a clear gateway to information about and access to the range of services that may be available to disabled families ... Far from service provision being integrated across the different agencies and professionals so that families experienced a seamless needs-led service, it was the absence of systematic services which came through most strikingly.' (2002, p. 251)

The families in this study were economically and socially deprived with resulting high levels of anxiety and depression.

Salway et al. (2008) confirm that people from ethnic minority groups are less likely to receive Disability Living Allowance. Among the reasons for this, they found negative past experiences of trying to claim for the allowance, poor information, and the greater social costs of revealing impairment in their communities.

Health and social care professionals are predominantly white and non-disabled, and receive little training concerning the needs and difficulties of disabled people from ethnic minority groups (French and Swain, 2008). It is almost impossible to be entirely free of racist beliefs and attitudes when living in a predominantly white society. Some of these attitudes and behaviour patterns may be conscious, while others are submerged. It may be that we attend to people from ethnic minority groups a little less than other people, that we do not expect as much of them, or that we give them a little less of our time. In many ways, the more subtle and submerged racism becomes the more difficult it is to deal with. Racist attitudes and behaviour within the health and social care services have the potential to permeate policy, practice and the interpretation of research data (Bhopal, 2007). An extreme example of this is the widespread involvement of medical professionals in the Nazi regime (Silver, 2003), as discussed in Chapter 1.

Race equality training, when skilfully undertaken by people from ethnic minority groups, can help people to become aware of their attitudes and behaviour in a relaxed and non-threatening environment. It is no longer viewed as acceptable to treat people from ethnic minority groups 'just like everyone else' or to take a 'why can't they be like us?' approach. True inclusion and equity in services is recognizing and responding to people's specific needs which forms the basis of client-centred approaches within health and social care.

Over twenty years ago, the Commission for Racial Equality stated that, 'Without equal employment opportunities it is unlikely that there will be equal opportunities in service delivery' (1988, p. 11). Nawaz (2006) agrees that those employed in health and social care should reflect the community that they serve. The discrimination faced by patients and clients from ethnic minority groups can also be faced by people who are seeking employment, which highlights the importance of equal opportunity and anti-discriminatory policies. Bhopal (2007) highlights the history of discrimination against nurses from ethnic minority groups who were denied state registration. He states, 'Fairness in employment is a fundamental component of equity in service delivery' (2007, p. 173). He also points out that high-quality monitoring of both recruitment and the utilization of services by patients and clients is necessary to develop services.

There are many advantages to employing staff from ethnic minority groups. They can, for instance, communicate with clients in their own languages and can contribute to the evaluation of the adequacy of services. It is important, though, that such staff do not become restricted in their role to 'race experts' or be channelled to work with particular groups of service users against their wishes (Dominelli, 2002). Neither should they replace service users from ethnic minority groups regarding user involvement and consultation. It is vital too that people from ethnic minorities are promoted into positions of power so that they can influence services (Audit Commission, 2004). Much the same can be said, of course, about disabled people and it follows from this that more disabled people from ethnic minority groups need to be employed in health and social care services.

Bhopal reminds us that most of the industrial world comprises multi-ethnic societies and that 'the whole world is destined to become multi-ethnic, probably within the next 20 or 30 years' (2007, p. x). His list of the overarching challenges to health and health care is shown in Box 8.7.

Box 8.7	Challenges to health and social care

- Understanding and responding to varying health behaviours, beliefs and attitudes
- Responding to differences in the pattern of disease and reducing inequalities where this is possible
- Maintaining high-quality communication despite language and cultural barriers
- Delivering services that are culturally sensitive
- Overcoming personal biases, stereotyped views, personal racism and institutional racism and inertia
- Ensuring equal opportunities in employment

(Adapted from Bhopal, 2007)

Butt's (2006) wide-sweeping suggestions for improving practice with people from minority ethnic groups are shown in Box 8.8.

Box 8.8	Improving health and social care practice for minority ethnic groups

- Implement a needs-led approach
- Implement a policy and monitoring framework to promote diversity
- Implement an ethnic record keeping and monitoring system that produces information that is used

- Plan for the delivery of services that promote diversity
- Build processes and a workforce that can implement effective engagement

(Adapted from Butt, 2006)

Conclusion

It is clear from the above account that, although progress is slowly being made, a great deal still needs to be done to provide disabled people, including those from ethnic minority groups, with sensitive and effective health and social care. The attitudes and behaviour of individual practitioners are vitally important in bringing about change, but management backing and the development of policy relating to resources, staff recruitment, and working practices must be made at every level of the organization if meaningful progress is to be achieved. It is essential that the 'voice' of clients, both individual and collective, directs any change that is made. This involves practitioners and policymakers in listening to individual clients, whose daily experiences are likely to be fundamentally different from their own, and to consult with organizations of disabled people at every stage of service planning and implementation, as discussed in Chapter 7. In the face of different forms of discrimination and multiple discrimination, as well as the vested interests that obstruct change, there can be no simple solution to developing health and social care policy and practice. Successful change will only result from collective commitment and action.

Reflective exercises

1. Addressing the health and social care needs of disabled people, including those from ethnic minorities, is a massive task which involves changing many aspects of society itself. It is, nonetheless, important that practitioners try to realize this goal in their own practice and places of work rather than becoming overwhelmed.

   With a colleague from a different profession to your own, discuss any three changes that could realistically be implemented in your workplace to improve the health of disabled people – including people from ethnic minorities. Think of health in its broadest sense to include biological, social and psychological elements. You may like to think of a change which focuses on each of these dimensions.

2. As we have discussed in this chapter, health equality depends on different professionals working together in an interdisciplinary way with disabled people themselves. Consider how this might happen in your place of work and compare your ideas with a health or social care professional

from another organization. You may like to consider some of the following factors:

(a) The priority given to disabled people
(b) Training issues
(c) Finance issues
(d) Cultural differences between professions

Consider ways in which health and social care services may forge links with the local community to improve the health and well-being of disabled people.

Suggestions for further reading

1. Ahmad, W.I.U. (ed.) (2000) *Ethnicity, Disability and Chronic Illness*. Buckingham, Open University Press

Gives a useful overview of practice with disabled and chronically ill people from ethnic minorities. It includes some interesting research studies and has a practical orientation, which is useful to professionals who wish to improve their practice in this area. Chapters 4 and 7 concern sickle cell disorder, Chapter 5 examines services for minority ethnic deaf people and Chapter 6 explores the language, communication and information needs of parents of severely disabled children from ethnic minority groups.

2. Bhopal, R.S. (2007) *Ethnicity, Race and Health in Multicultural Societies*. Oxford, Oxford University Press

Gives a detailed but very readable account of the health status of people from ethnic minority groups in multicultural societies. Its focus is broad, including epidemiology, health care planning, and health promotion. Chapter 6 on inequalities in health and Chapters 7 and 8 on principles and approaches to health and health care may be of particular interest. The book contains practical interactive exercises.

3. Siegrist, J. and Marmot, M. (eds) (2006) *Social Inequalities in Health: New evidence and policy implications*. Oxford, Oxford University Press

Gives a broad account of social inequalities in health and the policy implications. It covers the individual and psychological aspects of health inequalities as well as the social and political dimension and gives many examples of interventions to improve these inequalities. Chapter 2 on life course development of unequal health, Chapter 3 on the impact of social policy on health and Chapter 6 on socioeconomic position and health may be of particular interest.

4. Thompson, N. (2006) *Anti-discriminatory Practice* (4th edn). Basingstoke, Palgrave Macmillan

Provides a good, basic overview of anti-discriminatory practice in the social services. A major strength is that it covers many types of diversity, for instance gender, disability and ethnicity. It is a practical book that gives plenty of ideas for changing and improving practice. Of particular interest are Chapter 4 on ethnicity and racism and Chapter 6 on disability.

9 Families and 'Carers'

with Sarah Keyes

In this chapter we discuss:

- Services: policy and provision
- What parents want: a wish list
- Parental involvement: barriers and strategies

We would like to begin this chapter by recognizing that to cover all the relevant issues would require another book and we have had to take a particular focus. The title of the chapter signals such a broad arena that it raises the realization that disability touches all our lives. There are numerous situations which we do not directly address here but which you may encounter and will need to follow up. These include the experiences of ageing parents of disabled adults, partner/spousal carers, and families caring for older disabled people. Life course transitions is also a major topic and we deal only with transition to adulthood in this chapter. If you have a particular interest in this topic, you will find Priestley (2001) useful. We focus here on the experiences of parents of disabled children, with the hope that the issues raised are generalizable to experiences of other groups signalled by the title of this chapter. We begin by considering the concept of 'carer'.

The words from a disabled activist provide a good starting point for a critical examination of disabled people and caring in families:

> The words 'disabled people' rarely appear these days in policy
> discussions without the words 'and their carers' tagged on behind.
> Over the last decade there has been much research on 'informal carers'
> and increasing emphasis on their key role in the implementation of
> community care policies. But where is the experience of disabled
> people in all of this? Do they have nothing to offer a relationship other
> than a 'burden of care'? (Morris, 1993a, p. 10)

The words 'care' and 'carer' can, then, be deeply problematic to disabled people (see Chapter 7). They are associated with the notion of dependency, as the above quote suggests. A distinction is made between formal and informal care, though this distinction is not absolute, which is central to the debates, with enforced dependency on informal carers being challenged by the Independent Living Movement. The distinction has, perhaps, become clearer with the establishment of direct payments and personal assistants (PAs), the term PA being an expression of disabled people's rejection of the term carer. This is far from absolute, however, as some people who have acted as informal carers have gone on to act as PAs. In this chapter we focus on informal care in families, with a particular concentration on families with disabled children.

This is a difficult and controversial arena and has been for perhaps the past thirty years. Feminist perspectives have played a significant role in the debates, with some feminists viewing the provision of care, through unpaid work, as falling predominantly on women and thus furthering their oppression (Fawcett, 2000). It can be argued that the economics of community care are reliant on care being provided by family members, particularly female family members. More recently, questions have been raised about young people acting as carers particularly for disabled parents. It can be argued, however, that the focus is being put on the needs of the children of disabled parents without addressing the needs of disabled adults in their parenting role. Integral to this arena is the questionable notion that there are two categories of people: carers and cared for. Suffusing all these issues are questions regarding the rights of disabled people and their struggle for independent living. We shall return to this complex set of issues as we progress through the topics in this chapter.

We first outline the mandate for the improvement of services coming from national policy and research. While the former prioritizes partnership with carers, the latter suggests substantial dissatisfaction. The analysis here takes a broad approach in covering issues relating to the support of carers. The following two sections take a different basis. The focus is the views of parents (and/or guardians) of young disabled people, using a research project, the 'Evidence of Need' project at the Percy Hedley Foundation (PHF), conducted in 2007 by John Swain and Sarah Keyes. We first look at the parents' service needs, their 'wish list'. We then turn to barriers to the involvement in decision making in health and social care for carers, and strategies for overcoming such barriers. The chapter closes by summarizing possibilities for change.

Services: policy and provision

The Audit Commission report (2003), which was compiled with 'disabled children's voices at the heart', found that there was:

- a lottery of provision, with the services received depending 'largely on where they live' (p. 2). Too little provided too late, including families missing out on benefits that they are entitled to and having 'unacceptably long waits for interventions, equipment and adaptations' (p. 3)

■ a jigsaw puzzle of services, with families having to 'jump through a series of hoops' in order to get support (p. 3). Also, different services being used by the same family were found to be 'working to their own priorities', with a lack of joint planning.

It is not surprising then that the report referred to services for disabled children as 'Cinderella' services. However, the Audit Commission (2003, pp. 2–4) also found examples of good practice, which it suggests could be more widely implemented, including:

■ Involving disabled children and young people and their parents in making changes to the local map of services
■ Involving disabled children and young people in designing assessments that will 'put their views first'
■ Families being provided with support at the earliest opportunity
■ Involving parents and carers in training staff
■ Appointing a 'care co-ordinator' who would oversee the whole care package
■ Returning to the notion of inter-agency working, agencies which work together to establish joint teams for disabled children

More recently, the Department for Education and Skills (DfES, 2007), stated that the government has pledged improvement in three priority areas: access and empowerment, responsive services and timely support, and improving quality and capacity. This includes:

■ Making it clear what services disabled children and young people and their families can expect
■ Piloting individual budgets (see Chapter 5)
■ Engaging with service users
■ Making sure that disabled children are considered a priority, on both a local and a national level
■ Making sure that interventions are available at the appropriate stage in a child's development
■ Continuing to implement the Early Support Programme
■ Support during the transition into adulthood
■ More 'short breaks' for disabled children
■ Accessible childcare for parents who wish to work
■ Maximizing mobility
■ The commissioning of the Children's Workforce Development Council which will establish the skills and behaviours the workforce requires and identify gaps

Another theme that arose from a review of the relevant literature is that parents may have to fight for the services they need for their children (Audit

Commission, 2003), which inevitably means that the services children receive may be dependent on how articulate and willing or able to fight their parents are. In the words of a parent cited in the Audit Commission report:

'Even the people who work for social services told me, when I was practically in tears, and saying I am depressed and tired and worn out. They would sit there and calmly say to me "those who shout the loudest get all the attention". And that is when I thought, this is not good enough.' (2003, p. 2)

A delay in waiting for services can mean that, by the time they are available, they are no longer relevant (Audit Commission, 2003; DfES, 2007).

Financial support

Rickford (2000, p.18) states that, on average, caring for a disabled child costs three times more than for a non-disabled child, though this of course would depend on numerous factors including the child's impairment. Finance and funding is an issue that affects disabled children and young people and their families, both in terms of the services available to them, and the services they are able to use. According to the Department for Education and Skills, 29% of disabled children live in poverty (DfES, 2003). A Joseph Rowntree Foundation (JRF) study (Beresford and Oldman, 2002) found that three-quarters of families with a disabled child reported that their housing was inadequate. Moving on into adulthood, another JRF study (Burchardt, 2005) showed that, at age 26, disabled people were nearly four times as likely to be unemployed or involuntarily out of work as non-disabled people. Among those who were in employment, earnings were 11% lower than for their non-disabled counterparts with the same level of educational qualifications.

Direct payments given to carers of disabled children have become an option available to families with disabled young people, and local authorities now have a mandatory responsibility to offer this to families who may be eligible for this method of accessing services (Blyth and Gardner, 2007) (see Chapter 5 for a full coverage of direct payments and individual budgets). However, carers of disabled children have yet to access direct payments in significant numbers (Commission for Social Care Inspection, 2005). Blyth and Gardner (2007, p. 239) found that the 'overwhelming evidence' was that direct payments allow families to access services in a flexible way, and to choose services in a way that acknowledges both the needs of the child and the rest of the family. They suggest that what establishes direct payments within a local authority as a viable option is: the development of independent support services; 'champions' of the cause (both within the local authority and among recipients) who promote it; the willingness of local authorities to allow families to employ friends and family and the provision of resources such as staff training and a dedicated management post. Direct payments provide an opportunity for continuity of care. It is of note that a significant number of parents chose to use direct payments to fund support by families, friends and acquaintances (Scope, 2004).

The parent–professional relationship

Support from individual members of staff and professionals can make a difference in the lives of disabled children and young people and their families (Audit Commission, 2003). However, mothers in Read's study (2000) stated that contact with services were some of the most difficult and stressful experiences that they had (see also Duncan, 2003). Indeed, Runswick-Cole (2007) points out that the private lives of families with disabled children and young people become a lot more public as they are subject to the scrutiny of professionals and service providers. There are times when there are conflicts of interest between parents and professionals, or, perhaps more controversially, between the disabled child or young person and their parent or the professional (Davis, 2004). There is clearly a need for professionals to listen to each individual child, their aspirations and needs as they envisage them, and this inevitably requires time and flexibility on the part of the professional.

Highlighting the 'relative dearth' of research into disabled children in society, Case (2000) concludes that 'the parent–professional relationship remains one of disparity, with the professional persisting in the expert role' (p. 287). He suggests that a more negotiative, two-way relationship is needed, incorporating the needs and views of both parents and professionals.

It is important that the unique needs of each individual child, and the way in which these interact with the rest of the family, are considered (Sure Start, 2002). Coordination between the different professionals who come and go from their lives is something that is important to families with a disabled child (Dowling and Dolan, 2001). This has given rise to the idea of a 'one-stop-shop' (see below), where parents can access all that they need with comparatively less 'toing and froing'.

Networks of support

Having a disabled child in the family is something that affects the whole family (Dowling and Dolan, 2001). The Audit Commission report (2003, p. 5) found that 'in common with many other (studies) it is harder for disabled children, young people and their families to contribute to everyday life in the way that others take for granted', and that 'the whole family is vulnerable to social exclusion' (Audit Commission, 2003, p. 25). This depends on many factors including the child's type of impairment and also the support available to the family.

The idea of consideration of the whole family has not surprisingly generated concern for siblings, usually non-disabled siblings. Naylor and Prescott (2004), for instance, highlight the fact that support for siblings of disabled children remains underdeveloped. They suggest that there is a need for siblings to have an opportunity to talk about their experiences on an adult level; resolving frustrations, enabling self-expression and encouraging activities. While it is clear, however, that disablism can have implications for the family as a whole, thus including siblings, having disabled siblings is certainly not inevitably problematic (Burke, 2004).

Transition into adulthood

The processes of transition through childhood, adolescence and ultimately into adulthood are, for any young person, significant times (Frith, 1984; Olson et al., 1983). These times of change can be particularly significant for disabled children and young people and their families (Morris, 2002; Case, 2000). The literature suggests that many parents of disabled children are anxious about the future, in particular the transition from children's to adults' services (Audit Commission, 2003), many of which are scarcer and less comprehensive and coordinated than services for children and young people (Swain and Thirlaway, 1994).

Priestley states that 'there are many barriers to adult status for young disabled people' (2003, p. 89). The way in which services are provided for disabled young people can have an influence on the way in which they and their families approach and negotiate the transition process. Traditionally, services for many disabled people (including many adults) have been based on the idea of disabled people having a 'child-like' status, thus reinforcing dependency throughout life. More recently, there has been a move to develop services, especially for disabled young people, that cater for individual needs and promote autonomy, choice and participation, with a view to preparing them for life as a disabled adult. However, more needs to be done in this area of service development (Mercer, 2004). This would involve forward planning, putting the disabled child at the centre of any decisions made, involving the whole family and considering their economic, social and recreational needs. It would also involve the recognition that aspirations and needs can differ in any family, and the recognition that the views of disabled people can differ radically from those of their parents.

A greater level of communication and coordination between children's and adults' services, especially during the transition and the time leading up to it, is also needed (Morris, 2002). There is also a need for information explaining what choices are available to be presented in an accessible format (Morris, 2002). Morris (2002) also highlights the fact that many of the assessments aimed at evaluating young people's needs during and after the transition period focus on what they cannot do rather than what they are able to do. All support during the transition of the family requires flexibility by all involved due to the 'complex and multi-dimensional nature of disabled young people's transition towards "adulthood"' (Mitchell, 1999, p. 766). The recent report from the Department for Education and Skills (DfES, 2007) has pledged money to set up a transition support programme.

Disabled parents

Many disabled adults have roles as carers, as parents, grandparents and relatives (Wates, 2004). We focus specifically here on their experiences of services, but of course they have been integral to our discussions so far as parents of disabled children and as disabled young people who may become disabled parents themselves. As with many disabled parents of disabled children, Micheline Mason believes that she was in a good position as a parent:

'For me, it was the unknown factors of our life ahead which were frightening, not the known hand of cards with which I had been dealt. After all, I knew all about brittle bones already whereas most people know very little. For most, the reality of any impairment which is not one you have yourself, is a leap in the dark.' (Wates and Jade, 1999, p. 77)

The available evidence suggests that disabled parents face considerable barriers in receiving effective services for effective support as parents:

[A] detailed study of the policies and protocols revealed tensions not only at the level of co-ordinating structures, records, budgets, training, and so on, but, more fundamentally, between operational understandings of the two sets of legislation involved (specifically, the Children Act 1989 and legislation policy and practice guidance concerning disabled adults) in relation to each other. The report concluded that neither is being used to ensure that disabled adults' entitlement to support in fulfilling their parenting responsibilities is addressed as a matter of course by local authorities. (Olsen and Clarke, 2003, p. 13)

Not all disabled parents either want or seek support from health and social care services. It is frequently reported, however, that parents seeking support do not do so until they have reached crisis point, fearing that they will be seen as incompetent parents and, at the very worst, having the child removed from the family.

All too frequently disabled parents report that they cannot access resources and receive no attention from service providers unless and until the difficulties experienced within their families, sometimes as a direct result of the lack of timely support, attract potentially stigmatising labels such as 'child in need', 'child at risk', 'young carer' or yet more seriously (and by no means always appropriately in the opinion of the Social Services Inspectorate) trigger child protection procedures. (Wates, 2002, p. 12)

| Box 9.1 | **Experiences of a disabled parent** |

The following extract is taken from *A Different Kind of Parent*, a speech given at the Joseph Rowntree Foundation Taskforce Conference 'The Right Support' on 23 September 2003 by Reesha Armstead (see www.disabledparentsnetwork.org.uk). It provides examples of her encounters with professionals and her strategies for dealing with them.

'Imagine being told by a midwife that she wants to give your baby a bottle because it's easier than enabling you to breastfeed.

'Imagine going to your doctor for a postnatal check six weeks after giving birth. Imagine the doctor saying: "what are we going to do with you now? We can't let this happen again can we?"

'Imagine asking social services for help and being told by a child social worker that the best they can do is take your baby to a family centre for ten hours a day to be cared for away from you.

'I told the midwife in the hospital that she couldn't give my baby a bottle and went on to breastfeed her for a whole year. I told the doctor that he couldn't do anything with me and to cancel the appointment with the gynaecologist to discuss being sterilised because I wanted another baby.

'I told the child social worker that I couldn't accept her offer and asked her never to darken my door again. I then fought adult services for a direct payment to enable me to employ my own personal assistants to enable me to be a wife and mother. Actually they refused and I asked for a reassessment of my needs without mentioning the care of the baby. In other words I actually had to deny my child. It worked.

'It is the fact that I have had to prove myself that makes me a disabled parent. When will I just be able to be a Mum? Do you know?'

What parents want: a wish list

The 'Evidence of Need' project at the Percy Hedley Foundation (PHF) set out to listen to the views of parents of disabled children and young people, and the young people themselves, about the services that they were currently receiving and how they would like to see these services developed.

The PHF is a registered charity, situated on the outskirts of Newcastle upon Tyne. It plays a crucial role in the lives of children, students and adults with neurological, speech, language, sensory and communication difficulties within the North East community. The PHF schools are non-maintained special schools serving the needs of 13 local authorities in the North East and Cumbria as well as those further afield.

The Evidence of Need research project was unusual in that its sole purpose was to gather independently collected data to inform the development of PHF services. It was funded by the PHF and conducted by a team of researchers at Northumbria University. The project included semi-structured interviews lasting between half an hour and two hours, conducted with 20 parents currently using Percy Hedley services and 8 parents who have not used Percy Hedley services, contacted through Newcastle Special Needs

Network. Although not stipulated, the interviews were mainly conducted with mothers rather than fathers and the findings need to be interpreted in this light. All were asked for a 'wish list' of priorities for change and development in the services they receive or require.

A questionnaire was sent out to all families using, and some who had used, Percy Hedley services (a total of 220): 84 replies were received. The questionnaire presented a 'wish list' that had emerged from the interviews, in the form of quotes from parents who had been interviewed. Those filling in the questionnaire were asked to indicate whether or not they saw each recommendation as a priority, and to make further comments. The following analysis presents some key recurring themes, using quotes from the interviews and the questionnaires.

1. A one-stop-shop
Many of the comments were very positive about the idea:

> 'When you first have a child with a disability you haven't a clue what's out there ... it would be brilliant if there was like a shop ... I think that is the biggest thing that is missing.'

> 'Save time and journey to different places.'

2. The need for flexible residential accommodation
The main reason given was the lack of support and leisure activities over school holidays:

> 'School holidays are hard ... to handle a child with disability for 6 weeks is quite demanding.'

The flexibility of this as a service was emphasized by parents, recognizing that different families have different needs, and the same family has different needs at different times:

> 'To give the school a residential side to it I think is quite important for families ... I'm suggesting the ability to stay if it is appropriate ... I think it should be a residential situation that's varied so every child had a chance ... if the staff that knew the children during the day worked in it as well, people would be so confident.'

Many parents expressed the need for this provision in relation to their social and working lives:

> 'Some parents have to go out at night to visit a friend and this option suits well.'

Many also thought there would be benefits for their son or daughter:

'It would be great for our son to stay with his pals.'

Although this was a desire solely for part-time residential care, it is one of the points that many disabled people would contest.

3. The participation of parents in developing services
First and foremost parents emphasize their expertise in relation to their child:

> 'We know our children best and know what services they need. Also no one ever asks my son what he wants, they just say oh well, we have this and, well, that's usually it, take it or leave it. Both parents and children should have more involvement in what they need and want.'

Many of the parents' comments emphasized not only the importance of being involved in decision-making processes, but also their wish to have a say in the broadest range of the planning and monitoring of services:

> 'Make sure that issues are debated to ensure that parents are part of decision-making process rather than feeling that they should restrict their view to only slightly extend current practice.'

A theme that the parents repeatedly returned to at different points in this project (and to which we shall return later) was their fraternity and solidarity with other parents:

> 'In the early years I gained most of my information from other parents.'

4. The provision of out of school activities
A number of parents expressed concerns over the isolation of their child and lack of opportunities to develop friendships:

> 'He seldom goes to parties, and never for tea or sleepovers at friends' houses. He has missed that sort of "normal" child socialization that non-disabled children enjoy. Because schools are segregated and out of the way, parents never get to meet each other so we don't have chances to build up trust to let our kids go to their friend's house. I suppose parents are reluctant to invite their children's friends over for tea or sleepovers because we don't know their friends or the types of impairments they have so not sure about asking them over or that parents would want them to go to a "stranger's house".'

Some also spoke of their isolation from other parents:

> 'Parents miss the socialization with each other too.'

Distance and the special school system was clearly a problem for some families:

> 'Anything to help make up for the social exclusion which is a consequence of being shipped out of the local community to attend special school.'

5. Activities for the whole family

As with the above, there is a clear need for the development of such services, with a strong emphasis put on the involvement of non-disabled peers:

> 'I do feel that if my son has a more varied social network, i.e. non-disabled peers as well as disabled peers of various ages he progresses better.'

Again emphasis was also given to the possibility of spending time with other parents:

> 'One of the other things on my wish list would be where people met socially ... 'cause whenever we go to school we gain a lot from each other as families.'

The idea of including siblings seemed to be generally of importance:

> 'Things for the whole family, I think, to bring other members of the family, to help them to understand really ... And, again, I think things like, a sort of siblings group might be good for some people ... she gets asked to do things that other siblings would not get asked to do ... she's just kind of grown up with that ... I think it probably would be good for her to meet other children who are in the same situation and talk about things.'

> 'It is very difficult for the other children – they miss out on a lot because we can't do normal things like go to the cinema, even shopping can be difficult.'

6. An information service

The comments generally emphasize the need for such a service, with recurrent expressions of the lack of information and parents' struggles to get the information they require:

> 'You need to know everything no matter how small.'

> 'No one offers information, you have to go out and find it for yourself or learn the hard way through mistakes.'

'It feels that I always have to ask social services, they never give me any information.'

'These needs should be met by health visitors. It's often too little, too late when the child has started school.'

Again some parents put a strong emphasis on the need for information exchange between parents:

'Other parents often pass on the most useful things – tell you where to look – is there a way of facilitating that?'

7. Support for processes of transition to adulthood

The emphasis given to this clearly emerges from concern about lack of knowledge of future possibilities and the loss of established support systems as the young person moves towards adulthood:

'My son has a protected childhood. I'm scared for him when he turns an adult. I really don't know what will happen to him or what is out there for him.'

'And as he gets older, it is not just stopped dead there and he gets some sort of support so he becomes a functional adult as best as he can be and as happy as he can be.'

Their struggles for required services and their say in planning developments remain crucial to parents:

'As my son gets older, you find you have to fight even more for help. With no help or support life is bleak.'

'It's important that parents are involved as they will know what the issues are likely to be and can inform the services which we will need in the future.'

The need for continued support was expressed by many parents, with the ultimate aim of independent living for some:

'I would love [my daughter] to be able to live independently through the week and come home to her family when she wishes. What a fantastic idea!'

8. A support agency

The notion of a support agency was first explained by one of the parents in the project as follows:

'To me it is quite simple, we need somebody that sits in the middle and that takes in a whole host of people that want jobs as enablers or care support workers, and carers ... to set an agency up ... I want to set an agency up ... and these people we get in we'll train them in empowerment training, social model training, they get in-house training, CRB checks, and they'll be paid a decent wage so they'll be valued in their role as enablers ... and then we'll have another register of disabled people that want to have support workers through direct payments and they come to us and kind of match them ... who do you want to work for you ... it would be like a carematch.com kind of thing ... disabled people can even do it online ... to make it really easy to find support workers.'

The need for such a support agency was stressed in a number of different ways.

'Parents are not well trained in dealing with paperwork.'

'It is so hard to find enablers and we just have to take the only person that comes along. Direct payments are supposed to give disabled people more choice and freedom yet we have to advertise for carers/enablers and if you only have a few hours then hardly anyone comes. I think this kind of agency would take away all that hassle for disabled people and parents of disabled children.'

'I have found it difficult to find someone reliable and willing to take on the type of approach I would like. He either gets plonked in a chair or has everything done for him when he can do lots himself.'

'It's *incredibly* difficult to find carers who can sign adequately.'

'I cannot find suitable carers and the wage allowed is disgustingly low.'

A few comments suggested that parents would like to be supporters themselves.

'I would like to become a support worker/carer to someone with similar disabilities to my son's.'

Parental involvement: barriers and strategies

In this section, we draw on two discussion groups with parents in the PHF project and findings of previous research to analyse the possible barriers to and strategies for a say for parents in developing services.

The Audit Commission report (2003, p. 21) states that 'disabled children and their families very much want to be involved in the services being provided to them.' As well as highlighting the way in which parent–professional relationships have changed in recent years, Murray (2000, p. 683) highlights the needs for a stronger home–school relationship, and the need for partnership. She defines such partnerships as being ones where the disabled child or young person is valued and highlights the need for the parent's knowledge of their child to be seen as crucial.

Although it has received little attention in the literature, it is perhaps not surprising that the evidence suggests involvement in decision making is important for disabled parents:

> The JRF study of social services departments policies and protocols (Wates, 2002) showed that the involvement of local groups of disabled parents, with representation in some cases from disabled parents' national organisations, made an appreciable difference in terms of developing service designs that were more effectively linked in with the appropriate specialist adult services as well as children's services, less likely to be experienced as stigmatising, and better able to respond flexibly to family situations. (Wates, 2004)

The involvement in decision making about education was clearly of high priority to the Evidence in Need PHF project participants:

> 'With these kids, you have to have a closer connection with their education, because it's just so much going on … it is important, because every child is different, individual, and the services need developing.'

Many parents of disabled children benefit from support, both formal and informal, from parents in a similar position (Case, 2000; Morris, 2002). A particularly strong recurring theme in this project was the need for involvement with other parents:

> 'If you have somewhere where parents have had experience of something, if you have a central location for distributing, you get feedback from that parent, saying "this was good, this didn't work …" and then staff can look at a child with similar needs and can think "that'll work, or that's not gonna work for that child …" Instead of trying to find your own path, you can find people who've done a similar thing.'

> 'I think with parents, you naturally have a good rapport; they've got that empathy, so you automatically listen to what they're saying. They've always got something of some knowledge to tell you. I got nearly all of my knowledge from other parents when my son was born,

than you get from professionals, 'cause they hold all that really close to their chests, especially social workers.'

Recognition was given, however, to the practical difficulties of involving parents:

'The parents' meetings they had here were at hours that the parents couldn't make. They were brilliant, but they were at times that most of the parents couldn't make ... We're not all in this area.'

And suggestions were made about strategies to overcome such barriers to participation:

'I suppose one other way, again, is maybe to do something through the website, maybe a chat room or comments page or something where parents can ask questions: "I'm looking for a such and such for this particular problem, has anybody got any ideas?" Or again, you could do that through a newsletter. You could have a page for parents to put comments.'

A strong emphasis emerged on the social dimension of services, and the development of a network of families. The barriers that lead to the social exclusion of young disabled people have been researched and well documented across Europe (Susinos, 2007). Research carried out by Contact a Family Wales (Rees, 2002) found that several existing (independent) groups, which had been formed with a view to supporting the whole family, provided emotional and practical support and a source of information for parents as well as play and leisure activities for the whole family. Burke's (2008) work affirms that non-disabled siblings can perceive themselves as disabled by being a member of a family living with a disabled child. He developed the concept of 'disability by association', which addresses family ownership of the disabled child's impairment, like Goffman's (1963) notion of a courtesy stigma (Burke and Fell, 2007). One way of developing support for siblings is to organize joint activities, which give disabled children and young people and their siblings the opportunity to interact with those from other families (Chandler, 2003).

In the PHF project, the informal social context was seen as integral to service development:

'I think you do get disconnected from able-bodied families, because your needs are so different, so there is always the isolation of the family, between your friends and peers. You develop new friends and peers, of other disabled children. I think to increase the social aspects of the school, it's not just the social, but it's where people talk about issues or other services.'

'Another way of doing that is putting on events that children can attend, or families as a whole can attend, so maybe building into that, maybe at lunchtime, an informal chat, maybe put on a workshop or a question and answer session as part of that.'

Coordination between the different professionals who come and go from their lives is important to families with a disabled child:

'I think that would be a benefit, if you could come and see different professionals, all based in the same place. It's a lot easier for families, and also there's more chance of them actually talking to each other and there being a more integrated plan for each individual child.'

The move towards direct payments was clearly of high importance for many parents in the PHF project. While the provision of direct payments had opened up possibilities for families, the experiences of some parents spoke to the difficulties created by the established system. The employment of suitable carers and the responsibilities placed on parents by the system reverberated through the parents' discussions:

'I've just had to employ a girl, she's only 17. She's going to university in a year, and I've got to train her up before I can really get any respite, for her to take him out and do anything with him. So I'm having to go through all that, and fit her in my lifestyle, when really social services should be doing all that ... by the time you just get it right, she's gonna have to go. But they're the only ones that are willing to do it. It's took us two year to get two hours.'

'It is another responsibility, I must admit, doing the direct payments, if you're not numeracy-literate. It's like another job, to employ somebody, but on the good side of it, you get those who you want, and it's a bit more flexible on that side.'

Parents were clearly aware of the low rates of pay and the implications for them as employers, though, as so often with the provision of services, it emerged that there was a postcode lottery – rates of pay and time allowances differed from locality to locality:

'It's embarrassing, getting somebody in and saying "I expect you to do all this work for this amount of money, because social services won't give more".'

Even when parents had successfully obtained direct payments, the problems could be such that the money could not be used to benefit the family:

'The thing it does give you is flexibility, but if you haven't got people around you who you know, or can find, then really the flexibility's out the window, but you're left with nothing. In my case now, there's a massive amount of money sat in the bank account, £20,000 that they're just gonna take all back, because I can't find someone.'

Overall, the views expressed by parents in the Evidence of Need project in general reflected those documented through recent projects examining parental views. It is clear that they are the views of parents whose experiences are that of segregated provisions, as with so many families with disabled children, and the consequences regularly emerge in their day-to-day experiences. It is clear too, and perhaps unsurprising in this context, that their views can differ from those of many disabled adults. These parents take the viewpoint of carers aspiring for the best for their children in a segregated context over which they had no choice (apart from different segregated provisions).

Conclusion

In this chapter we have attempted to analyse the views and experiences of carers of disabled people, including disabled people themselves. This has included documenting the voices of parents of disabled children. It is evident that families are unique and generalization can only be tentative, but there are recurring themes which speak significantly to the development of services. The participation of parents in the planning and decision-making processes is crucial. Disabled parents, in particular, can fall between the stools of policy and legislation, being both disabled and parents of a disabled child. Furthermore, the participation of parents needs to be considered as collective rather than simply individual. A high priority also needs to be given to the involvement of families as a whole, including siblings. Strategies for the development of participation need to take account of social as well as more formal contact between professionals and parents and their families. It is in this context that the carers' perspective challenges 'Cinderella' services for the families of young disabled people. The National Carers Strategy statement provides a positive conclusion to the chapter:

If carers are to have the same opportunities as everyone else in society, and to be able to have a life outside caring, we need to improve support and recognition for what they do. That means improving health and social care support, ensuring that carers are able to access education and leisure opportunities, and making sure that people with caring responsibilities have the chance to work flexibly so as to combine work with their caring roles. For the many children and young people who support parents or other family members it means making sure that they are not providing unreasonable levels of care, and that they have the support they need to learn, to develop and to thrive. (DH, 2008)

Reflective exercises

1. Consider the provision of services for the families of disabled children, taking particular account of the wish list of parents covered earlier in this chapter. List possible major improvements to services, bearing in mind particularly the segregated nature of provisions at the Percy Hedley Foundation (and other institutions for disabled young people) and the implications this can have for families.
2. Focus next on the transition to adulthood for young disabled people. It is a complex time including possibilities of moving towards independent living, becoming a parent and earning a living. In considering the implications for the provision of services, you will need to take into account discussions in previous chapters as well as the present one.
3. Finally, consider the improvement of services for disabled parents. In doing so you might look back to the experiences of Reesha Armstead outlined in Box 9.1. With a colleague from a different profession, discuss any three changes that could realistically be implemented in your workplace to improve the provision of services for disabled parents.

Suggestions for further reading

1. Olsen, R. and Clarke, H. (2003) *Parenting and Disability: Disabled parents' experiences of raising children*. Bristol: The Policy Press

   This book reports on the first comprehensive study of parenting, disability and mental health, which examines the views of parents and children in 75 families. It advocates measures to support disabled parents and their families by promoting and supporting relationships within the family.

2. Wates, M. and Jade, R. (eds) (1999) *Bigger Than The Sky: Disabled women on parenting*. London: The Women's Press

   Although this book is older than most recommended texts, it remains a unique and highly valuable anthology. It is the first collection by disabled women to explore the issues of parenting. They challenge rigid, limiting views of what it means to be a disabled woman, and indeed of what a parent is and does.

3. Read, J. (2000) *Disability, the Family and Society: Listening to mothers*. Buckingham, Open University Press

   Explores mothers' perspectives about the ways that they find themselves acting as mediators between their children and a world that can be hostile to their interests. It takes as its starting point a study in which mothers from diverse backgrounds detail the ways in which they attempt to represent their children to the world, and the world to their children in both formal and informal interactions.

Conclusion

In this book we have looked towards a social model for inter-agency working. As you will have seen, the social model has a foundation in critique. It is a direction of thinking that challenges the individual model of understanding disability, including the medical model and associated tragedy model. Within this, it takes a critical stance towards the provision, policy and practice of health and social care. This is not to deny the fact that disabled people require effective health and social care, as do non-disabled people. Nor is it about criticizing individual professionals, beyond the commonsense judgement that some do a better job than others. Within the social model, the analysis is directed towards society, lack of justice, and lack of equality built into society – or institutional discrimination. It is as a system, then, that the social model casts a critical eye upon health and social care services.

Critical, however, does not mean negative. As a service provider, the social model can be engaged with through critical reflective practice, which includes the:

- Recognition and questioning of power relations, structures and ideologies that limit people's freedom
- Promotion of people's control over decision-making processes that shape their lives
- Promotion of people's struggles against repression and 'man-made' sufferings, and supporting the removal of barriers to equal opportunities
- Promotion of full participatory citizenship for all

The voices of disabled people, the involvement of service users, are prioritized at all levels. At the broadest, this is disabled people's control over day-to-day decision making in their lives. This will include a say in the decision making over treatment by professionals, the management of services, and policymaking, again at all levels. Furthermore, the analysis of ways in which services are run by disabled people for disabled people (in CILs) highlights differences from those of traditional statutory and voluntary services in what they offer, how the service is delivered and the underlying ethos and philosophy. This provides a concrete example of how the social model of disability can be put into practice in the context of services.

We have, then, been building an understanding of the development of inter-agency working underpinned by the social model of disability. It is a complex and controversial process of changing service provision and practice, requiring considerable thought, and we hope this text has fuelled your thinking.

One of our tasks as authors is to try to ensure that this text does not date – it is 'up to date'. This is never easy and we are writing at a time when change is coming. It is a time of global recession and a new coalition has come to power in the UK. It is a time when looking to the future is difficult, complex and uncertain. We know that the next four years in the UK will see cuts in services and benefits, but how these will affect the day-to-day lives of disabled people we cannot know in any detail, particularly from the viewpoint of disabled people as prioritized in this text. We believe, however, that the issues we have discussed will become further exacerbated rather than alleviated over the coming years. The task of establishing a social model of inter-agency policy and practice will remain deeply important to disabled people and their families and 'carers', but perhaps increasingly difficult to establish. And we end with the hope that we have contributed to the development of justice, equality and the full participatory citizenship of disabled people.

References

Abelow Hedley, L. (2006) The Seduction of the Surgical Fix, in E. Parens (ed.) *Surgically Shaping Children: Technology, Ethics and the Pursuit of Normality* (Baltimore: The John Hopkins University Press).

Acheson, D. (1998) *Independent Inquiry Into Inequalities in Health* (London: TSO).

Ager, W. and McPhail, M. (2008) Issues of Power in Service User and Carer Involvement: Partnership, Processes and Outcomes, in M. McPhail (ed.) *Service User and Carer Involvement* (Edinburgh: Dunedin Academic Press).

Ahmad, W. and Atkin, K. (eds) (1996) *'Race' and Community Care* (Buckingham: Open University Press).

Ahmad, W. and Bradby, H. (2008) Locating Ethnicity And Health: Exploring Concepts and Contexts, in W.I.U. Ahmad and H. Bradby (eds) *Ethnicity, Health and Health Care* (Oxford: Blackwell).

Ahmad, W.I.U., Atkin, K. and Chamba, R. (2000) 'Causing Havoc Among Their Children': Parental And Professional Perspectives On Consanguinity And Childhood Disability, in W.I.U. Ahmad (ed.) *Ethnicity, Disability and Chronic Illness* (Buckingham: Open University Press).

Anionwu, E. and Atkin, K. (2001) *The Politics of Sickle Cell and Thalassaemia* (Buckingham: Open University Press).

Anstey, K.W. (2008) A Critique of Arguments Supporting Disability Avoidance, *Disability and Society*, 23(3): 235–46.

Appleyard, B. (1999) *Brave New Worlds: Genetics and the Human Experience* (London: Harper Collins).

Armstrong, D. (2003) *Experiences of Special Education: Re-evaluating policy and Practice Through Life-stories* (London: Routledge).

Asch, A. (2001) Disability, Bioethics and Human Rights, in G. Albrecht, K.D. Seelman and M. Bury (eds) *Handbook of Disability Studies* (London: Sage).

Asthana S. and Halliday J. (2006) *What Works in Tackling Health Inequalities?* (Bristol: Policy Press).

Atkin, K., Ahmad, W.I.U. and Anionwu, E. (1998) Screening and counselling for Sickle Cell Disorders and Thalasseamia: The Experience of Parents and Health Professionals, *Social Science and Medicine*, 47: 1639–51.

Atkin, K., Ahmad, W.I.U. and Anionwu, E.N. (2000) Service Support for Families Caring for a Child with Sickle Cell Anaemia or Beta Thalassaemia Major: Parents Perspectives, in W.I.U. Ahmad (ed.) *Ethnicity, Disability and Chronic Illness* (Buckingham: Open University Press).

Atkin, K., French, S. and Vernon, A. (2004) Health Care for People from Ethnic Minority Groups, in S. French and J. Sim (eds) *Physiotherapy: A Psychosocial Approach* (3rd edn) (Oxford: Elsevier).

Atkinson, D. (ed.) (1993) *Past Times: Older People With Learning Difficulties Look Back On Their Lives* (Buckingham: Open University Press).

Atkinson, D. (1998) *The Life Story Interview* (London: Sage).

Atkinson, D. (1999) *Advocacy: A Review* (York: Joseph Rowntree Foundation).

Atkinson, D. (2002) Self-Advocacy and Research, in B. Gray and R. Jackson (eds) *Advocacy and Learning Disability* (London: Jessica Kingsley).

Atkinson, D. and Williams, F. (eds) (1990) *'Know Me As I Am': An Anthology Of Prose, Poetry And Art By People With Learning Difficulties* (London: Hodder and Stoughton).

Atkinson, D., McCarthy, M., Walmsley, J. et al. (eds) (2000) *Good Times, Bad Times: Women With Learning Difficulties Telling Their Stories* (Kidderminster: British Institute of Learning Disability).

Audit Commission (2002) *Equality and Diversity – Learning from Audit, Inspection and Research* (London: Audit Commission).

Audit Commission (2003) *Services for Disabled Children. A Review of Services for Disabled Children and Their Families* (London: The Audit Commission).

Audit Commission (2004) *The Journey to Race Equality* (London: The Audit Commission).

Bahl, V. (1993) Access to Health Care for Black and Ethnic Minority Elderly People: General Principles, in A. Hopkins and V. Bahl (eds) *Access to Health Care for Black and Ethnic Minorities* (London: Royal College of Physicians).

Baker, S. (2006) A Disabled Mother's Story, in J. Leece and J. Bornat (eds) *Developments in Direct Payments* (Bristol: Policy Press).

Ballantyne, E. and Muir, A. (2008) In Practice: From the Viewpoint of Occupational Therapy, in S. French and J. Swain (eds) *Disability on Equal Terms: Understanding and Valuing Difference in Health And Social Care* (London: Sage).

Banton, M. and Singh, G. (2004) 'Race', Disability and Oppression, in J. Swain, S. French, C. Barnes and C. Thomas (eds) *Disabling Barriers – Enabling Environments* (2nd edn) (London: Sage).

Barnes, C. (1991) *Disabled People in Britain and Discrimination: A Case for Anti-Discrimination Legislation* (London: The Hurst Company).

Barnes, C. (1994) Images of Disability, in S. French (ed.) *On Equal Terms: Working with Disabled People* (Oxford: Buttterworth-Heinemann).

Barnes, C. (1996) Theories of Disability and the Origins of the Oppression of Disabled People in Western Society, in L. Barton (ed.) *Disability and Society: Emerging Issues and Insights* (London: Longman).

Barnes, M. (2003) Bringing Difference Into Deliberation? Disabled People, Survivors and Local Governance, *Policy and Politics*, 30(3): 319–31.

Barnes, C. and Mercer, G. (2006) *Independent Futures: Creating User-led Disability Services in a Disabling Society* (Bristol: Policy Press).

Barnes, C. and Mercer, G. (eds) (1996) *Exploring the Divide: Illness and Disability* (Leeds: The Disability Press).

Barnes, C. and Mercer, G. (eds) (1997) *Doing Disability Research* (Leeds: The Disability Press).

Barnes, C. and Mercer, G. (eds) (2004) *Disability Policy and Practice – Applying the Social Model* (Leeds: Disability Press).

Barnes, C. and Roulstone, A. (2005) 'Work' Is A Four-Letter Word: Disability, Work And Welfare, in A. Roulstone and C. Barnes (eds) *Working Futures? Disabled People, Policy and Social Inclusion* (Bristol: Policy Press).

Barnes, C., Mercer, G. and Shakespeare, T. (1999) *Exploring Disability: A Sociological Introduction* (Cambridge: Polity Press).

Barton, L. (2001) *Disability, Struggle and the Politics of Change* (London: David Fulton).

Barton, L. (2004) The Disability Movement: Some Observations, in J. Swain, S. French, C. Barnes and C. Thomas (eds) *Disabling Barriers – Enabling Environments* (2nd edn) (London, Sage).

Barton, L. (2008) *From Exclusion To Inclusion: Barriers And Possibilities In Relation To Disabled Learners* (bidok.uibk.ac.at/library/barton-inclusion.html).

Beeton, K. (2008) An Exploration of the Quality of Life of Adults with Haemophilia, in J. Swain and S. French (eds) *Disability on Equal Terms* (London, Sage).

Begum, N. (1996) Doctor, Doctor … Disabled Women's Experience of General Practitioners, in J. Morris (ed.) *Encounters with Strangers: Feminism and Disability* (London: The Women's Press).

Beresford, B. and Oldman, C. *The Housing Needs of Disabled Children: The national evidence* (York: Joseph Rowntree Foundation).

Beresford, P. (2003) *It's Our Lives: A Short Theory Of Knowledge, Distance and Theory* (London: Citizen Press).

Beresford, P. (2007) *The Changing Roles and Tasks of Social Work from Service Users' Perspective* (London: Shaping Our Lives).

Beresford, P. and Campbell, J. (1994) Disabled People, Service Users, User Involvement and Representation, *Disability and Society*, 9(3): 315–25.

Beresford, P. and Croft, S. (2000) User Involvement, in M. Davies (ed.) *The Blackwell Encyclopaedia of Social Work* (Oxford: Blackwell).

Beresford, P., Croft, S., Evans, C. and Harding, T. (1997) Quality in Personal Social Services: The Developing Role of User Involvement in the UK, in A. Evans, K. Haverinen, K. Leichsering and G. Wistow (eds) *Developing Quality in Personal Social Services* (Aldershot: Ashgate).

Berkman, L.F. and Melchior, M. (2006) The Shape of Things to Come: How Social Policy Impacts Social Integration and Family Structure to Produce Population Health, in J. Siegrist and M. Marmot (eds) *Social Inequalities in Health: New Evidence And Policy Implications* (Oxford, Oxford University Press).

Bewley, C. (2000) Care Managers Can be Champions for Direct Payments, *Care Plan*, 6(4): 13–16.

Bewley, C. and Glendinning, C. (1994) *Involving Disabled People in Community Care Planning* (York: Joseph Rowntree Foundation).

Bhopal, R.S. (2007) *Ethnicity, Race and Health in Multicultural Societies* (Oxford, Oxford University Press).

Bhopal, R.S. and White, M. (1993) Health Promotion for Ethnic Minorities: Past, Present and Future, in W.I.U. Ahmad (ed.) *'Race' and Health in Contemporary Britain* (Buckingham: Open University Press).

Blakemore, K. (1998) *Social Policy: An Introduction.* (Buckingham: Open University Press).

Blakemore, K. and Johnson, J. (2009) What Future for Health and Social Care?, in Book 6, The Shaping of Care Services, Open University Course K101 *Understanding Health and Social Care* (Milton Keynes: Open University).

Blyth, C. and Gardner, A. (2007) 'We're Not Asking For Anything Special': Direct Payments and the Carers of Disabled Children, *Disability and Society*, 22(3): 235–49.

Boazman, S (1999) Inside Aphasia, in M. Corker and S. French (eds) *Disability Discourse* (Buckingham: Open University Press).

Boazman, S. (2002) I Had No Way Of Communicating That I Was Still A Bright, Intelligent Whole Human Being, *Good Housekeeping*, November, pp. 93–4.

Booth, T. and Booth, W. (1998) *Growing up with Parents who have Learning Difficulties* (London: Routledge).

Bornat, J. (2006) Introduction, in J. Leece and J. Bornat (eds) *Developments in Direct Payments* (Bristol: Policy Press).

Borsay, A. (2005) *Disability and Social Policy in Britain since 1750: A History of Exclusion* (Basingstoke: Palgrave Macmillan).

Boxall, R., Jones, M. and Smith, S. (2002) Advocacy and Parents with Disabilities, in D.C. Race (ed.) *Learning Disability: A Social Approach* (London: Routledge).

Bradshaw, P.L. (2008) Service User Involvement in the NHS in England: Genuine User Participation Or Dogma-Driven Folly? *Journal of Nursing Management*, 16: 673–81.

Brandon, D. (2000) Advocacy, in D. Martin (ed.) *The Blackwell Encyclopaedia of Social Work* (Oxford: Blackwell Publishers).

Branfield, F. (2007) *User Involvement in Social Work Education* (London: Shaping Our Lives National User Network).

Branfield, F. and Beresford, P. (2006) *Making User Involvement Work: Supporting Service User Involvement and Knowledge* (York: Joseph Rowntree Foundation).

Braye, S. (2000) Participation and Involvement in Social Care: An Overview, in H. Kemshall and R. Littlechild (eds) *User Involvement and Participation in Social Care* (London: Jessica Kingsley).

Brechin, A. (2000) Introducing Critical Practice, in A. Brechin, H. Brown and M. A. Eby (eds) *Critical Practice in Health and Social Care* (London: Sage).

Brechin, A. and Swain, J. (1986) *Shared Action Planning: A Skills Workbook* (Milton Keynes: Open University Press).

Brechin, A., Brown, H. and Eby, M.A. (eds) (2000) *Critical Practice in Health and Social Care* (London: Sage).

Brignell V. (2009) Assisted Death (30th Jan, www.newstatesman.com).

Bristol Royal Infirmary Inquiry (2001) (www.bristol-inquiry.org.uk).

Brooks, R. (ed.) (2007) *Public Services at the Crossroads: Executive Summary* (London: Institute for Public Policy Research).

Brown, H. (2000) Challenges from Service Users, in A. Brechin, H. Brown and M. A. Ely (eds) *Critical Practice in Health and Social Care* (London: Sage).

Brown, V. (2009) Rubbish Society: Affluence, Waste and Values, in S. Taylor, S. Hitchliffe, J. Clark and S. Bromley (eds) *Making Social Lives* (Milton Keynes: The Open University).

Browne, L. (1990) *Survey of Local Authorities Direct Payments* (London: RADAR).

Burchardt, T. (2005) *The Education and Employment of Disabled Young People* (York: Joseph Rowntree Foundation).

Burke, P. (2004) *Brothers and Sisters of Disabled Children* (London: Jessica Kingsley).

Burke, P. (2008) *Disability and Impairment: Working with Children and Families* (London: Jessica Kingsley Publishers).

Burke, P. and Fell, B. (2007) Childhood Disabilities and Disadvantage: Family Experiences, in P. Burke and J. Parker (eds) *Social Work and Disadvantage: Addressing the Roots of Stigma through Association* (London: Jessica Kingsley Publishers).

Bury, M. (1997) *Health and Illness in a Changing Society* (Routledge: London).

Butler, J. and Calhan, M. (1999) Health and Social Policy, in J. Baldock, N. Manning, S. Miller and S. Vickerstaff (eds) *Social Policy* (Oxford: Oxford University Press).

Butt, J. (2006) *Are We There Yet? Identifying the Characteristics of Social Care Organisations that Successfully Promote Diversity* (London: Social Care Institute for Excellence).

Butt, J., Bignall, T. and Stone, E. (2000) *Directing Support: Report From a Workshop on Direct Payments and Black and Minority Ethnic Disabled People* (York: Joseph Rowntree Foundation).

Campbell, P. (1996) The History of the User Movement in the United Kingdom, in T. Heller, J. Reynolds, R. Gomm, R. Muston and S. Patterson (eds) *Mental Health Matters: A Reader* (Basingstoke: Macmillan).

Campbell, J. (2006a) Stop Trying to Kill Us Off (9th May, www.guardian.co.uk).

Campbell, J. (2006b) Direct Payments: The Heart of Independent Living, in J. Leece and J. Bornat (eds) *Developments in Direct Payments* (Bristol: Policy Press).

Campbell, J. and Oliver, M. (1996) *Disability Politics: Understanding Our Past, Changing Our Future* (London: Routledge).

Carmichael, A. (2004) The Social Model, The Emancipatory Paradigm and User Involvement, in C. Barnes and G. Mercer (eds) *Implementing the Social Model of Disability: Theory and Research* (Leeds: The Disability Press).

Carr, S. (2004) *Has Service User Participation Made a Difference to Social Care Services?* (London: Social Care Institute for Excellence).

Carr, S. (2008) *Personalisation: A Rough Guide*, Report 20 (London: Social Care Institute of Excellence).

Case, S. (2000) Refocusing on the parent: what are the social issues of concern for parents of disabled children? *Disability and Society*, 15(2): 271–92.

Chamba, R. and Ahmad, W.I.U. (2000) Language, Communication and Information: The Needs Of Parents Caring For a Severely Disabled Child, in W.I.U. Ahmad (ed.) *Ethnicity, Disability and Chronic Illness* (Buckingham: Open University Press).

Chandler, S. (2003) *We're Listening. A Consultation With Families Of Disabled Children On How They Would Like Resources Allocated In 2003-2006* (Birmingham: Contact a Family, West Midlands).

Chappell, A.L. (1997) From Normalisation to Where? in L. Barton and M. Oliver (eds) *Disability Studies: Past, Present And Future* (Leeds: The Disability Press).

Charlton, J.I. (2000) *Nothing About Us Without Us: Disability Oppression and Empowerment* (Berkeley: University of California Press).

Choppin, E. (2006) Outcry Over Proposed Killing of Disabled Babies, *Disability Now*, December, p. 1.

Clark, A. (2006) A Reflective Challenge, in L. Addy (ed.) *Occupational Therapy Evidence in Practice for Physical Rehabilitation* (Oxford: Blackwell).

Clark, A., Giarchi, G.G. and Ford, D. (2010) *Disability, Policy and Practice: Issues for Health and Social Care Practitioners* (London: Jessica Kingsley).

Clark, H. (2006) 'It's Meant That, Well, I'm Living A Life Now': Older People's Experience Of Direct Payments, in J. Leece and J. Bornat (eds) *Developments in Direct Payments* (Bristol: Policy Press).

Clark, L. (2002) *Liverpool Central Primary Care Trust Accessible Health Information: Project Report*, www.leeds.ac.uk/disability-studies.

Clements, T. (2002) Exploring the Role of Values in the Management of Advocacy Schemes, in B. Gray and R. Jackson (eds) *Advocacy and Learning Disability* (London: Jessica Kingsley).

Closs, A (1998) Quality Of Life Of Children and Young People With Serious Medical Conditions, in C. Robinson and K. Stalker (eds) *Growing Up With Disability* (London: Jessica Kingsley).

Cohen, B. (2005) Inter-Agency Collaboration In Context: The 'Joining-Up' Agenda. in A. Glaister and B. Glaister (eds) *Inter-Agency Collaboration – Providing for Children* (Edinburgh: Dunedin Academic Press).

Cole, A., McIntosh, B. and Whittaker, A. (2000) *Developing New Lifestyles With Disabled People* (York: Joseph Rowntree Foundation).

Commission for Racial Equality (1988) *Racial Equality in Social Service Departments* (London: Commission for Racial Equality).

Commission for Social Care Inspection (2005) *Performance Assessment Framework* (www.cqc.org.uk).

Connelly, N. and Seden, J. (2003) What Service Users Say About Services: The Implications For Managers, in J. Henderson and D. Atkinson (eds) *Managing Care In Context* (London: Routledge).

Cooper, M. (1997) Mabel Cooper's Life Story, in D. Atkinson, M. Jackson and J. Walmsley (eds) *Forgotten Lives: Exploring The History Of Learning Disability* (Kidderminster: British Institute of Learning Disability).

Cooper, M., Ferris, G. and Coventry, M. (2000) Croydon Lives, in D. Atkinson, M. McCarthy, J. Walmsley, M. Cooper et al. (eds) *Good Times, Bad Times: Women With Learning Difficulties Telling Their Stories* (Kidderminster: British Institute of Learning Disabilities).

Corker, M (1996) *Deaf Transitions: Images and Origins of Deaf Families Deaf Communities and Deaf Identities* (London: Jessica Kingsley)

Cotterill, P. and Letherby, G. (1993) Weaving stories: personal autobiographies in feminist research. *Sociology* 27(1): 67–79.

Croft, S. and Beresford, P. (2002) Service Users' Perspectives, in M. Davies (ed.) *Companion to Social Work* (2nd edn) (Oxford: Blackwell).

Crow, L (1996) Including all of our Lives: Renewing the Social Model Of Disability, in J. Morris (ed.) *Encounters with Strangers: Feminism and Disability* (London: The Women's Press).

Dahl, E, Fritzell, J. and Lahelma, E.(2006) Welfare State Regimes and Health Inequalities, in J. Siegrist and M. Marmot (eds) *Social Inequalities in Health: New Evidence and Policy Implications* (Oxford: Oxford University Press).

Dahlgren, G. and Whitehouse, M. (1991) *Policies and Strategies to Promote Social Equity in Health* (Stockholm: Institute for Futures Studies).

Darke, P. (2004) The Changing Face of Representation of Disability in the Media, in J. Swain, S. French, C. Barnes and C. Thomas (eds) *Disabling Barriers – Enabling Environment* (2nd edn) (London: Sage).

Davis, K. (2004) The Crafting of Good Clients, in J. Swain, S. French, C. Barnes and C. Thomas (eds) *Disabling Barriers – Enabling Environment* (2nd edn) (London: Sage).

Dawson, C. (2000) *Independent Successes: Implementing Direct Payments* (York: Joseph Rowntree Foundation).

Department of Health, Long Term Conditions (www.dh.gov.uk).

DfES (Department for Education and Skills) (2003) Every Child Matters (available at www.education.gov.uk/consultations/downloadableDocs/EveryChildMatters.pdf).

DfES (2007) *Aiming High for Disabled Children: Better Support for Families* (London: HM Treasury).

DH (Department of Health) (1991) *The Patient's Charter* (London: Department of Heath).

DH (1997) *The NHS: Modern, Dependable* (London: Department of Heath).

DH (2000) *The Health and Social Care Bill* (London: TSO).

DH (2001a) *The Expert Patient: A New Approach To Chronic Disease Management For The 21st Century* (London: Department of Health).

DH (2001b) *Valuing People: A New Strategy for Learning Disability in the 21st Century* (Cm 5086) (London: Department of Health).

DH (2003) *Priorities Framework (2003–2006)* (London: Department of Heath).

DH (2004a) *Chronic Disease Management: A Compendium of Information* (London: Department of Health).

DH (2004b) *Choosing Health: Making Healthy Choices Easier* (London: TSO).

DH (2005a) *National Service Framework for Long Term Conditions* (London: TSO).

DH (2005b) *Supporting People with Long Term Conditions: An NHS and social care model to support local innovation and integration* (London: TSO).

DH (2006) *Our Health, Our Care, Our Say: A New Direction For Community Services,* White Paper (Cm 6737) (London: TSO).

DH (2007a) *Making Decisions: The Independent Mental Capacity Advocate (IMCA) Service* (London: Department of Health).

DH (2007b) *Putting People First: A Shared Vision and Commitment to the Transformation of Adult Social Care* (2007) (London: Department of Health).

DH (2007c) *Supporting People with Long Term Conditions* (London: Department of Health).

DH (2008) *Carers at the Heart of 21st Century Families and Communities: A Caring System on Your Side, A Life of Your Own* (London: Department of Health).

DH (2009a) *The NHS Constitution: The NHS Belongs To Us All* (London: Department of Health).

DH (2009b) *The Second Year of the Independent Mental Capacity Advocacy Service 2008/2009* (London: Department of Health).

DH and DOE (Department of the Environment) (1992). *Housing and Community Care* (London: HMSO).

DH and Her Majesty's Treasury (2002) *Tackling Health Inequalities* (London: TSO).

Dimmock, A.F. (1993) *Cruel Legacy: An Introduction to the Record of Deaf People In History* (Edinburgh: Scottish Workshop Publications).

Dinhan, A. (2005) Empowered or Over-empowered? The Real Experience of Participation in the UK's New Deal for Communities, *Journal of Community Development*, 40(3): 301–12.

Disabled Parents Network (www.DisabledParentsNetwork.org.uk).

Dominelli, L. (1997) *Anti-Racist Social Work* (2nd edn) (Basingstoke: Macmillan).

Dominelli, L. (2002) *Anti-Oppressive Social Work: Theory and Practice* (Basingstoke: Palgrave).

Douglas, J., Komaromy, C. and Robb, M. (2004) *Diversity and Difference*, Communication, Unit 6, K205, Communication and Relationships in Health and Social Care (Milton Keynes: The Open University).

Dow, J. (2008) Our Journey: Perspectives From People Who Use Services, in M. McPhail (ed.) *Service User and Carer Involvement* (Edinburgh: Dunedin Academic Press).

Dowling, M. and Dolan, L. (2001) Families With Children With Disabilities – Inequalities and The Social Model, *Disability and Society*, 16(1): 21–35.

Dowson, S. and Whittaker, A. (1993) *The Role of the Advisor in Supporting People with Learning Difficulties in Self-Advocacy Groups* (London: Values into Action).

Doyal, L. (1991) *The Political Economy of Health* (London: Pluto Press).

DPI (Disabled People's International) (2000) *Disabled People Speak on the New Genetics*, DPA Europe Position Statement on Bioethics and Human Rights (London: Disabled People's International).

Drake, R. (1996) A Critique of the Role of Traditional Charities, in L. Barton (ed.) *Disability and Society: Emerging Issues and Insights* (London: Longman).

Drake, R. (1999) *Understanding Disability Policies* (London: Macmillan).

DRC (Disability Rights Commission) (2004a) *Policy Statement on Social Care and Independent Living* (London: Disability Rights Commission).

DRC (2004b) *Disability Rights Commission's Response to the Human Genetics Commission Consultation Choosing the Future – Genetics and Reproductive Decision Making* (London: Disability Rights Commission).

DRC (2006) *Equal Treatment: Closing the Gap* (London: Disability Rights Commission).

Duffy, J. (2008) *Looking Out from the Middle: User Involvement in Health and Social Care in Northern Ireland* (London: Social Care Institute for Excellence).

Duncan, N. (2003) Awkward Customers? Parents and Provisions for Special Educational Needs, *Disability and Society*, 18(3): 341–56.

Duster, G. (1990) *Backdoor to Eugenics* (New York: Routledge).

Eberstadt, N. and Satel, S. (2004) *Health and the Income Inequality Hypothesis* (Washington: The AEI Press).

Evans, C. (1996) From Those Who Know: The Role Of Service Users, in Hanvey C. and Philpot T. (eds) *Sweet Charity: The Role and Workings of Voluntary Organisations* (London: Routledge).

Evans, C. (1999) Gaining Our voice: The Development Patterns of Good Practice in User Involvement, *Managing Community Care*, 7(2): 7–13.

Evans, S.E. (2004) *Forgotten Crimes: The Holocaust and People with Disabilities* (Chicago: Ivan R. Dee).

Evans, C., Carmichael, A. and members of the Direct Payment Best Value Project Group of Wiltshire and Swindon Users' Network (2002) *Users' Best Value: A Guide To User Involvement Good Practice In Best Value Reviews* (York: Joseph Rowntree Foundation).

Ewles, L. and Simnett, I. (2003) *Promoting Health: A Practical Guide* (5th edn) (London: Bailliere Tindall).

Fawcett, B. (2000) *Feminist Perspectives on Disability* (Harlow: Pearson Education Limited).

Fergusson, I. (2008) Concluding Thoughts: Frustrations and Possibilities, in M. McPhail (ed.) *Service User and Carer Involvement* (Edinburgh: Dunedin Academic Press).

Fergusson, I. and Ager, W. (2008) Ways of Knowing, in M. McPhail (ed.) *Service User and Carer Involvement* (Edinburgh: Dunedin Academic Press).

Fernando, S. (1989) *Race and Culture in Psychiatry* (London: Routledge).

Finkelstein, V. (1990) A Tale of Two Cities, *Therapy Weekly*, 16(34): 6–7.

Finkelstein, V. (1991) Disability: An Administrative Challenge? (The Health And Welfare Heritage), in M. Oliver (ed.) *Social Work: Disabled People and Disabling Environments* (London: Jessica Kingsley).

Finkelstein, V. (1998) Emancipating Disability Studies, in T. Shakespeare (ed.) *The Disability Reader: Social Science Perspectives* (London: Cassell).

Finkelstein, V. (2004) Modernising Services? in J. Swain, S. French, C. Barnes and C. Thomas (eds) *Disabling Barriers – Enabling Environments* (2nd edn) (London: Sage).

Finlay, W.M.L., Walton, C. and Antaki, C. (2008) Promoting Choice and Control in Residential Services for People with Learning Disabilities, *Disability and Society*, 23(4): 349–60.

Flick, U. (1998) *An Introduction to Qualitative Research* (London: Sage).

Flynn, R. (2002) *Short Breaks: Providing Better Access and More Choice for Black Disabled Children and Their Parents* (Bristol: Policy Press).

French, S. (1990) The Advantages of Visual Impairment: Some Physiotherapists' Views, *The New Beacon*, 74(872): 1–6.

French, S. (1994) The Disabled Role, in S. French (ed.) *On Equal Terms: Working With Disabled People* (Oxford: Butterworth-Heinemann).

French, S. (1996) Out of Sight, Out of Mind: The Experience and Effect of a 'Special' Residential School, in J. Morris (ed.) *Encounters with Strangers: Feminism and Disability* (London: The Women's Press).

French, S. (1999) Multidisciplinary Teams, in J. Swain and S. French (eds) *Therapy and Learning Difficulties: Advocacy, Participation and Partnership* (Oxford: Butterworth-Heinemann).

French, S. (2001) *Disabled People and Employment: A Study of the Working Lives of Visually Impaired Physiotherapists* (Aldershot: Ashgate).

French, S. (2004a) Defining Disability: Implications for Physiotherapy Practice, in S. French and J. Sim (eds) *Physiotherapy: A Psychosocial Approach* (3rd edn) (Oxford: Butterworth-Heinemann).

French, S (2004b) Enabling Relationships in Therapy Practice, in J. Swain, J. Clark, K. Parry, S. French and F. Reynolds, Enabling *Relationships in Health and Social Care: A Guide For Therapists* (Oxford: Butterworth-Heinemann).

French, S. (2005) Don't Look!: The History of Education for Partially Sighted Children, *British Journal of Visual Impairment,* 23(3): 108–13.

French, S. and Swain, J. (1999) Conclusion: Reflections on Therapy and Learning Difficulties, in J. Swain and S. French (eds) *Therapy and Learning Difficulties: Advocacy, Participation and Partnership* (Oxford: Butterworth-Heinemann).

French, S. and Swain, J. (2001) The Relationship Between Disabled People and Health and Welfare Professionals, in G. Albrecht, H.D. Seelman and M. Bury (eds) *Handbook of Disability Studies* (London: Sage).

French, S. and Swain, J. (2002) The Perspective of the Disabled People's Movement, in M. Davies (ed.) *The Blackwell Companion to Social Work* (2nd edn) (Oxford: Blackwell).

French, S. and Swain, J. (2004) Whose Tragedy? Towards a Personal Non-Tragedy View of Disability, in J. Swain, S. French, C. Barnes and C. Thomas (eds) *Disabling Barriers – Enabling Environments* (2nd edn) (London: Sage).

French, S. and Swain, J. (2007) User Involvement in Services for Disabled People, in R. Jones and F. Jenkins (eds) *Management, Leadership and Development in the Allied Health Professions: An Introduction* (Oxford: Radcliffe).

French, S. and Swain, J. (2008) *Understanding Disability: A Guide for Health Professionals* (Edinburgh: Elsevier).

French, S. with Swain, J., Atkinson, D. and Moore, M. (eds) (2006) *An Oral History of the Education of Visually Impaired People: Telling Stories For Inclusive Futures* (Lampeter: Edwin Mellen Press).

Frith, S. (1984) *The Sociology of Youth* (Ormskirk: Causeway Press).

Garth, B. and Aroni, R. (2003) 'I Value What You Have To Say': Seeking the Perspective of Children With a Disability, Not Just Their Parents', *Disability and Society,* 18(5): 561–76.

Gee, M. and McPhail, M. (2008) The Voice of Service Users and Carers in Universities, in M. McPhail (ed.) *Service User and Carer Involvement* (Edinburgh: Dunedin Academic Press).

Gelling, J. (2006) Being a Guinea Pig for Direct Payments, in J. Leece and J. Bornat (eds) *Developments in Direct Payments* (Bristol: Policy Press).

Ghaye, T. (2000) Empowerment Through Reflection: Is This a Case of the Emperor's New Clothes? in T. Ghaye, D. Gillespie and S. Lillyman (eds) *Empowerment Through Reflection: The Narratives Of Healthcare Professionals* (Dinton: Quay Books).

Ghaye, T. and Lillyman, S. (2000) *Reflection: Principles And Practice For Healthcare Professionals* (Dinton: Mark Allen).

Gillespie-Sills, K. and Campbell, J. (1991) *Disability Equality Training: Trainers' Guide* (London: Central Council for Education and Training in Social Work).

Glasby, J. and Dickinson, H. (2008) *Partnership Working in Health and Social Care* (Bristol: Policy Press).

Glasby, J. and Littlechild, R. (2002) *Social Work and Direct Payment* (Bristol, Policy Press).

Glasby, J. and Littlechild, R. (2006) An Overview of the Implementation and Development of Direct Payments, in J. Leece and J. Bornat (eds) *Developments in Direct Payments* (Bristol: Policy Press).

Glasby, J. and Littlechild, R. (2009) *Direct Payments and Personal Budgets: Putting Personalisation into Practice* (Bristol: Policy Press).

Glasby, J., Glendinning, C. and Littlechild, R. (2006) The Future of Direct Payments, in J. Leece and J. Bornat (eds) *Developments in Direct Payments* (Bristol: Policy Press).

Glendinning, C. (2006) Direct Payments and Health, in J.Leece and J. Bornat (eds) *Developments in Direct Payments* (Bristol: Policy Press).

Goble, C. (2002) Professional Consciousness and Conflict in Advocacy, in B. Gray and R. Jackson (eds) *Advocacy and Learning Disability* (London: Jessica Kingsley).

Goble, C. (2004) Dependence, Independence and Normality, in J. Swain, S. French, C. Barnes and C. Thomas (eds) *Disabling Barriers – Enabling Environments* (2nd edn) (London: Sage).

Goffman, E. (1963) *Stigma: Notes On The Management Of Spoiled Identity* (Englewood Cliffs: Prentice Hall).

Goodley, D. (2000) *Self-Advocacy in the Lives of People with Learning Difficulties* (Buckingham: Open University Press).

Goss, S. and Miller, C. (1995) *From Margin to Mainstream: Developing User- and Carer-Centred Community Care* (York: Joseph Rowntree Foundation).

Gould, N. (1996) Introduction: Social Work Education And The 'Crisis Of The Professions', in N. Gould and I. Taylor (eds) *Reflective learning for social work* (Aldershot: Arena).

Gove, J. and Watt, S. (2004) Identity and Gender, in K. Woodward (ed.) *Questioning Identity: Gender, Class, Ethnicity* (London: Routledge).

Gray, B. and Jackson, R. (2002) Introduction, in B. Gray and R. Jackson (eds) *Advocacy and Learning Disability* (London: Jessica Kingsley).

Greenhalgh, T., Voisey, C. and Robb, N. (2008) Interpreted Consultations as 'Business-as-Usual'? An analysis of Organisational Routines in General Practice, in W.I.U. Ahmad and H. Bradby (eds) *Ethnicity, Health and Health Care* (Oxford: Blackwell).

Hafferty, F.W. (2006) Professions, in G. L. Albrecht (ed.) *Encyclopedia of Disability*, Vol. 3 (Thousand Oaks: Sage).

Halliday Willey, L. (1999) *Pretending To Be Normal: Living With Asperger's Syndrome* (London: Jessica Kingsley).

Ham, C. (1999) *Health Policy in Britain* (4th edn) (Basingstoke: Palgrave).

Hampton, S. (2005) Family Eugenics, *Disability and Society*, 20(5): 553–62.

Hargreaves, S. (2007) Gaps between UK Social Groups in Infant Mortality are Widening, *British Medical Journal*, 384(7589): 335.

Hasler F. (2004) Direct Payments, in J. Swain, S. French, C. Barnes and C. Thomas (eds) *Disabling Barriers – Enabling Environments* (2nd edn) (London: Sage).

Hasler F. (2006) Holding the Dream: Direct Payments and Independent Living, in J. Leece and J. Bornat J. (eds) *Developments in Direct Payments* (Bristol: Policy Press).

Hasler, F., Campbell, J. and Zarb, G. (1999) *Direct Routes to Independence: A guide to Local Authority Implementation and Management of Direct Payments* (London: Policy Studies Institute).

The Health, Social Care and Well-being Strategies (Wales) Regulations (2003) (London: TSO).

Heaton, M. (1998) Listen, You Might Hear Something, *Outlook*, June 15:12.

Herefordshire Centre of Independent Living (2009) (www.herefordshire-cil.com).

Heywood, F. (2006) The Assessment Process, in S. Clutton, J. Grisbrooke and S. Pengelly (eds) *Occupational Therapy in Housing: Building on Firm Foundations* (London: Whurr Publishers).

Higgins, M. and Swain, J. (2009) *Disability and Child Sexual Abuse: Lessons From Survivors' Narratives for Effective Protection, Prevention and Treatment* (London: Jessica Kingsley).

Hirsch, H. (1998) Culture and Disability: The Role of Oral History, in R. Perks and A. Thomson (eds) *The Oral History Reader* (London: Routledge).

Holman, A. with Bewley, C. (1999) *Funding Freedom 2000: People With Learning Difficulties Using Direct Payments* (London: Values into Action).

Home Office (2005) *Race Equality in Public Services* (London: The Home Office).

House, J.S. (2001) Understanding Social Factors and Inequalities in Health: 20th Century Progress and 21st Century Prospects, *Journal of Health and Social Behaviour*, 43, June: 125–42.

Hughes, B. (2004) The Disappearing Body, in J. Swain, S. French, C. Barnes and C. Thomas (eds) *Disabling Barriers – Enabling Environments* (London: Sage).

Hughes, B. (2009) Wounded, Monstrous Objects: A Critique of the Disabled Body in the Sociological Imagery, *Disability and Society*, 24(4): 399–410.

Hughes B. and Paterson K. (1997) The Social Model of Disability and the Disappearing Body: Towards a Sociology of Impairment, *Disability and Society*, 12: 225–40.

Humphries, S. and Gordon, P. (1992) *Out of Sight: The Experience Of Disability 1900–1950* (Plymouth: Northcote House).

Hunter, S. and Tyne, A. (2001) Advocacy in a Cold Climate: A Review of Some Citizen Advocacy Schemes in the Context of Long-Stay Hospital Closure, *Disability and Society*, 16(4): 561.

Hurst, R. (2000) To Revise or Not to Revise, *Disability and Society*, 15(7): 1083–7.

Husson, T. (2001) *Reflections: The Life and Writings of a Young Blind Woman in Post-Revolutionary France* (New York: New York University Press).

IFF Research (2008) *Employment Aspects and Workforce Implications of Direct Payments* (London: IFF Research).

Illich, I. (1976) *Limits to Medicine. Medical Nemesis: The Expropriation of Health* (Harmondsworth: Penguin).

Imrie, R. (2006) *Accessible Housing: Quality, Disability and Design* (Abingdon: Routledge).

Ingstad, B. and Reynolds Whyte, S. (eds) (1995) *Disability and Culture* (Los Angeles: University of California).

Jones, K. (2000) *The Making of Social Policy in Britain* (London: The Athlone Press).

Jones, L. (2000) Behavioural and Environmental Influences on Health, in J. Katz, A. Peberdy and J. Douglas (eds) *Promoting Health: Knowledge and Practice* (2nd edn) (Basingstoke: Palgrave).

Jordan, B. (2001) Tough Love: Social Work Social Exclusion and the Third Way, *British Journal of Social Work*, 31: 527–46.

Kent, D. (2000) Somewhere a Mocking Bird, in E. Parens and A. Asch *Prenatal Testing and Disability Rights* (Washington, DC: Georgetown University Press).

Kerr, A. and Shakespeare, T. (2002) *Genetic Politics: From Eugenics and Genome* (Cheltenham: New Clarion Press).

Kim, H.S. (1999) Critical Reflective Inquiry for Knowledge Development in Nursing Practice, *Journal of Advanced Nursing* 29(5): 1205–12.

Kitcher, P. (1996) *The Lives to Come: The Genetic Revolution And Human Possibilities* (New York: Simon and Schuster).

Knight, B., Sked, A. and Garrill, J. (2002) *Breaking the Silence: Identification of the Communication and Support Needs of Adults with Speech Disabilities in Newcastle* (Newcastle: The Centre for Research and Innovation in Social Policy).

Koch, T. (2000) Life Quality Versus the Quality of Life: Assumptions Underlying Prospective Quality of Life Instruments in Health Care Planning *Social Science and Medicine*, 51(3): 419–27.

Kroll, D. (1990) Equal Access to Care, *Nursing Times*, 86(23): 72–3.

Ladd, P. (1990) Language Oppression And Hearing Impairment, in The Book of Readings of The Disability Equality Pack *Disability – Changing Practice* (K665x) (Milton Keynes: Open University).

Langan, M. (1998) The Restructuring of Health Care, in G. Hughes and G. Lewis (eds) *Unsettling Welfare: The Reconstruction of Social Policy* (London: Routledge).

Lapper, A. (2005) *My Life in My Hands* (London: Simon and Schuster).

Lawton, J., Ahmad, N., Hanna, L., Douglas, M. and Hallowell, N. (2006) Diabetes Service Provision: A Qualitative Study of the Experiences and Views of Pakistani and Indian Patients With Type 2 Diabetes, *Diabetic Medicine*, 23(9): 1003–7.

Leadbeater, C. (2004) *Personalisation Through Participation: A New Script for Public Services* (London: Demos).

Leadbeater, C., Bartlett, J. and Gallagher, N. (2008) *Making it Personal* (London: Demos).

Leon, D. and Walt, G. (2001) Poverty, Inequality and Health in International Perspective: A Divided World? in D. Leon and G. Walt (eds) *Poverty, Inequality and Health: An International Perspective* (Oxford: Oxford University Press).

Lester, H. and Glasby, J. (2006) *Mental Health Policy and Practice* (Basingstoke: Palgrave Macmillan).

Levin, E. (2004) *Involving Service Users and Carers in Social Work Education* (London: SCIE).

Lewis, D.R. and Phillips, J. (1997) Leisure, in B. Gates (ed.) *Learning Disabilities* (Edinburgh: Churchill Livingstone).

Lewis C. (2009) My Life is Unbearable – Don't Fix it, Just Kill Me (29th May, www.heresycorner.blogspot.com).

Lindow, V. (1999) Power, Lies and Injustice: The Exclusion of Service User Voices, in M. Parker (ed.) *Ethics and Community in the Health Care Professions* (London: Routledge).

Longmore, P.K. and Umansky, L. (eds) (2001) *The New Disability History* (New York: New York University Press).

Lovell, T. and Cordeaux, C. (1999) *Social Policy for Health and Social Care* (London: Hodder and Stoughton).

Machenbach, J.P. (2006) Socio-economic Inequalities in Health in Western Europe: From Description, To Explanation To Intervention, in J. Siegrist and M. Marmot (eds) *Social Inequalities in Health: New Evidence and Policy Implications* (Oxford: Oxford University Press).

MacKay, R. (2003) Tell Them Who I Was: The Social Construction Of Aphasia, *Disability and Society*, 18(6): 811–26.

MacPherson, W. (1999) *The Stephen Lawrence Inquiry*, Report of an Inquiry by William MacPherson of Cluny (London: TSO).

Marks, D. (1999) *Disability: Controversial Debates and Psychosocial Perspectives* (London: Routledge).

Mason, D. (2000) *Race and Ethnicity in Modern Britain* (Oxford: Oxford University Press).

Mason, M. (2000) *Incurably Human* (London: Working Press).

Mason, M. and Rieser, R. (1992) The Limits of 'Medicine', in R. Rieser and M. Mason (eds) *Disability Equality in the Classroom: A Human Rights Issue* (2nd edn) (London: Disability Equality in Education).

McCarthy, M. and Thompson, D. (1995) No More Double Standards: Sexuality and People with Learning Difficulties, in T. Philpot and L. Ward (eds) *Values and Visions: Changing Ideas In Services For People With Learning Difficulties* (Oxford: Butterworth-Heinemnann).

McKnight, J. (1995) *The Careless Society* (New York: Basic Books).

McNally, S.J. (1997) Representation, in B. Gates (ed.) *Learning Disabilities* (Edinburgh: Churchill Livingstone).

McPhail, M. and Ager, W. (2008) Introduction: Good Intentions in a Messy World, in M. McPhail (ed.) *Service User and Carer Involvement* (Edinburgh: Dunedin Academic Press).

McSloy, N. (2008) Expert Knowledge: A Carer's Perspective, in M. McPhail (ed.) *Service User and Carer Involvement* (Edinburgh: Dunedin Academic Press).

Mello-Baron, S., with Moore, A. and Moore, I. (2003) Mental Health: New World, New Order, New Partnerships? in J. Horwath and S.M. Shardlow (eds) *Making Links Across Specialisms: Understanding Modern Social Work Practice* (Lyme Regis: Russell House Publishing).

Mencap (2004) *Treat Me Right: Better Healthcare for People with a Learning Disability* (London: Mencap).

Mencap (2007) *Death By Indifference* (London: Mencap).

Mercer, G. (2004) User-Led Organisations: Facilitating Independent Living, in J. Swain, S. French, C. Barnes and C. Thomas (eds) *Disabling Barriers – Enabling Environments* (2nd edn) (London: Sage).

Middleton, L. (1999) *Disabled Children: Challenging Social Exclusion* (Oxford: Blackwell).

Mitchell, D., Traustadóttir, R., Chapman, R. et al. (2006) *Exploring Experiences of Advocacy by People with Learning Disabilities: Testimonies of Resistance* (London: Jessica Kingsley).

Mitchell, P. (1997) The Impact of Self-Advocacy on Families, *Disability and Society*, 12(1): 43–56.

Mitchell, W. (1999) Leaving Special School: The Next Step and Future Aspirations, *Disability and Society*, 14(6): 753–69.

Morris, D. (2000) A Few Thoughts on Independent Living, in S. Vasey (ed.) *The Rough Guide to Managing Personal Assistants* (London: The National Centre for Independent Living).

Morris, J. (1991) *Pride Against Prejudice: Transforming Attitudes to Disability* (London: The Women's Press).

Morris, J. (1993a) *Community Care or Independent Living?* (York: Joseph Rowntree Foundation).

Morris, J. (1993b) *Independent Lives: Community Care and Disabled People* (Basingstoke: Macmillan Press).

Morris, J. (2002) Moving into Adulthood, in *Foundations*. Joseph Rowntree Foundation (www.jrf.org.uk).

Morris, S. (2006) Twisted Lies: My Journey in an Imperfect Body, in E. Parens (ed.) *Surgically Shaping Children: Technology, Ethics and the Pursuit of Normality* (Baltimore: The John Hopkins University Press).

Murray, P. (2000) Disabled Children, Parents and Professionals: Partnership on Whose Terms? *Disability and Society*, 15(4): 683–98.

Naidoo, J. and Wills, J. (2008) *Foundations of Health Promotion* (Oxford: Elsevier).

Nancarrow, S.A., Vernon, W. and Johns, A. (2004) 'The Squeaky Wheel Gets the Grease': Engaging Service Users In Organisational Change, *Journal of Interprofessional Care*, 18(2): 141–51.

National Council for Civil Liberties (1951) *50,000 Outside the Law: An Examination of the Treatment of those Certified as Mentally Defective* (London: National Council for Civil Liberties).

Nawaz, S. (2006) Improving Access to Services for Black and Minority Ethnic Disabled Children, *Journal of Adoption and Fostering*, 30(3): 52–9.

Naylor, A. and Prescott, P. (2004) Invisible Children? The Need for Support Groups for Siblings of Disabled Children, *British Journal of Special Education*, 31(4): 199–206.

Nazroo, J. (1998) *The Health of Britain's Ethnic Minorities* (London: Policy Studies Institute).

Nazroo, J., Jackson, J., Karlsen, S. and Tornes, M. (2008) The Black Diaspora and Health Inequalities in the US and England: Does Where You Go and How You Get There Make a Difference? in W.I.U. Ahmad and H. Bradby (eds) *Ethnicity, Health and Health Care* (Oxford: Blackwell).

NHS Direct Wales – Encyclopaedia (www.nhsdirect.wales.nhs.uk/encyclopaedia/e/article/expertpatients).

NHS Executive (1997) *Priorities and Planning Guidance for the NHS* (Leeds: NHS Executive).

NHS Scotland (2005) *Long Term Conditions Action Team Report* (www.sehd.scot.nhs.uk).

Not Dead Yet UK (www.notdeadyetuk.org/).

Nuffield Council on Bioethics (2006) *Critical Care Decisions in Fetal and Neonatal Medicine*: Ethical issues (www.nuffieldbioethics.org).

Oakley, A. (1981) Interviewing Women: A Contradiction in Terms, in H. Robert (ed.) *Doing Feminist Research* (London: Routledge and Keegan Paul).

Office of the Deputy Prime Minister (2005) *Sustainable Communities: People, Places and Prosperity. A five year plan from the Office of the Deputy Prime Minister* (London: TSO).

Oliver, M. (1993a) Disability and Dependency: A Creation of Industrial Societies, in J. Swain, V. Finkelstein, S. French and M. Oliver (eds) *Disabling Barriers – Enabling Environment* (London: Sage).

Oliver, M. (1993b) *What's So Wonderful About Walking?* Inaugural Professorial Lecture, 9th February (London: Greenwich University).

Oliver, M. (1996a) *Understanding Disability: From Theory to Practice* (Basingstoke: Macmillan).

Oliver, M. (1996b) Defining Impairment and Disability: Issues at Stake, in C. Barnes and M. Mercer (eds) *Exploring the Divide: Illness and Disability* (Leeds: The Disability Press).

Oliver, M. (1998) Theories of Disability in Health Practice and Research, *British Medical Journal,* 317: 1446–9.

Oliver, M. (2004) If I Had a Hammer: The Social Model In Action, in J. Swain, S. French, C. Barnes and C. Thomas (eds) *Disabling Barriers – Enabling Environments* (2nd edn) (London: Sage).

Oliver, M. (2009) *Understanding Disability: From Theory to Practice* (2nd edn) (Basingstoke: Palgrave Macmillan).

Oliver, M. and Barnes, C. (1998) *Disabled People and Social Policy: From Exclusion To Inclusion* (London: Longman).

Oliver, M. and Sapey, B. (2006) *Social Work with Disabled People* (3rd edn) (Basingstoke: Palgrave Macmillan).

Oliver, M. and Zarb, G. (1997) The Politics of Disability: A New Approach, in L. Barton and M. Oliver (eds) *Disability Studies: Past, Present and Future* (Leeds: The Disability Press).

Olsen, R. and Clarke, H. (2003) *Parenting and Disability: Disabled Parents' Experiences of Raising Children* (Bristol: The Policy Press).

Olson, D., McCubbin, H., Barnes, H. et al. (1983) *Families: What Makes Them Work?* (Beverley Hills: Sage).

O'Sullivan, T. (2000) Decision Making in Social Work, in M. Davies (ed.) *The Blackwell Encyclopaedia of Social Work* (Oxford, Blackwell Publishers).

Ovretveit, J. (1997) How Patient Power and Client Participation Affect Relations Between Professionals, in J. Ovretveit, P. Mathias and T. Thompson (eds) *Interprofessional Working for Health and Social Care* (Basingstoke: Palgrave).

Palmer, G., McInnes, T. and Kenway, P. (2007) *Monitoring Poverty and Social Exclusion* (York: Joseph Rowntree Foundation).

Palmer, N., Peacock, C., Turner, F. et al. (1999) Telling People What You Think, in J. Swain and S. French (eds) *Therapy and Learning Difficulties: Advocacy Participation and Partnership* (Oxford: Butterworth-Heinemann).

Parens, E. and Asch, A. (2000) The Disability Rights Critique of Prenatal Genetic Testing: Reflections and Recommendations, in E. Parens and A. Asch (eds) *Prenatal Testing and Disability Rights* (Washington: Georgetown University Press).

Parr, S., Byng, S., Gilpin, S. et al. (1997) *Talking About Aphasia* (Buckingham: Open University Press).

Pearson, C. (2006a) Direct Payment in Scotland, in J. Leece and J. Bornat (eds) *Developments in Direct Payments* (Bristol: Policy Press).

Pearson, C. (2006b) Changing Cultures of Care in Scotland: The Experience of Two Local Authorities, in C. Pearson (ed.) *Direct Payments and Personalisation of Care* (Edinburgh: Dunedin Academic Press).

Pearson, C. (2006c) Supporting Roles, in C. Pearson (ed.) *Direct Payments and Personalisation of Care* (Edinburgh: Dunedin Academic Press).

Pearson, C. (2006d) The Future of Direct Payment in Scotland, in C. Pearson (ed.) *Direct Payments and Personalisation of Care* (Edinburgh: Dunedin Academic Press).

Pearson, C. and Riddell, S. (2006) Introduction: The Development of Direct Payment in Scotland, in C. Pearson (ed.) *Direct Payments and Personalisation of Care* (Edinburgh: Dunedin Academic Press).

Perez, W. and Flynn, M. (2009) User Involvement (www.intellectualdisabilty.info/).

Pfeiffer, D. (2000) The Devils are in the Details: The ICIDH2 and the Disability Movement, *Disability and Society,* 15:1079–82.

Pilgrim, D. and Rogers, A. (1999) *A Sociology of Mental Health and Illness* (2nd edn) (Buckingham: Open University Press).

Pochin, M. (2002) Thoughts from a UK Citizen Advocacy Scheme, in B. Gray and R. Jackson (eds) *Advocacy and Learning Disability* (London: Jessica Kingsley).

Poll, C., Duffy, S., Hatton C. et al. (2006) *A report on In Control's 1st phase 2003–2005* (London: In Control Publications).

Potts, M. and Fido, R. (1991) *'A Fit Person To Be Removed': Personal Accounts of Life in a Mental Deficiency Institution* (Plymouth: Northcote House).

Pound, C. (2004) Dare to be Different: The Person and The Practice, in J.F. Duchan and S. Byng (eds) *Challenging Aphasia Therapies: Broadening the Discourse and Extending the Boundaries* (Hove: The Psychology Press).

Pound, C. (2008) Communication Disability: Exploring New Personal And Professional Narratives, in J. Swain and S. French (eds) *Disability on Equal Terms* (London: Sage).

Power, C. and Kuh, D. (2006) Life Course Development of Unequal Health, in J. Siegrist and M. Marmot (eds) *Social Inequalities in Health: New Evidence and Policy Implications* (Oxford: Oxford University Press).

Priestley, M. (1998) *Disability Politics and Community Care* (London: Jessica Kingsley).

Priesley, M. (2001) *Disability and the Life Course: Global Perspectives* (Cambridge: Cambridge University Press).

Priestley, M. (2003) *Disability: A Life Course Approach* (Cambridge: Polity).

Prime Minister's Strategy Unit (2005) *Improving the Life Chances of Disabled People.* A joint report with Department of Work and Pensions, Department of Health, Department for Education and Skills, Office of the Deputy Prime Minister (London: Cabinet Office).

Public Administration Committee (2008) *User Involvement in Public Services*, 6th Report of Session 2007–08, House of Commons (London: TSO).

Putnam, R.D. (2000) *Bowling Alone: The Collapse and Revival Of American Community* (New York: Simon and Schuster).

Quershi, T., Berridge, D. and Wenman, H. (2000) *Where to Turn?* (London: National Children's Bureau/Joseph Rowntree Foundation).

Qulsom, F., Bywaters, P., Ali, Z., Wallace, L., and Singh, G. (2002) Disadvantage and Discrimination Compounded: The Experience of Pakistani and Bangladeshi Parents of Disabled Children in the UK, *Disability and Society*, 17(3) 237–53.

Read, J. (1996) What We Want from Mental Health Services, in J. Reed and J. Reynolds (eds) *Speaking Our Minds: An Anthology* (Basingstoke: Macmillan).

Read, J. (2000) *Disability, The Family and Society: Listening to Mothers.* (Buckingham: Open University Press).

Rees, S. (2002) *Parent Support Groups – From Parent Support To Providing Services.* (Cardiff: Contact a Family Wales) (www.cafamily.org.uk).

Reine, I., Novo, M. and Hammarstrom, A. (2004) Does the Association Between Ill Health and Unemployment Differ Between Young People and Adults: Results From a 14 Year Follow Up Study with a Focus on Psychological Health and Smoking, *Public Health*, 118(5): 337–45.

Rembis, M.A. (2009) Redefining Disability in the Genetic Age, New 'Eugenics' and the Future of Impairment, *Disability and Society*, 24(5): 585–98.

Reynolds, F. (2004) The Professional Context, in J. Swain, J. Clark, K. Parry, S. French and F. Reynolds, *Enabling Relationships in Health and Social Care: A Guide for Therapists* (Oxford: Butterworth-Heinemann).

Rice, B. and Robson, P. (2006) *Tipping Point: User Involvement Project*, Executive Summary (London: University of East London/ RADAR).

Rickford, F. (2000) The Forgotten Families, *Community Care*, 6–12 July, pp. 18–20.

Riddell, S. (2006) Direct Payment and the Marketisation of Care in Scotland, in C. Pearson (ed.) *Direct Payments and Personalisation of Care* (Edinburgh: Dunedin Academic Press).

Robinson, L. (2004) Beliefs, Values and Inter-cultural Communication, in M. Robb, S. Barrett, C. Komaromy and A. Rogers (eds) *Communication, Relationships and Care: A Reader* (London: Routledge).

Robinson, M. (2001) *Communication and Health in a Multi-Ethnic Society* (Bristol: Policy Press).

Robson, P., Begum, N. and Locke, M. (2003) *Developing User Involvement: Working Towards User Centred Practice In Voluntary Organisations* (Bristol: Policy Press).

Rolfe, G., Freshwater, D. and Jasper, M. (2001) *Critical Reflection for Nursing and the Helping Professions* (Basingstoke: Palgrave).

Rolph, S. (2002) *Reclaiming The Past: The Role of Local MENCAP Societies in the Development of Community Care in East Anglia* (Milton Keynes: Open University).

Rooney, S. (2002) Social Inclusion and People with Profound and Multiple Disabilities: Reality or Myth? in D.C. Race (ed.) *Learning Disability: A Social Approach* (London: Routledge).

Runswick-Cole, K. (2007) 'The Tribunal Was The Most Stressful Thing: More Stressful Than My Son's Diagnosis Or Behaviour': The Experiences Of Families Who Go To The Special Educational Needs And Disability Tribunal *Disability and Society*, 22(3): 315–28.

Russell, M. (1998) *Beyond Ramps: Disability at the End of the Social Contract* (Monroe: Common Courage Press).

Ryan, T. and Holman, A. (1998) *Able and Willing: Supporting People With Learning Difficulties to Use Direct Payments* (London: Values into Action).

Ryan, J. and Thomas, F. (1990) *The Politics of Mental Handicap*, revised edition (London: Free Association Books).

Salway, S., Platt, L., Harriss, K. and Chowbey P. (2008) Long Term Health Conditions and Disability Living Allowance: Exploring Ethnic Differences and Similarities in Access, in W.I.A. Ahmad and H. Bradby (eds) *Ethnicity, Health and Health Care* (Oxford: Blackwell).

Saxton, M. (2000) Why Members of the Disability Community Oppose Prenatal Diagnosis and Selective Abortion, in E. Parens and A. Asch (eds) *Prenatal Testing and Disability Rights* (Washington: Georgetown University Press).

Schalick, W.O. (2006) Interdisciplinary Teams, in G.L. Albrecht (ed.) *Encyclopedia of Disability* (Thousand Oaks: Sage).

SCIL (Southampton Centre for Independent Living) (2000) *A Brief Introduction* (Southampton: SCIL).

SCIL (2005) The Twelve Basic Needs (Online) Available at http://www.southamptoncil.co.uk Southampton.

SCIL Annual Report, 2004–2005 (Southampton: SCIL).

SCIL Annual Report, 2007–2008 (Southampton: SCIL).

Scope (2004) *In the Driving Seat. Direct Payments for your Child* (London: Sage).

Seymour, J., Payne, S., Chapman, A. and Holloway, M. (2008) Hospice or Home? Expectations of End-Of-Life Care Among White and Chinese Older People in The UK, in W.I.U. Ahmad and H. Bradby (eds) *Ethnicity, Health and Health Care* (Oxford: Blackwell).

Shakespeare, T. (2000) *Help* (Birmingham: Venture Press).

Shakespeare, T. (2008) Disability, Genetics and Eugenics, in J. Swain and S. French (eds) *Disability on Equal Terms* (London: Sage).

Shakespeare, T., Gillespie-Sells, K. and Davies, D. (1996) *The Sexual Politics of Disability* (London: Cassell).

Siegnal, J. and Theorell, T. (2006) Socio-economic Position and Health: The Role of Work and Employment, in J. Siegrist and M. Marmot (eds) *Social Inequalities in Health: New Evidence and Policy Implications* (Oxford: Oxford University Press).

Siegrist, J. and Marmot, M. (2006) Social Inequalities in Health: Basic Facts, in J. Siegrist and M. Marmot (eds) *Social Inequalities in Health: New Evidence and Policy Implications* (Oxford: Oxford University Press).

Silver, J.R. (2003) The Decline of German Medicine, 1933–1944, *Journal of the Royal College of Physicians*, 33: 54–66.

Simons, K. (1992) *Sticking Up for Yourself: Self-Advocacy and People With Learning Difficulties* (York: Joseph Rowntree Foundation).

Smith, B. and Goldblatt, D. (2004) Whose Health Is It Anyway? in S. Hinchliffe and K. Woodward (eds) *The Natural and the Social: Uncertainty, Risk, Change* (2nd edn) (London: Routledge).

Smith, R. (2009) Three Babies Aborted Every Day Due to Down's Syndrome (26th October, www.telegraph.co.uk).

Smith, R. (2006) Our Baby Twins were Designed to be Healthy, *London Lite*. Monday 17th November, p. 19.

Smyth, L. (2006) The Freedom of Direct Payments, in J. Leece and J. Bornat (eds) *Developments in Direct Payments* (Bristol: Policy Press).

Snyder, S.L. and Mitchell, D.T. (2006) Eugenics. in G. Albrecht (ed.) *Encyclopedia of Disability*, Volume 2 (Thousand Oaks: Sage).

Social Exclusion Unit (2004) *Breaking the Cycle* (London: Office of the Deputy Prime Minister).

Spedding, F., Harkness, E., Townson, L. et al. (2002) The Role of Self Advocacy: Stories From a Self-Advocacy Group Through The Experiences Of Its Members, in B. Gray and R. Jackson (eds) *Advocacy and Learning Disability* (London: Jessica Kingsley).

Stalker, K. and Robinson, C. (2008) Learning Disabilities, in M. Davies (ed.) *The Blackwell Companion to Social Work* (3rd edn) (Oxford: Blackwell).

Stanley, K. (2005) The Missing Million: The Challenges of Employing More Disabled People, in A. Roulstone and C. Barnes (eds) *Working Futures: Disabled People, Policy and Social Inclusion* (Bristol: Policy Press).

Steptoe, A. (2006) Psychological Processes Linking Socio-economic Position with Health, in J. Siegrist and M. Marmot (eds) *Social Inequalities in Health: New Evidence and Policy Implications* (Oxford: Oxford University Press).

Stevens, S. (2006) The First Ten Years of Direct Payments: A Personal Experience, in J. Leece and J. Bornat (eds) *Developments in Direct Payments* (Bristol: Policy Press).

Stewart, A. (2006) How Direct Payments Changed My Life, in J. Leece and J. Bornat (eds) *Developments in Direct Payments* (Bristol: Policy Press).

Stiker, H. (1997) *A History of Disability* (Ann Arbor: University of Michigan Press).

Stone, E. (1999a) Disability and Development in the Majority World, in E. Stone (ed.) *Disability and Development: Learning From Action and Research on Disability in the Majority World* (Leeds: The Disability Press).

Stone, E. (1999b) Modern Slogan, Ancient Script: Impairment and Disability in the Chinese Language, in M. Corker and S. French (eds) *Disability Discourse* (Buckingham: Open University Press).

Stuart, O. (1993) Double Oppression: An Appropriate Starting Point? in J. Swain, V. Finkelstein, S. French and M. Oliver (eds) *Disabling Barriers – Enabling Environments* (London: Sage).

Sumsion, T. (2005) Promoting Health Through Client Centred Occupational Therapy Practice, in A. Scriven (ed.) *Health Promoting Practice: The Contribution of Nurses and Allied Health Professionals* (Basingstoke: Palgrave Macmillan).

Sure Start (2002) *Supporting Families Who Have Children with Special Needs and Disabilities* (Nottingham: Department for Education and Skills).

Susinos, T. (2007) 'Tell Me In Your Own Words': Disabling Barriers And Exclusion in Young Persons, *Disability and Society*, 22(2): 117–27.

Sutherland, A.T. (1981) *Disabled We Stand* (London: Souvenir Press).

Swain, J. (2005) European Disability Action Mainstream Tool (EDAMAT) – Focus Group Report. Unpublished.

Swain, J. and French, S. (2000) Towards an Affirmation Model of Disability, *Disability and Society*, 15(4): 569–82.

Swain, J. and French, S. (2004) Researching Together: A Participatory Approach, in S. French and J. Sim (eds) *Physiotherapy: A Psychosocial Approach* (Oxford: Butterworth-Heinemann).

Swain, J. and French, S. (2008) Affirming Identity, in J. Swain and S. French (eds) *Disability on Equal Terms* (London: Sage).

Swain, J. and Thirlaway, C. (1994) Families in Transition, in S. French (ed.) *On Equal Terms: Working with disabled people* (Oxford: Butterworth-Heinemann).

Swain, J., Gillman, M. and French, S. (1998) *Confronting Disabling Barriers: Towards Making Organisations Accessible* (Birmingham: Venture Press).

Swain, J., French, S. and Cameron, C. (2003) *Controversial Issues in a Disabling Society* (Buckingham: Open University Press).

Swain, J., French, S., Barnes, C. and Thomas, C. (eds) (2004) *Disabling Barriers – Enabling Environments* (2nd edn) (London: Sage).

Swain, J., Clark, J., Parry, K., French, S. and Reynolds, F. (2004) *Enabling Relationships in Health and Social Care: A Guide for Therapists* (Oxford: Butterworth-Heinemann).

Swain, J., French, S. and Thirlaway, C. (2005) Independent Evaluation: Developing User Involvement in Leonard Cheshire. Unpublished.

Taylor, M. (2008) Disabled in Images and Language, in J. Swain and S. French (eds) *Disability on Equal Terms* (London: Sage).

Thomas, C. (1999) *Female Forms: Experiencing and Understanding Disability* (Buckingham: Open University Press).

Thomas, C. (2007) *Sociologies of Disability and Illness: Contested Ideas in Disability Studies and Medical Sociology* (Basingstoke: Palgrave Macmillan).

Thompson, N. (1998) *Promoting Equality: Challenging Discrimination and Oppression in the Human Services* (Basingstoke: Macmillan).

Thompson, N. (2006) *Anti-discriminatory Practice* (4th edn) (Basingstoke: Palgrave Macmillan).

Thompson, P. (2000) Introduction, in J. Bornat, R. Perks, P. Thompson and J. Walmsley (eds) *Oral History, Health and Welfare* (London: Routledge).

Timmins, N. (2001) *The Five Giants: A Biography of the Welfare State* (London: Harper Collins).

Tope, R. and Thomas, E. (2007) *Health and Social Care Policy and the Interprofessional Agenda* (London: Health Economics Research Centre).

Townson, L., Macauley, S., Harkness, E. et al. (2007) Research Project on Advocacy and Autism, *Disability and Society*, 22(5): 523–36.

Turner, M. and Beresford, P. (2005) *User Controlled Research: Its Meaning and Potential* (Bristol: Shaping Our Lives and Centre for User Participation, Bristol University).

Twigg, J. (1999) Social Care, in J. Baldock, N. Manning, S. Miller and S. Vickerstaff (eds) *Social Policy* (Oxford: Oxford University Press).

UN (United Nations) (1993) Standard Rules on the Equalization of Opportunities for Persons with Disabilities (www.un.org/documents/ga/res/48/a48r096.htm).

UPIAS (Union of the Physically Impaired Against Segregation) (1976) *Fundamental Principles of Disability* (London: Union of the Physically Impaired Against Segregation).

Vasey, S. (1992) Disability Culture: It's a Way of Life, in R. Rieser and M. Mason (eds) *Disability Equality in the Classroom: A Human Rights Issue* (London: Disability Equality in Education).

Vasey, S. (ed.) (2000) *The Rough Guide to Managing Personal Assistants* (London: The National Centre for Independent Living).

Vernon, A. (1996) Fighting Two Different Battles: Unity Is Preferable To Enmity, *Disability and Society*, 11(2): 285–90.

Vernon, A. and Swain, J. (2002) Theorising Divisions and Hierarchies: Towards a Commonality or Diversity? in C. Barnes, M. Oliver and L. Barton (eds) *Disability Studies Today* (Cambridge: Polity Press).

Wallcraft, J. (1996) Becoming Fully Ourselves, in J. Reed and J. Reynolds (eds) *Speaking Our Minds: An Anthology* (Basingstoke: Macmillan).

Walmsley, J. (1998) Life History Interviews with People with Learning Disabilities, in R. Perks and A. Thompson (eds) *The Oral History Reader* (London: Routledge).

Walmsley, J. (2002) Principles and Types of Advocacy, in B. Gray and R. Jackson (eds) *Advocacy and Learning Disability* (London: Jessica Kingsley).

Walmsley, J. (2006) Organisation, Structure and Community Care, 1971–2001, in J. Welshman and J. Walmsley (eds) *Community Care in Perspective: Care, Control and Citizenship* (Basingstoke: Palgrave Macmillan).

Walmsley, J., Bornat, J. and Goodley, D. (2002) *Advocacy and Campaigning*, Open University Course, K202, Care Welfare and Community, Workbook 7, Unit 22 (Milton Keynes: Open University).

Walmsley, J. and Johnson, K. (2003) *Inclusive Research with People with Learning Difficulties: Past, Present And Future* (London: Jessica Kingsley).

Ward, L. (1995) Equal Citizens: Current Issues for People with Learning Difficulties and Their Allies, in T. Philpot and L. Ward (eds) *Values and Visions: Changing Ideas in Services for People with Learning Difficulties* (Oxford: Butterworth-Heinemann).

Waterfield, J. (2004) Professions and Professional Work, in S. French and J. Sim (eds) *Physiotherapy: A Psychosocial Approach* (Oxford: Butterworth-Heinemann).

Waters, J. and Duffy, S. (2007) *Individual Budgets: Report on Individual Budget Integration* (London: In Control Publications).

Wates, M. (2002) *Supporting Disabled Adults in their Parenting Role* (York: York Publishing Services).

Wates, M. (2004) Righting the Picture: Disability and Family Life, in J. Swain, S. French, C. Barnes and C. Thomas (eds) *Disabling Barriers – Enabling Environments* (2nd edn) (London: Sage).

Wates, M. and Jade, R. (eds) (1999) *Bigger Than The Sky: Disabled Women on Parenting* (London: The Women's Press).

Watson, J.D. (2000) *A Passion for DNA: Genes, Genomes and Society* (Oxford: Oxford University Press).

Watters, C. (1996) Representations and Realities: Black People, Community Care and Mental Illness, in W.I.U. Ahmad and K. Atkin (eds) *Race and Community Care* (Buckingham: Open University Press).

Welshman, J. (2006) Ideology, Ideas and Care in the Community, 1848–1871, In J. Welshman and J. Walmsley (eds) *Community Care in Perspective: Care, Control and Citizenship* (Basingstoke: Palgrave Macmillan).

Wendell, S. (1996) *The Rejected Body: Feminist Philosophical Reflections on Disability* (London: Routledge).

Wendell, S. (1997) Towards a Feminist Theory of Disability, in L. Davis (ed.) *The Disability Studies Reader* (London: Routledge).

Whalley Hammell, K. (2006) *Perspectives on Disability and Rehabilitation: Contesting Assumptions; Challenging Practice* (Edinburgh: Churchill Livingstone).

Wilder, E. (2006) *Wheeling and Dealing: Living with Spinal Cord Injury* (Nashville: Wanderbilt University Press).

Wiles, F. (2008) Diverse Communities and Resources for Care, Open University course K101 *Understanding Health and Social Care*, Block 3 (Milton Keynes: Open University).

Williams, B., Copestake, P., Eversley, J. and Stafford, B. (2007) *Experiences and Expectations of Disabled People* (London: Office for Disability Issues).

Williams, V. (2006) The Views and Experiences of Direct Payment Users, in C. Pearson (ed.) *Direct Payments and Personalisation of Care* (Edinburgh: Dunedin Academic Press).

Williams, V. and Holman, A. (2006) Direct Payments and Autonomy: Issues for People with Learning Difficulties, in J. Leece and J. Bornat (eds) *Developments in Direct Payments* (Bristol: Policy Press).

Williams-Findlay, R.B. (2003) *Our Voice in Our Future* (York: Joseph Rowntree Foundation).

Wolfensberger, W. (1977) *A Multi-Component Advocacy/Protection Scheme* (Toronto: Canadian Association for the Mentally Retarded).

Wolfensberger, W. (1994) The Growing Threat to the Lives of Handicapped People in the Context of Modernistic Values, *Disability and Society* 9(3): 395–413.

World Health Organization (1980) *International Classification of Impairments, Disabilities and Handicaps* (ICIDH) (Geneva: World Health Organization).

World Health Organization (2001) *International Classification of Functioning, Disability and Health* (ICIDH-2) (Geneva: World Health Organization).

Wright, S. (1999) 'Having A Go': User Involvement in the GOLD Programme, *Research and Policy Briefings from the Mental Health Foundation*, 1(9).

Yeandle, S., Escott, K., Grant, L. and Batty, E. (2008) Women and Men Talking about Poverty, in J. Johnson and C. De Souza (eds) *Understanding Health and Social Care: An Introductory Reader* (2nd edn) (London: Sage).

Zarb, G. and Nadash, P. (1994) Cashing in on Independence: Comparing the Costs and Benefits of Cash and Services (York: Joseph Rowntree Foundation).

Index